INFANTS AT RISK:
Assessment of Cognitive Functioning

INFANTS AT RISK:
Assessment of Cognitive Functioning

Edited by
RICHARD B. KEARSLEY
NEW ENGLAND MEDICAL CENTER HOSPITAL
IRVING E. SIGEL
EDUCATIONAL TESTING SERVICE

LAWRENCE ERLBAUM ASSOCIATES, PUBLISHERS
1979   Hillsdale, New Jersey

DISTRIBUTED BY THE HALSTED PRESS DIVISION OF
JOHN WILEY & SONS
New York   Toronto   London   Sydney

Lawrence Erlbaum Associates, Inc., Publishers
62 Maria Drive
Hillsdale, New Jersey 07642

Distributed solely by Halsted Press Division
John Wiley & Sons, Inc., New York

Library of Congress Cataloging in Publication Data

Main entry under title:

Infants at risk.

"Outcome of a conference sponsored by the National
Foundation-March of Dimes."
    1. Mentally handicapped children — Testing Congresses.
2. Cognitive disorders — Testing — Congresses.   3. Infant
psychology — Testing — Congresses.   I. Kearsley, Richard B.
II. Sigel, Irving E.
RJ506.M4I52   618.9'28'588   78-23246
ISBN 0-470-26574-4

Printed in the United States of America

Contents

Foreword

The conference from which these papers were selected reflected a desire on the part of The National Foundation and the Georgia Warm Springs Foundation to consider whether to enlarge the base of their research support. Although heretofore the emphasis of the Foundation has been directed towards the medical and biological sciences, it is increasingly evident that a broader based, interdisciplinary approach is timely. The papers in this volume indicate that the interaction of professionals from various disciplines focused on a common set of problems extends the perspective of the investigators as well as the practitioners. Each of the participants at the original conference not only represented a particular discipline or area of clinical work, but also considered the applicability of his or her work in dealing with high–risk children. It is apparent that researchers and practitioners need one another. For example, information about the family's orientation toward the high–risk child may be important in understanding the rate and quality of language development. On the other hand, understanding the sequence of language development may be of value to practitioners in diagnosing the status of the child. In all of this, there is the need for conceptualizing the high–risk syndrome, understanding the methods and procedures for diagnosis, and ultimately evolving methods of treatment that are consistent with such findings.

The need for cross-disciplinary research and communication is evident in these days of knowledge explosion and increased concern for the well being of children at risk. It is impossible for any one discipline to solve the problems of this high-risk population, because the syndrome involves not only the children themselves, but also their families. The complexity of the syndrome is evident in the multiple handicaps that involve the child and impose a continuing strain on the family's resources. As such, their solution requires the best efforts of the various medical and behavioral specialties. Unfortunately, at this time no one discipline can assess or treat the whole child. The physician, the psychologist, the speech therapist, the physical therapist, and the parent counselor each play but a part to enable the child to maximize his potential and to help the family cope. Thus, the challenge is extended to the various areas for research to enhance the knowledge base so that more effective methods of treatment can be made available. Because more effective treatment involves planning the child's social and educational experiences, it becomes even more important to include educators and parents in this joint enterprise.

The National Foundation and the Georgia Warm Springs Foundation recognize the complexity of the issue and feel that bringing together members from the various disciplines is a first step towards improving communication and sharing knowledge, which in turn may contribute to the modification of practices and procedures designed to help these children. Of course, new research ideas can emerge from such interactions because the laboratory researcher now has a chance to learn what the practitioner is up against and the kinds of questions that such professionals feel need answering.

GABRIEL STICKLE
SAMUEL J. AJL

Preface

This volume of papers is the outcome of a conference sponsored by The National Foundation-March of Dimes. Its purpose was to sample the "state of the art" within the behavioral sciences, particularly that concerned with infancy and early cognitive development, and to explore the degree to which this body of knowledge could improve the diagnosis and treatment of premature and other high-risk infants. The papers selected for inclusion in this volume reflect the advance in our understanding of early growth and development that has resulted from over 20 years of basic research concerned with the perceptual, cognitive, and learning capabilities of infants and young children. Of equal importance, they indicate the need to expand the traditional biological model that has guided the clinical management of high-risk infants to accommodate a broader perspective of the developmental needs of such children.

The subsequent decision of the Foundation to initiate a program of social and behavioral research designed to foster closer collaborative relationships between physicians and behavioral scientists and to facilitate the clinical application of the results of basic research within the behavioral sciences is, in large measure, a tribute to the quality of the contributions made by the conference participants. Some of the papers delivered at the conference are not included. These other papers provided more technically oriented information that was useful during the conference discussions in reaching general conclusions and in formulating policy recommendations for The National Foundation's support of research in this area.

As the papers demonstrate, the detailing of the course of human development, not only from the perspective of the children, but also from the broader view of the children and their social and psychological environment, enhances our understanding of the unfolding nature of children, particularly those life-space features that impact upon the direction of future development. Several of the papers address basic issues of early development from the perspective of the normal infant in an effort to provide a model of the possible course of emerging skills and competences that offers interested practitioners and researchers a guide against which to monitor the development of atypical children. Other papers reflect a growing awareness of the inadequacies of traditional measures used to infer the intellectual status of high-risk and handicapped children and suggest alternative procedures that appear to provide a more accurate assessment of the cognitive capabilities of such children.

The papers do contain details of experimental procedures that may appear to be an unnecessary encumberance of detail. This emphasis on methodology has been included not only to further the reader's understanding of these research findings, but also to provide specific examples of laboratory procedures that have been or may be adapted for diagnostic purposes. For those interested only in outcomes, these details might be skimmed; however, our purpose in compiling this volume is to provide, wherever possible, a solid empirical base for the conclusions offered.

Of equal importance is the search for a new paradigm that is of heuristic value in advancing our understanding of the problems surrounding high-risk infants as well as in creating new diagnostic and therapeutic procedures. These papers offer a note of optimism about the developmental outcome of such infants. By directing attention to the social and cognitive potential of children and by establishing intervention procedures derived from a behavioral framework, interested practitioners may be able to provide parents with a more positive set of expectations about the future of their child than that offered by a deficit-oriented model of disease. This does not imply that all the problems surrounding high-risk infants have been solved or that every child identified as having a biological handicap will develop into a totally capable individual. Rather, it emphasizes the position that acceptance of the inevitability of inadequate performance of these children is not a valid point of view.

No doubt some readers will disagree with the perspective taken here. Such disagreement, however, should be based on evidence. To that end, the authors make every effort to distinguish between suggestions that are speculative in nature and those that are based on sound data. Lipsitt's observations concerning crib death and Zelazo's discussion of perceptual–cognitive interaction strategies exemplify this point of view. Where Lipsitt offers a behavioral model as a source of understanding the pathogenesis of crib death, Zelazo demonstrates the applicability of a set of assessment strategies for defining a course of behavioral treatment. This juxtaposition of speculation and hard data reflects the fact that we are in the beginning stages of applying a behavioral model and its supporting research methodology to the diagnosis and care of high-risk children. Thus, the mission of this volume is to demonstrate that a large corpus of scientific knowledge and an array of behavioral methods are presently available and are of potential clinical value in more accurately defining the degree of children's disability as well as the level of their various competences. In addition, this collection of papers provides some guidance for subsequent intervention based on corrective procedures designed to enhance children's potential to function with increasing degrees of adequacy.

The conference was organized by the editors of this volume, who gratefully acknowledge the sponsorship of The National Foundation and the Georgia Warm Springs Foundation, the efforts of the conference participants, and the continuing support of Samuel Ajl and Gabriel Stickle.

RBK

IES

INFANTS AT RISK:
Assessment of Cognitive Functioning

1 The Newborn as Informant

Lewis P. Lipsitt
Brown University

The newborn's psychobiological status is a product of congenital, prenatal, and birth conditions. Hereditary factors interact with intra-uterine biochemical factors, and both sets of conditions can be further complicated by obstetrical circumstances. By capitalizing on clinical–pediatric and behavioral assessment procedures, we should be able to carry out psychophysiological assessments on the newborn that will clearly reflect the course of and hazards inherent in embryonic and fetal development. Because specific prenatal hazards often have enduring effects, the newborn should be able to tell us whether things have gone badly or well. The neonate could become our collaborator in helping to forecast future developmental problems, and under the best of such circumstances might provide information about the probable success of various remedial interventions. The behavior of the newborn, in short, might provide the best, most valid indices of the "condition of the organism" that can be obtained. This dream is possible because so many advances have been made over the past two decades in the recording and understanding of sensory functioning, central nervous system integrity, and behavioral plasticity.

It is not too early for the behavioral scientist to apply already existing technologies for the benefit of infants born following a hazardous pregnancy. We should be better able to detect the character of the insufficiencies incurred and to plan the best possible remediation procedures for the problems discovered through close studies of sensory and learning processes in the young infant.

Many neonatal laboratories now use polygraphic recording procedures to document impairments due to prematurity, oxygen deprivation, and other perinatal conditions that tend to place infants in developmental jeopardy.

Although it is well known that prematurity and anoxia contribute heavily to various developmental anomalies, including cerebral palsy, mental retardation, epilepsy, and school problems (Drillien, 1964; Sameroff & Chandler, 1975), much research remains to be done to develop the best clues for the early detection and amelioration of these conditions (Gluck, 1974; Lipsitt, 1977).

This paper reviews several areas of behavioral investigation of the newborn, with emphasis on those procedures that have shown special promise for the eventual better detection of neonatal aberrations and their sequelae. The promising techniques to be considered are those that have yielded interesting and stable individual-difference data in groups of normal infants and provided some preliminary findings suggesting that they may have special use in detecting early deficits related to later cognitive functioning. The propositions to be considered are:

1. Careful measurement of sucking behavior in the normal newborn, when appropriated for use with premature, small for dates, and otherwise stressed infants can have special value, particularly if questions are asked about patterns of response, rather than merely about whether the infant has a particular response in its repertoire. It should be more illuminating to ask not only whether the infant can hear or suck, but also whether the psychophysical curve relating the baby's response to various stimulus intensities matches that for other infants of the same age. We thus not only ask whether the infant detects a new taste, but also whether its adaptation to the new taste resembles that of normal infants who show an orderly accommodation of responses to different concentrations of sweet fluid.

2. The detection of sensory and behavioral deficit will probably be facilitated by the intensive study of habituation, which capitalizes upon the organism's accommodation to external stimuli. The infants are asked not only to detect a light of moderate intensity, but to report on changes in their defensive or orienting "attitude" toward repetitive presentations of the same stimulus. The inability of infants to show psychophysiological change to such redundant stimulation has been shown in preliminary studies to be a mark of nervous-system (probably cortical) immaturity or central nervous system (CNS) damage.

3. Stimulation of premature infants with special procedures for providing extra experience has suggested that infants who may be predicted on an actuarial basis to be retarded or to show some deficit later in life might benefit from compensatory stimulation. Such extra input, in anticipation of the predicted deficit, could succeed in mitigating the loss.

4. There are presently some indications that the so-called "sudden infant death syndrome" (crib death) is a disorder of development that might have some anticipatory components detectable during the earliest days of life. The early leads into an understanding of this matter require much additional

work, because we cannot know the possibilities until the plausible existing hypotheses have been pursued. The supposition is put forward here that at least some crib deaths, which occur mostly between 2 and 4 months of age, may be due to a failure to undergo critical experiences during the first 2 months of life. By the age of 2 to 4 months, many responses that were initially unconditioned or obligatory become executed on an operant or more "voluntary" basis. During the early months, the infant must learn to engage in "respiratory retrieval responses" in order to respond properly to potentially lethal threats of respiratory occlusion.

POLYGRAPHIC STUDIES OF THE NEWBORN'S SUCKING AND HEART RATE

Recent advances in the use of polygraphic recording in infant research, and the exquisite sensitivity and responsivity of the newborn to exteroceptive stimulation, have led to considerable progress in our understanding of the sensory and learning capabilites of the newborn. The developmental psychologist's capability for conducting refined assessments of the neonate's sensorium has brought us closer to doing informative longitudinal studies, both short- and long-term. These investigations are necessary not only to discover whether certain very early experiences may have a lasting effect upon the behavior and well being of the baby, but also to find whether stimulus interventions may have salubrious consequences for a child who might otherwise manifest a later developmental deficit. It is not too early for us to hope that it might be possible to provide immunity, through behavioral techniques, against some sorts of developmental anomalies. First, however, it is necessary to seek solid documentation of the sensory capacities and behavioral repertoire of the very young infant (Lipsitt, 1977).

In this spirit, a number of studies have been carried out in my laboratory at Women and Infants Hospital of Rhode Island to find out, for example, about the neonate's capacity for discriminating odors and tastes. Through both of these senses the newborn relates closely with the world in the first hours following birth. Our studies have generated some data relating to the approach and avoidance style of the newborn, the differences among newborns in such styles, and the reactions of babies to stimuli that adults would regard as pleasant and unpleasant. In this section, several studies are reviewed from which the inexorable conclusion is drawn that the baby is keenly sensitive in the first few hours of life to subtle changes in gustatory stimulation.

The baby acts on its discrimination of these taste changes either to promote the perpetuation of the taste or to suppress it, depending largely upon sweetness. In short, the newborn is a hedonic creature who responds to the incentive–motivational properties of reinforcers with both motor changes in behavior, such as in sucking and swallowing, and autonomic behavioral changes. The autonomic aspects of these behavioral consequences of pleasant and unpleasant stimulation, such as the accompanying heart-rate changes, are, of course, the rudiments of affect. There is no mistaking the most avid manifestations of such affect, as when the infant goes quickly quiet when offered a sweet fluid. Mothers do indeed respond sympathetically and reciprocally to these behaviors in their newborns by, for example, moving to promote the baby's search for the nipple and the sweet taste or by helping the baby to escape momentary respiratory occlusion when awkwardly positioned. Mothers and fathers usually respond quickly with looking, touching, and lifting when the baby cries; this is, in fact, a good example of the infant and its caretakers "pleasuring" each other.

Our studies of neonatal taste are carried out in a special crib, housed in a white, sound-attentuated chamber with temperature about 80° Fahrenheit. Ambient light is about 50 foot-candles. Breathing is monitored by a Phipps and Bird infant pneumobelt around the abdomen and respiration and body activity recorded continuously on a Grass polygraph. Hewlett–Packard electrodes are placed on the chest and leg, permitting polygraphic monitoring of the primary heart rate, which is then integrated by a Hewlett–Packard cardiotachometer and recorded on another channel.

Sucking is recorded on one of the polygraph channels, using a "suckometer," which consists of a stainless-steel housing with a pressure transducer, over which a commercial nipple is pulled. A polyethylene tube runs into the nipple from a pump source and delivers fluid under the experimenter's control and, in most of our studies, on demand of the subject. When delivering, the pump ejects into the nipple-end a tiny drop of fluid contingent upon the execution of a sucking response of preset amplitude. The size of this drop for each criterion suck is usually 0.02 ml although in some studies in which the effect of the magnitude of the drop is under study, the drop amount may be varied from 0.01 ml to 0.04 ml. See Figures. 1.1 and 1.2.

The situation is arranged such that the infant may receive no fluid for sucking, or might receive a fluid such as sucrose or dextrose in any desired concentration. Contingent upon sucking, one drop of fluid is ejected into the baby's mouth for each suck. A polygraph event marker records fluid ejections during fluid delivery periods or the occurrence of a criterion suck during no-fluid conditions. A 74 dB background white noise assures a fairly constant acoustical environment in the infant chamber.

The laboratory nurse initially makes contact with the mother to explain the research program and obtain informed consent. When the infant is brought to the laboratory for testing, the electrodes and pneumobelt are applied and the infant is swaddled and placed on its left side. The nipple is inserted, supported by a cushion to enable recording without touching the baby. During the first few sucking bursts on the nipple, no fluid is

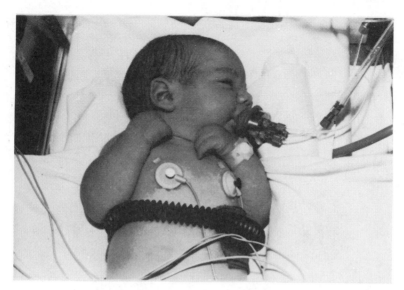

FIG. 1.1.   Two-day-old infant prepared for recording of respiration, heart rate, and sucking.

delivered, and the experimenter calibrates the equipment. Preamplifier sensitivity is adjusted for each infant so that the average sucking amplitude results in a 5 cm excursion of the polygraph pen. The threshold criterion is then set at half this excursion, and only those responses exceeding that minimum are considered as criterion responses.

Newborns characteristically suck in bursts of responses separated by rests. Burst length and rest length both constitute individual-difference variables under no-fluid conditions, i.e., some newborns engage in reliably longer bursts and pauses than others. Both of these parameters, as well as the sucking rate within bursts, however, are significantly influenced by the conditions that are prearranged as the consequences of an infant's behavior. With a change from a no-fluid condition to a fluid-sucking condition or from sucking for a less-sweet solution to a sweeter solution, several behavioral consequences characteristically occur. There is a tendency for the sucking bursts to become longer, for the inter-burst intervals to become shorter, and for the inter-suck intervals to become longer. Thus, sucking rate within bursts becomes slower with increasing sweetness of the fluid, and the infant takes fewer and shorter rest periods.

Contrast Effects

The aforementioned regularities of response in relation to the incentive–reinforcement conditions imposed upon the infants during polygraphic testing make it possible (a) to explore the effects of a previous taste experience upon the infant's response during a subsequent taste experience

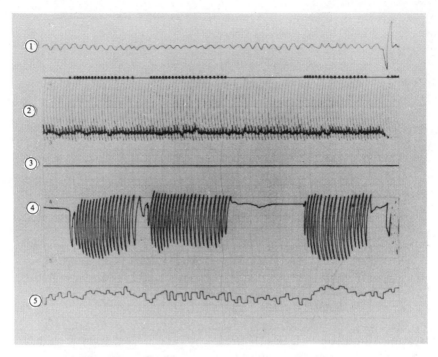

FIG. 1.2. Polygraph recording of (1) respiration, (2) electrocardiogram, (3) blank channel, (4) sucking, and (5) electrocardiotachometer, with digital representation between channels 1 and 2 of the sucking responses recording in channel 4.

and (b) to investigate the interrelationships of these various sucking-response parameters and their relationship to certain other response measures, such as heart rate. Kobre and Lipsitt (1972) tested infants for 2 minutes on the nipple without any fluid delivery whatever. Subjects in this study were rejected for further study if they had a mean sucking rate lower than 30 per minute during the 2 minute period. The 25 subjects remaining were divided into five groups. A total of 20 minutes of responding was recorded for each subject in four successive 5-minute periods. Between each period the nipple was removed for 1 minute to allow the tube to be flushed with water and the child to be picked up.

These 25 infants, most 3 days old, received one of five reinforcement regimens for the 20-minute period. One group received only sucrose. A second group received water throughout, and a third received sucrose and water, alternated twice, in 5-minute units. A fourth group received no fluid throughout the four 5-minute periods and was compared with a group that received sucrose alternated with no fluid in 5-minute periods.

Frequency polygons of the inter-response times, or inter-suck intervals, were printed out on the console of an on-line PDP-8 computer. Comparison of the first three groups revealed that sucking rate within bursts slows down for a fluid-sucking condition relative to no-fluid sucking and that sucking rate becomes still slower for sweet-fluid sucking relative to sucking for plain distilled water. Thus, there is an orderly progression from no fluid to plain water to 15% sucrose sucking, with sucking response becoming slower and slower as the incentive value of the reinforcement delivered consequent upon the response increases. Also, under the sucrose condition, the infants invested a larger number of responses during a comparable period of time than under either the water or no-fluid condition. This effect, which was a consequence of the infant taking fewer rest periods under the higher incentive condition, also occurred in the comparison of responses emitted for water compared with no fluid.

In this study, the infants who sucked for sucrose throughout the 20-minute testing period emitted significantly more responses per minute than did the group that received water throughout the 20-minute period. Moreover, both groups showed stable response rates for their respective fluids through the four blocks of 5 minutes each. The most interesting finding in this experiment, however, concerned subjects who were alternated from one 5-minute period to another between sucrose and water, or between sucrose and no fluid. These groups showed marked effects attributable to the alternating experiences. For example, when sucking for sucrose, the sucrose/water group was essentially comparable to the group sucking for sucrose throughout. When switched to water, however, response rate during each of those 5-minute periods was significantly lower than in their counterpart controls in the water-throughout group. Thus, when newborns have experience in sucking for sucrose, an immediately subsequent experience with water "turns them off." They display their apparent "aversion" for the water by a marked reduction in instrumental behavior that would put that fluid in their mouths. When the consequence of the response is changed, as from water to sucrose, response rate goes back to a normal level. The infant thus optimizes taste-incentive experiences by modulating oral behaviors pertinent to their occurrence.

The same type of effect occurred in the sucrose/no-fluid group, which showed lower response rates when sucking for no fluid after experience in sucking for sucrose. These negative contrast effects were reliable, and there is no reason to suppose that the phenomenon is not widespread throughout the range of incentive conditions to which neonates would be normally subjected. We would expect such effects to occur whenever the infant is called upon to "compare and contrast" two levels of incentive, such as formula vs. plain water or breast-milk vs. a sweeter formula.

Newborns, then, seem strikingly affected in their subsequent behavior by experiences within the immediately previous 5 minutes. The negative contrast effect demonstrated here is one of the most rudimentary types of behavioral alteration due to experiential circumstances. As with neonatal habituation to olfactory stimulation (Engen & Lipsitt, 1965), the suggestion is that memorial processes are already working in the newborn, such that there is a lasting impression made, admittedly of unknown duration, of the experience endured. These are the beginnings of learning processes.

Relations Between Sucking Behavior and Heart Rate

We now know that at least some aspects of the motor behavior of the newborn are modulated to accord with the incentive conditions to which the baby is exposed. Several studies have reinforced this impression and have further provided us with data on the rudiments of affect in the neonate in the form of changes in autonomic responding depending on incentive conditions.

A study of 44 normal full-term newborns, 24 males and 20 females, was conducted on two consecutive days using the same polygraphic techniques (Lipsitt, Reilly, Butcher, & Greenwood, 1976). On the first day of testing, the mean age of the infants was 54 hours and, on the second day, 78 hours. Eleven of the infants were breast-fed and the remainder bottle-fed.

Immediately following calibration of the apparatus, a period of 10 minutes of sucking was recorded for each infant in five successive periods, each of 2 minutes duration. Three of these periods were spent sucking for no fluid, followed by two periods of 15% sucrose-sucking. About 35 seconds intervened between periods, during which time a computer printed out the inter-response time data (IRT) for the preceding period. The nipple was not removed between periods, and the infant continued sucking under the same condition as in the preceding period. The beginning of a period, following the 35-second print-out, was initiated after the infant stopped sucking for at least 2 seconds and after the end of a burst. Following the second sucrose period, the nipple was removed. A 2-minute period of polygraph recording then ensued during a "resting" state, defined as quiescent and with regular respiration, in which the infant neither sucked nor was stimulated in any way.

The results suggest a very interesting interplay between the sucking response and heart rate. They further substantiate a process supporting our supposition that a "savoring mechanism" seems to be operative in the earliest days or even minutes of life.

The computer print-out at the end of each 2-minute period provided a frequency distribution of sucking IRTs in 100 msec bins for inter-suck intervals under 2 seconds. The mean IRT could be calculated from the print-out, using the midpoint of the bin as its numerical representation.

The sucking data from this study essentially replicated those of the previously reported study in showing that under no-fluid sucking, significantly more rest periods (defined as IRTs greater than 2 seconds) were engaged in than for 15% sucrose sucking, fewer responses per burst occurred for no-fluid sucking, and both the modal and mean IRT for no-fluid sucking were reliably shorter than for sucrose sucking. In addition, more responses per minute were emitted for sucrose than under the no-fluid condition.

A feature of the data that was rather a surprise was the seemingly paradoxical increase in heart rates during sucrose-sucking conditions where the sucking rate within bursts was slower. This effect, like all of the sucking-parameter effects, occurred on both the first and second days of the study. During basal recording, the heart-rate mean was approximately 116 beats per minute. When sucking for no fluid, the rate rose to 124, and when sucking for sucrose the rate rose further to 147. Thus, although sucking rate within burst was *reduced* when the infant sucked for sucrose, heart rate nevertheless increased reliably. Moreover, correlations from first to second day of testing indicated that heart rate is a stable individual difference variable under all three conditions but, interestingly, the correlation coefficient rose from 0.29 to 0.46 to 0.71 in going from basal to no fluid to sucrose-sucking, respectively. (An incidental suggestion from this finding is that heart rate as an individual difference variable will have greater utility when measured under a high-incentive sucking condition.)

One interpretation of the increased heart rate during the sucrose period over the water-sucking period could be that while sucking under the higher incentive condition, more sucks per minute are emitted and fewer rest periods occur even though sucking rate is slower within bursts; thus, there could be greater over-all energy expenditure during the high-incentive condition, accounting for the higher heart rates as secondary to this energizing phenomenon. Inspection of the polygraph records from the Lipsitt et al. (1976) study indicated quite clearly that the enhanced heart rate during sucrose-sucking bursts, relative to no-fluid bursts, could not be attributed to a generalized increase in heart rate over the entire period of sucrose sucking. The fact is that within a few sucks of the switch in conditions from no fluid to sucrose or from water to sucrose, the enhanced heart rate could already be seen. That is, it takes only a few seconds or a few sucks for the effect of the sweet taste on the tongue to be reflected in the higher heart rate. This observation was substantiated in a subsequent study by Crook and Lipsitt (1976) who showed that the enhanced heart-rate effect under sweet-sucking conditions can be documented even when length of the sucking burst is controlled and heart rates are considered only during actual sucking and not during inter-burst intervals. A detailed analysis in the Crook and Lipsitt study of heart rate and sucking was made possible by tape recording each interbeat interval and each intersuck interval for subsequent processing by a small computer. Because heart rate accelerates to a stable level at the start of a sucking burst, this period of acceleration was excluded from analysis. Thus, only bursts of 12 or more sucks were considered, and for any such burst the heart rate within it was taken as the mean rate between the eighth and final suck. This method of analysis concentrates upon the asymptotic heart-rate level under differential incentive conditions.

In the Crook and Lipsitt study, half of the 22 full-term newborns sucked for 9 minutes in three blocks of 3 minutes, first receiving a 0.02 ml drop of 5% sucrose for each criterion suck, then no fluid contingent upon such sucks, and finally a 0.02 ml drop of 15% sucrose for each suck. The other half received these conditions in reverse order. Regardless of the order in which the two nutrient conditions were administered, inter-suck intervals were longer under the sweeter condition, but heart rate was also higher.

In another recent study, Crook (1976) carefully documented the effects of quantity of the response-contingent fluid upon sucking rhythm and heart rate to complement the extensive data now available on sweetness. The temporal organization of neonatal nutritive sucking and heart rate were studied in two consecutive 4-minute periods to analyze the effects of two quantities of response-contingent fluid. In this study of 53 full-term infants with uncomplicated delivery (23 males and 30 females between 48 and 72 hours old), one group experienced only the larger amount (0.03 ml per suck), a second experienced the smaller (0.01 ml per suck), and two other groups experienced both in counterbalanced order. Crook found that cumulative pausing time and inter-suck intervals were both affected by the amount of fluid delivered at each response, just as with variations in sweetness. At the start of sucking bursts, heart rate accelerated to a stable level, and within-burst heart rates were higher with increased quantity of contingently delivered fluid.

Thus, sweetness and amount of fluid operate upon the baby in essentially identical ways, and it might be said that sweetness and amount of fluid are essentially collapsible incentive–motivational variables. It is tempting to infer further that the "pleasures of sensation" (Pfaffmann, 1960) control certain features of the newborn's motor behavior and autonomic nervous system processes.

HABITUATION IN THE NEWBORN

Habituation involves the gradual diminution of response, where response decrement due to sensory or motor fatigue can be ruled out, to an initially effective stimulus under conditions of repetitive stimulation. Through habituation, the infant can inform us not only that a given stimulus has been perceived, but that repetition of the stimulus is of no vital consequence, i.e., poses no threat calling for continued alerting or other defensive behavior. Moreover, response to a novel stimulus following habituation to a now-familiar stimulus yields information about the infant's discriminative capacities (Engen & Lipsitt, 1965). It has been shown that various responses, such as heart-rate acceleration and deceleration, bodily motility, sucking interruption, and respiratory disruption are subject to progressive response decrement under the habituation procedure. Frequently, several response systems may simultaneously habituate. Habituation can be demonstrated in human newborns, very likely in all sensory modalities, although there does remain a trace of controversiality about it.

Recovery from habituation is demonstrable with the passage of time since last stimulation and under conditions involving the introduction of a stimulus that is discrepant from the habituating stimulus. This response to novelty, combined with the capacity of the neonate to disregard innocuous stimulation after several repetitions, clearly reveals the neonate as a competent processor of stimulation and as an organism that benefits from experience. It is likely that the relative novelty of stimuli, to which the newborn is sensitive, is pertinent to the ease with which conditioning takes place. It is therefore of considerable interest for developmental psychologists to explore the effects of different types of stimulus familiarization (habituation training) or subsequent conditioning processes. Too little of that sort of work has been done (Cantor, 1955; Cantor & Cantor, 1964, 1965).

In a series of experiments in my laboratory (Engen & Lipsitt, 1965; Engen, Lipsitt, & Kaye, 1963), we delivered olfactory stimuli to the newborn simply by placing before the infant's nostrils a Q-tip dipped in one or another odorant such as anise oil or asafetida. The newborn child does respond respiratorily and with changes in heart rate to such olfactory stimulation. Under most circumstances, the infant's response includes respiratory disruption, heart-rate acceleration, and bodily movement measured on a stabilimeter. When stimulation by these odorants is repeated, the response declines markedly in even as few as 10 trials. The newborn habituates quickly to olfactory stimuli. These infants, all within the first 4 days of life, are first habituated to a given odorant, whereupon we present an alternate odorant without violation of the temporal sequencing of the stimuli. This procedure results in dishabituation or response recovery. Thus, the newborns can tell us which odorants they are sensitive to, both by their initial reactions to stimuli and by their recovery behavior after habituation. The infants "report" to us when they can discriminate the difference between two stimuli. If habituation to anise oil occurs and we then switch to asafetida, the habituated response will recover, informing us that the discrimination has been made.

In an elaboration of this procedure, we have admininstered mixed odorants to the newborns. After habituation to the mixture, we administer either component separately in the same diluent. In this situation, dishabituation does occur, indicating that the baby discriminates between the component odors and the mixture of both odorants combined. This latter study suggests that we are dealing not with a peripheral phenomenon, but rather with a central nervous system function or sensory integration.

It needs to be added that there may be some odorants, particularly those that are especially critical to the infant's early interactions with the mother, that do not easily habituate. Indeed, there is the suggestion that the odor of the mother herself may continue to draw orienting response and visual gaze from the infant as early as 10 days of age (Macfarlane, 1975).

Habituation relates to memory functions that are mediated by the brain. It should be possible, therefore, to improve our armamentarium of psychometric and psychophysical procedures for identifying deficiencies of the central nervous system by incorporating measures of habituation in our test battery. Lewis (1967) has in fact shown that impaired infantile habituation is related to low Apgar scores obtained in the delivery room and that poor habituation performance is related to other indices of possible brain damage. Similarly, hydrocephalic and anencephalic infants may show no habituation at all (Brackbill, 1971; Wolff, 1969). Thus, it seems reasonable to suppose that cognitive functioning is first affected by adverse perinatal circumstances and second, that it is closely associated with the ability of the very young infant to habituate to repetitive stimulation. One of the earliest and most systematic studies of habituation processes of infants, especially with relevance to the infant born at risk, was conducted in the Soviet Union (Bronshtein, Antonova, Kamenetskaya, Luppova, & Sytova, 1960). In these studies, a habituation technique involving the sucking response was used to document that infants born under conditions of excessive cranial pressure or with the umbilical cord around the neck display deficiencies in habituation. The infants were presented with stimuli while sucking. In normal infants momentary interruptions of sucking behavior occur with the intrusion of stimuli such as sounds or lights, and with repetitive presentations of the same stimulus, a reduction of interruptions in sucking occurs. With infants born at risk, however, many more trials of the interruptive stimulus were required to habituate the sucking-suppression response. Similarly, a study of average evoked responses in Down's syndrome infants, age 8 days to 1 year, showed that relative to normal infants matched in age, no significant response decrement occurred.

Bowes, Brackbill, Conway, and Steinschneider (1970) have shown that maternal anesthesia has a definite effect upon the capacity of the infant for habituation. Infants were tested at 2 and 5 days of age. Those whose mothers received relatively high dosages of anesthesia required as many as four times the number of trials to habituate as those who received little medication. Interestingly, these differences persisted as least to 1 month of age. It is challenging for child developmentalists to explore the mechanisms whereby such early effects of perinatal conditions manifest themselves at later ages. It maybe that later developmental conditions are affected indirectly rather than directly by perinatal conditions, such as amount of maternal anesthesia. A baby that is lethargic and unresponsive at birth might inhibit the "natural" responsiveness of the mother in such a way that subsequent mother–infant interactions will have been cumulatively delimited by the infant's initial under-responsiveness.

Of special interest is the fact that infants and mothers are reciprocally interactive with one another. The early habituation process, which is so natural to normal infants and which seems to be deficient in infants with birth stresses or nervous-system anomalies, can be exceedingly important in the early interactions between the infant and mother. It is through the process of mutual stimulation that familiar and novel events are experienced. Novel stimulation is typically introduced by the adult after habituation to some stimulus has occurred. In the case of infants deficient in habituation, all stimuli tend to be experienced similarly; there is no distinction between familiar and novel stimulation.

TEACHING THE LOW BIRTH-WEIGHT BABY

It is a commonplace assumption today that infants born prematurely, small for gestational age, or otherwise at risk within the first days and weeks of life can be stimulated in special ways to optimize cognitive and adaptive behavioral development (Barnard, 1976). This assumption is due in part to the considerable advances made over the past 20 years in the understanding of normal infant behavior and development (Lipsitt, 1977; Lipsitt, Mustaine, & Zeigler, 1977). It also stems from the heroic empirical efforts of a rather small number of behavioral investigators who have been fortunate to be productively associated with neonatal intensive care units. These observers called attention to the possibly injurious aspects of the nursery environment, such as the isolation of the baby from normal environmental stimulation often for weeks (Rothschild, 1967), the lack of opportunity for physical contact with a human caretaker (Klaus & Kennell, 1970), the prevailing loud and monotonous roar of the incubator (Lipsitt, 1971), and the diminished handling and other opportunities for stimulation from which learning to cope might follow (Hasselmeyer, 1969; Siqueland, 1969; Solkoff, Yaffe, Weintraub, & Blase, 1969). The best indications from this now-burgeoning literature on experiential effects in premature infants is that it is not a waste of time to arrange reciprocating interactions between small babies and their caretakers. Sensory-motor advances beyond the usual seem to be made in infants provided with extra stimulation in the high-risk nursery, and these gains are reflected in later developmental tasks and tests.

Some of the studies conducted with small babies have demonstrated that rather minimal exposure to extra stimulation during the neonatal period can have prolonged and profound effects on later behavior (e.g., Klaus & Kennell, 1976), so much that one must wonder about the mechanisms by which such large effects are mediated. There are indications in this regard that the introduction of special regimens of handling and other types of stimulation for the small baby has an immediate effect in altering the baby's behavior and may in addition change the caretaker's own behavior in relation to the child. The infant that is more alert and responsive will undoubtedly call forth more attention, caressing, and playing activities from the caretaker than the listless, lethargic, disinterested, and uninteresting baby. A model of child–caretaker interaction assuming that reciprocating relationships do occur at all developmental levels is appropriate. Such a model would predict that even a minor advance in the behavior of a young infant might evoke ever more complicated and curious behaviors in the caretaker. Thus, both immediately and perhaps a week later, the caretaker would attempt to elicit somewhat more sophisticated responses from the infant than would otherwise have been the case. One behavior recruits another, and each developmental advance in the baby provides the caretaker with the impetus to promote still further advances at later ages. It is of interest that most adults in their interactions with infants tend to operate at the frontiers of the baby's capabilities, often seeking to promote the occurrence of behaviors that are at the moment just below the threshold of the infant's capabilities. It is this natural tendency on the part of parents and other adults in the infant's environment that keeps most infants "on their toes," i.e., attuned to novel stimulation and in a state of readiness to benefit from experience. Unfortunately, it is only quite recently that these natural tendencies of adults have been capitalized upon in the newborn nursery.

Among the studies that have thus far demonstrated that some extra added attention to the stimulus needs of the newborn can have felicitous effects upon developmental outcome are those of Kennell, Klaus, and their colleagues (Kennell et al., 1974; Klaus et al., 1972). They arranged for mothers of newborns to have close physical contact with their infants for 1 hour after delivery and many times in the ensuing days of hospitalization. Control mothers were simply subjected to the usual routine of the hospital with regard to mother–infant contact: "a glance at their baby shortly after birth, a short visit 6 to 12 hours after birth for identification purposes, and then 20- to 30-minute visits for feeding every four hours during the day" (Kennell et al., 1974, p. 173). One month later observations of the mothers and their infants confirmed that those mothers who had had extra interaction during the period of hospitalization engaged in more demonstrative affection and generally showed more attention to their infants than did the control mothers. Follow-up data of a sort that has been all too rare after such manipulative studies showed that the mother–infant pairs with the neonatal head-start still interacted more when the children were 2 years of age, and the mothers tended even to speak differently to their youngsters!

Such follow-up studies as those by Klaus, Kennell, and their colleagues should help to illuminate more clearly the processes by which long-term gains of modest experiential enrichment are achieved. In all likelihood, the positive and sometimes even startling effects that have been achieved in this area will appear less like magic under closer scrutiny. As previously suggested, early stimulation of an infant may produce a more interested and inquisitive infant who then essentially calls for more stimulation as he or she matures. Solkoff et al. (1969) examined immediate and subsequent effects of handling premature infants during the earliest days of life. Both behavioral and physical measures were taken on 10 low birth-weight infants. Five of these infants were stroked in their incubators 5 minutes in every hour of the day over a period of 10 days. The five controls simply received routine nursery care. The researchers found that the handled infants became more active and alert, regained their birth weights faster, and were rated as healthier in terms of indices of growth and development than were the control babies. When the experimenters obtained information about the 10 infants at 7 to 8 months of age, the handled infants were described as more interested in stimulation than were the controls.

Another such study (Solkoff & Matuszak, 1975) involved the use of the Neonatal Behavioral Assessment Scale (Brazelton, 1973) administered to 11 premature infants (mean gestational age 31 weeks) who were still in the intensive care unit of the hospital in which they were born. Six of these infants received a short period of extra handling during each 16-hour nursing shift over a period of 10 days. The five control babies received only routine care. Both groups were administered the assessment scale on a before and after basis. Although there were no differences in the mean weight gain of the two groups, the handled infants showed positive changes (i.e., toward maturational improvement on 11 of the scale's items) whereas the control infants showed such changes on only 2 such items.

DEVELOPMENTAL JEOPARDY AND CRIB DEATH

We have seen the considerable recent successes in exploring the sensory capabilities and response repertoire of the newborn. Spurred on by these successes, developmental psychologists, psychophysiologists, and pediatricians have taken an increasing interest in using the new information about infant behavior and individual differences for the better detection of developmental deficits. A considerable literature has begun to appear on the assessment of perinatal risk and the determination of the sequelae of such risk. The issue of risk has become of more intense concern in part because of medical and technological advances that have enabled the fetologist and neonatologist to rescue for prolonged survival an infant that, only a few short years ago, would have been likely to die. The continuum of reproductive casualty (Pasamanick & Knobloch, 1961), then, still exists, but the cutoff point for survival has shifted sharply. There is great concern today that the very small, very premature babies that are now saved for survival may be in very special jeopardy for non-fatal developmental anomalies, such as learning disabilities and behavior disorders.

Psychologists are especially interested in high-risk infants whose futures may be marked for developmental jeopardy, because it is quite possible that behavioral interventions and compensations may help to avoid the hazards for which these infants seem destined.

It is my purpose here to elaborate upon a specific group of at-risk infants; those who are victims of the sudden infant death syndrome. Some infants show an apparent deficiency in their response to the threat of respiratory occlusion or the blockage of respiratory openings. I believe this problem may be related to crib death, but not directly through an inadequate unconditioned response. Instead, it may be due to a congenital aberration leading to an experiential deficiency that puts the infant in special danger with respect to the sudden infant death syndrome.

Normal newborn infants have a well-organized and readily elicited constellation of defensive responses that are made when aversive stimulation becomes intolerable or when there is even the suggestion of a threat to the blockage of the respiratory passages. This response, which has been incorporated as a test item in both the Graham (1956) and Brazelton (1973) scales, can be critical for survival. It is present on a reflexive basis in the very young infant, although indeed there are striking individual differences in the rapidity and vigor with which the response is elicited. My intention here is only to make the point that behavioral reciprocity between the infant and its environment must work in such a way that between birth and 2 months of age the infant must gain experience in retrieving its respiratory passages for breathing freely. If this is not done, at the critical age between 2 and 4 months of age, when so many basic biological reflexes begin to evolve into voluntary and operant behaviors, the infant may be in special jeopardy through not "knowing how" to adjust its posture and clear its respiratory passages for the continuation of breathing. If the response deficiency lasts a sufficiently long period of time, as in cases of repetitive apnea, especially during "rapid eye movement" (REM) sleep (Steinschneider, 1976), the baby may become anoxic and ultimately comatose before the appropriate defensive behavior is executed.

Although the contention espoused here is largely speculative, there is considerable presumptive evidence suggesting that babies at risk for crib death do have such a deficiency that, if not compensated for, could conceivably provide a pathway to the sudden infant death syndrome. The remaining remarks in this section are relevant to this notion.

The idea of behavioral reciprocity is, as stated, not limited to the communication of one psychobiological system of the infant with another of its systems. It also involves reciprocating relationships between the infant and another person in its life. The mother–infant interaction especially is a two-way affair, and this entire subject of reciprocating relationships deserves much greater attention than it has received. English pediatrician Mavis Gunther (1955, 1961) made some close observations of the fascinating ways in which the nursing mother and her infant affected each other reciprocally, immediately after birth and quite possibly with lasting effects. The nursing couple is comprised of a pair of persons that happen to be, so it seems, excellent operant conditioners of one another. Gunther has described the situation in which the nursing newborn often finds itself. When the newborn is suckling at the breast, its nostrils periodically and fortuitously become occluded. This results in an aversive reaction on the part of the infant, involving various manifestations of withdrawal from the nipple and breast. The newborn ordinarily sucks with a secure pressure seal between its lips and the nipple. Unlatching from the breast is not accomplished easily, particularly by a hungry infant. When threatened with nasal occlusion, therefore, the baby first engages in minor head movements, swaying the head from side-to-side and pulling its head backwards. Sometimes these actions succeed in freeing the nasal passages for breathing. If these maneuvers do not succeed, however, the normal infant executes a more vigorous pattern of behavior, such as arm waving and pushing against the mother's breast, this being often accompanied by facial vasodilation. Ultimately, if none of these maneuvers succeeds in wresting the infant free of the offending object, crying occurs. Under such circumstances, the baby is reinforced for retreating from the breast rather than remaining at it. Gunther described some instances in which the infant was observed to show reluctance when put to the breast after such an apparently aversive experience. Although Gunther does not phrase the sequence of activities as such, the stimulating event, the resulting reaction, and the subsequent aversion to the feeding situation may be easily conceptualized as one of the operant learning.

Aversive behavior occurs in human infants under conditions in which biological threat exists. In its milder forms, such behavior is manifested in the autonomic and withdrawal responses to intense stimulation, such as bright lights, noxious tactile stimuli, unpleasant odorants and tastes, trigeminal stimulants, and loud noises. The amount of active response to such stimulation is directly proportional to stimulus intensity, with very intense stimulation culminating in crying.

Angry behavior may be defined in terms of the presence and vigor of autonomic and withdrawal response to noxious stimulation. Aggressive behavior, in contrast, may be taken to refer to responses of the baby, in the presence of anger, that have the function of thwarting perpetuation of the instigating noxious stimulation. In ordinary feeding circumstances, such defensive behavior can be fortuitously directed against the mother. Stimulation that supports or threatens respiratory occlusion tends to elicit a response pattern consisting of five components, which may be viewed as a fixed action pattern beginning with mild responsivity and proceeding toward extreme arousal if the stimulus condition is not removed. The five steps involved, as noted earlier, are (a) side-to-side head waving; (b) head withdrawal, with backward jerks and grimacing; (c) facial vasodilation; (d) arm jabbing; and (e) crying. The continuum of response is here defined as angry behavior, which can be seen to abate when the threatening or noxious stimulation is reduced.

Such behavior often occurs in the natural course of infant feeding. When anger in the newborn results from respiratory occlusion, the action pattern has the effect of freeing the respiratory passages by displacing the offending object or by impelling the mother to adjust her feeding position. The freeing from occlusion constitutes a reinforcement condition that can increase the probability of its occurrence under this and similar future conditions. The anger response may occur subsequently with a shorter latency, or even anticipatorily to less intense but similar stimulating conditions. Still later in ontogeny, it may occur without direct (exteroceptive) instigation at all. Moreover, such "aggressive" behavior may be mediated by anger generated from circumstances entirely different from those in which the behavior has been first learned. The learning mechanisms involved in the acquisition of aggressive behavior are those presumed to be implicated in other forms of instrumental learning. Initially, a congenital response pattern (anger) is elicited by experiential circumstances conducive to its expression. Components of that action pattern are selectively reinforced, following which these behaviors (now called aggressive) are learned and perpetuated through periodic practice, with reinforcement renewed on subsequent occasions.

The foregoing comments are, as must be appreciated, entirely speculative and theoretical, except for their evidential basis in the observations of Gunther and others who have documented the infantile response to brief respiratory occlusion in the natural feeding situation. The thesis relating this type of behavior to the possible development of aggression is presented as a heuristic model of reciprocating relationships between mother and infant as well as for the "content", the verification of which is largely wanting. The following elaborations are presented in the same spirit.

From the earliest moments after birth, newborns engage in systematic, replicable, congenital patterns of behavior, which enter immediately into a reciprocating relationship with the environment. The moment a baby is born, stimuli impinge on its receptors, producing changes in the infant's behavior that in turn alter the effective stimulation from the environment. Experience has an immediate effect on the baby, and the baby immediately alters the world in which it lives.

Part of the newborn's behavioral repertoire is an important tendency to divert threats to its biological safety. Numerous aversive responses can be observed to noxious stimulation. A sudden increase in illumination occurring in the vicinity of the infant's open eyes, for example, causes the lids to close. If the skin surface is touched with great pressure or is pricked by a pointed object, the infant withdraws the offended part of its anatomy from the stimulus. If a noxious trigeminal stimulant is presented, the baby turns its head from the locus of the stimulation and shows by facial expression and vocalization that the experience is disturbing. On stimulation with bitter quinine, withdrawal of the tongue occurs. Each of the sensory modalities of the newborn can be excessively stimulated to produce its own aversive style of response, always culminating in crying when lesser manifestations of aversion fail to enable escape.

The absence of or deficiency in the respiratory occlusion response may be related to the occurence of the still unexplained "crib death" that takes the lives of a large number of infants at around 2 and 3 months of age. Many infants who succumb to crib death are known to have had a mild cold, usually described as "sniffles," for a day or several days prior to their death. Still others have been diagnosed on autopsy as having pneumonitis, presumably not so serious as to cause death. It is an empirical problem for developmental psychologists and psychobiologists to determine whether respiratory occlusion, and the failure to make appropriate adjustive responses to such occlusion, are pertinent factors in such deaths. Throat-clearing responses in the older child and adult are so prevalent and facile that, as with so many mature and fairly universal behaviors, we do not concern ourselves much with their ontogeny. It is possible, however, that just as learning (and failure to learn) are important antecedents of lifesaving responses (and their absence) in other spheres of human activity, so also is the learning of maneuvers to prevent respiratory occlusion necessary for the survival of the infant.

It is not inconceivable that a modicum of early practice is required for the infant to achieve a suitable level of "respiratory retrieval" when faced with the threat of occlusion. The infants who achieve the required minimum of practice are perhaps those whose experience at retrieval has been most frequent and most vigorous. These would be the infants who at birth and shortly thereafter have vigorous responses to the threat of a respiratory occluding stimulus; i.e., most practice in this situation is probably self-administered, as the baby lies in the crib, especially in the prone position, and moves around among blankets, hands, and other objects that are so readily brought to the mouth by the infant's own arms. In this connection, one wonders whether the lethargy of response displayed by the "failure-to-thrive infant" may not have had its earliest representation in a deficiency of this and similar neonatal response patterns or in the failure of opportunity to practice early congenital patterns of behavior.

SUMMARY

I have presented the thesis that newborn children may be considered to be informants about their own developmental condition. As when capitalizing upon information theoretically available from any informant, it is important to formulate the important questions and to pose them in such a way as to facilitate a response. Newborn infants can report upon their own condition by being asked to respond to environmental challenges. We can find out in this way that the neonate can see, hear, taste, smell, and feel. By presenting a challenge, we can also find out whether the child is capable of responding defensively.

The introduction of a taste on the tongue reveals much about the ability of the infant to suck, swallow, and discriminate one taste from another. Monitoring heart rate may even reveal whether the infant enjoys an experience. Thus, the study of diverse psychological processes of infants, including habituation, conditioning, discrimination, and all types of sensory and motor functions, can help to identify babies whose early behavior and development may have been compromised by perinatal hazards. It is important to study offspring resulting from adverse conditions of pregnancy in order to better understand the causes of fetal and neonatal aberrations. It is perhaps of even greater urgency that we understand better the psychobiological nature and significance of infancy in order to identify as early as possible those deficiencies that can best be compensated for at earlier ages. Our strongest ally in this endeavor is the infant, who should be observed closely and asked smart questions.

ACKNOWLEDGMENTS

Much of the research reported here was supported by the W. T. Grant Foundation. The author is indebted to Bernice Reilly, for her inestimable help in the design and execution of our neonatal studies over a 10 year period, and to Patricia Daniel and Helen Haeseler for helpful readings of an earlier draft of this manuscript.

REFERENCES

Barnard, K. E. Nursing: High risk infants. In T. D. Tjossem (Ed.), *Intervention Strategies for High Risk Infants and Young Children.* Baltimore: University Park Press, 1976.

Bowes, W. A., Brackbill, Y., Conway, E., & Steinschneider, A. Obstetrical medication and infant outcome: A review of the literature. *Monographs of the Society for Research in Child Development,* 1970, **35**, 3–25.

Brackbill, Y. The role of the cortex in orienting: Orienting reflex in an anencephalic human infant. *Developmental Psychology,* 1971, **5**, 195–201.

Brazelton, T. B. *Neonatal Behavioral Assessment Scale.* Philadelphia: William Heinemann Medical Books, 1973.

Bronshtein, A. T., Antonova, T. G., Kamenetskaya, N. H., Luppova, V. A., & Sytova, V. A. On the development of functions of analyzers in infants and some animals at the early stage of ontogenesis. In *Problems of evolution of physiological functions.* USSR: Academy of Science (U. S. Department of Health, Education, and Welfare, Translation Service), 1960.

Cantor, G. N. Effects of three types of pretraining on discrimination learning in preschool children. *Journal of Experimental Psychology,* 1955, **49**, 339–342.

Cantor, G. N., & Cantor, J. H. Effects of conditioned-stimulus familiarization on instrumental learning in children. *Journal of Experimental Child Psychology,* 1964, **1**, 71–78.

Cantor, G. N., & Cantor, J. H. Discriminative reaction time performance in preschool children as related to stimulus familiarization. *Journal of Experimental Child Psychology,* 1965, **2,** 1-9.

Crook, C. K. Neonatal sucking: Effects of quantity of the response-contingent fluid upon sucking rhythm and heart rate. *Journal of Experimental Child Psychology,* 1976, **21,** 539-548.

Crook, C. K., & Lipsitt, L. P. Neonatal nutritive sucking: Effects of taste stimulation upon sucking rhythm and heart rate. *Child Development,* 1976, **47,** 518-522.

Drillien, C. M. *The growth and development of the prematurely born infant.* Baltimore: Williams & Wilkins, 1964.

Engen, T., & Lipsitt, L. P. Decrement and recovery of responses to olfactory stimuli in the human neonate. *Journal of Comparative and Physiological Psychology,* 1965, **59,** 312-316.

Engen, T., Lipsitt, L. P., & Kaye, H. Olfactory responses and adaptation in the human neonate. *Journal of Comparative and Physiological Psychology,* 1963, **56,** 73-77.

Gluck, L. Perinatology: State of the art. *Contemporary Obstetrics and Gynecology,* 1974, **3,** 125-159.

Graham, F. K. Behavioral differences between normal and traumatized newborns. I. The test procedures. *Psychological Monographs,* 1956, **70,** (20, Whole No. 427).

Gunther, M. Instinct and the nursing couple. *Lancet,* 1955, **1,** 575.

Gunther, M. Infant behavior at the breast. In B. Foss (Ed.), *Determinants of infant behavior.* London: Methuen & Co., 1961.

Hasselmeyer, E. G. *Behavior patterns of the premature infant* (PHS Doc. No. 840). Washington, D. C.: U. S. Department of Health, Education, and Welfare, Public Health Service, Division of Nursing, 1969.

Kennell, J. H., Jerauld, R., Wolfe, H., Chesler, D., Kreger, N. C., McAlpine, W., Steffa, M., & Klaus, M. H. Maternal behavior one year after early and extended postpartum contact. *Developmental Medicine and Child Neurology,* 1974, **16,** 172-179.

Klaus, M. H., Jerauld, R., Kreger, N. C., McAlpine, W., Steffa, M., & Kennell, J. H. Maternal attachment: Importance of the first post-partum days. *New England Journal of Medicine,* 1972, **286,** 460-463.

Klaus, M. H. & Kennell, J. H. Mothers separated from their newborn infants. *Pediatric Clinics of North America,* 1970, **17,** 1015-1037.

Klaus, M. H., & Kennell, J. H. *Maternal-infant bonding.* St. Louis: C. V. Mosby, 1976.

Kobre, K. R., & Lipsitt, L. P. A negative contrast effect in newborns. *Journal of Experimental Child Psychology,* 1972, **14,** 81-91.

Lewis, M. The meaning of a response, or why researchers in infant behavior should be oriental metaphysicians. *Merrill-Palmer Quarterly,* 1967, **13,** 7-18.

Lipsitt, L. P. Learning ability and its enhancement. In J. H. Menkes & R. J. Schain (Eds.), *Learning disorders in children. Report of the Sixty-First Ross Conference on Pediatric Research.* Columbus, Ohio: Ross Laboratories, 1971.

Lipsitt, L. P. The study of sensory and learning processes of the newborn. In J. Volpe (Ed.), *Clinics in perinatology* (Vol. 4, No. 1) Philadelphia: W. B. Saunders, 1977.

Lipsitt, L. P., Mustaine, M. G., & Zeigler, B. Effects of experience on the behavior of the newborn. *Neuropadiatrie,* 1977, **8,** 107-133.

Lipsitt, L. P., Reilly, B. M., Butcher, M. J., & Greenwood, M. M. The stability and interrelationships of newborn sucking and heart rate. *Developmental Psychobiology,* 1976, **9,** 305-310.

Macfarlane, A. Olfaction in the development of social preference in the human neonate. *Parent-infant interaction.* London: CIBA Foundation Symposium 33, 1975.

Pasamanick, B., & Knobloch, H. Epidemiological studies on the complications of pregnancy and the birth process. In G. Caplan (Ed.), *Prevention of mental disorder in children.* New York: Basic Books, 1961.

Pfaffmann, C. The pleasures of sensation. *Psychological Review,* 1960, **67,** 253–268.

Rothschild, B. F. Incubator isolation as a possible contributing factor to the high incidence of emotional disturbance among prematurely born persons. *Journal of Genetic Psychology,* 1967, **110,** 287–304.

Sameroff, A. J., & Chandler, M. J. Reproductive risk and the continuum of caretaking casualty. In F. D. Horowitz (Ed.), *Review of child development research.* Chicago: The University of Chicago Press, 1975.

Siqueland, E. R. *The development of instrumental exploratory behavior during the first year of human life.* Paper presented at the meeting of the Society for Research in Child Development, Santa Monica, California, 1969.

Solkoff, N., & Matuszak, D. Tactile stimulation and behavioral development among low-birthweight infants. *Child Psychiatry and Human Development,* 1975, **6,** 33–37.

Solkoff, N., Yaffe, S., Weintraub, D., & Blase, B. Effects of handling on the subsequent developments of premature infants. *Developmental Psychology,* 1969, **1,** 765–768.

Steinschneider, A. *Implications of the sudden infant death syndrome for the study of sleep in infancy.* Paper presented at a symposium on crib death at the meeting of the American Psychological Association, Washington, D. C. 1976.

Wolff, P. H. What we must and must not teach our young children from what we know about early cognitive development. In *Planning for better learning.* Philadelphia: William Heinemann Medical Books, 1969.

2 Visual Cognition in Early Infancy

Marshall M. Haith
University of Denver

Webster defines cognition as "any mental operation by which we become aware of objects of thought or perception." The goal of this conference is to identify existing approaches to the study of cognition in the first 5 years of life. Webster's interpretation does not precisely capture scientific usage, but it is still doubtful whether the human newborn has sufficient mental capacity, by anyone's definition, to qualify as a "cognitive creature." Thus, you might ask why I plan to discuss research on newborns and young infants. The answer is that I accept Piaget's (1936) assertion that cognition, whatever it may be, does not suddenly emerge at some particular age. Rather, thinking ability is based on early sensorimotor experience. Thus, a full understanding of cognitive development requires knowledge about how precognitive sensorimotor activity unfolds, and birth is a logical starting point.

The principal concern in our laboratories has been visual activity, an area that has unique advantages for studying both cognition and development from the earliest days. Visual activity is an obviously useful object of study for research on visual sensitivity and visual processing. The eye is the only distal receptor that creates a temporal pattern of action as it fixates successive points in the visual field. A record of the sequence of fixations tells us, potentially, what information a baby has to work with; however, the value of visual activity for studying cognition transcends the eye's role in seeing and even the opportunity it presents to inventory the visual information the baby has sampled. It is important to remember that it is the brain that drives the eye and not the other way around. Thus, fixation patterning can also indicate what the organism is attempting to do. This perspective on visual activity suggests consideration of how information-seeking and inspecting activities are organized, topics that are somewhat foreign to the field of early infancy. Efforts have been devoted much more toward developmental evaluation of the integrity of the sensory systems and which dimensions of visual stimuli control the infant's attention. Although it is somewhat oversimplifying to draw a dichotomy between these two uses of visual behavior — as a marker of stimulus sensitivity or as an index of biological organization—the organization of information-seeking activity may be of greater importance, because it is through such activity that the food for cognition is acquired. Part of my concern in the discussion to follow is how newborns are biologically organized to acquire visual information from their world, and how this organization changes with experience.

In addition to the substantive reasons for studying early visual activity, there are pragmatic considerations. The basic aspects of visual activity from birth to maturity are remarkably similar. Newborns and adults open and close their eyes, adjust the pupillary opening appropriately for changing light levels, make firm fixations, and use rapid, saccadic eye movements to secure new fixation points. Of course, development does occur. One never sees in normal adults the occasional out-of-control eye movements observed in newborns, and the time parameters of eye movement and fixation do change with age, as does the smoothness of visual tracking. Still, with the exception of sucking, no other system in the newborn matches the speed and motoric sophistication of the visual system, and no other motor system changes less with age. Therefore, a study of visual activity over age permits unparalleled stability in measurement indices and, thereby, sidesteps a major problem with many other measures of cognitive development.

The work described in this chapter concerns both the newborn period (1 to 4 days) and the period of infancy from 3 weeks to 4 months of age. Because I want to communicate future direction as well as progress to date, I range broadly from reporting studies that have been executed and completely analyzed, to research in progress, to observations in pilot work, to ideas on the drawing board. First, I describe our techniques for studying visual behavior and then address questions about vision to which our research is pertinent.

METHODS FOR STUDYING VISUAL ACTIVITY

The techniques for studying visual activity described here have resulted from a number of developments over the past 15 years. Because these developments have been reviewed elsewhere (Haith, 1969), I concentrate here on the state of the art and current developments. The procedures can be broken down into three phases: recording, measuring, and analyzing.

Recording

The infant's visual activity is recorded in a situation similar to that shown in Figure 2.1. As the infant lies on a baby holder in a metal-framed wooden cabinet, an overhead TV camera records the eye image. A metal platform supports the TV camera and six lamps that surround it. The lamps (Bausch & Lomb illuminators) are positioned precisely so that their beams converge at the eye after passing through infrared (3 Polaroid HN7 filters) and heat filters (Corning 7–69) that render them invisible and cool. The camera is equipped with an infrared-sensitive tube. An advantage of using infrared light is that the illumination required for recording is not dependent on the level of visible illumination that is used to light the stimulus. We can record the eye in absolute darkness. This is especially important for newborn work, because newborns tend to close their eyes even in moderate light. A second purpose of this lighting arrangement is to create reflections on the newborn's eye that can be recorded by the camera. Because the positions of the lamps in the baby's visual field are precisely set, we can later determine

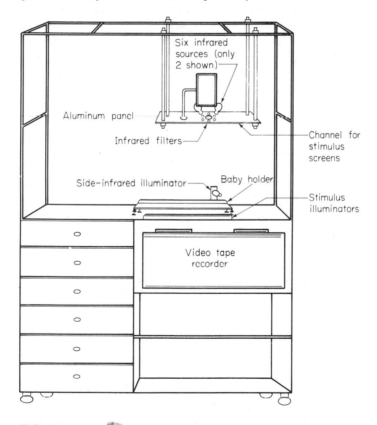

FIG. 2.1.   Illustration of the apparatus used. Infrared lights provide illumination for recording of the image of the eye via the infrared TV camera onto videotape. Stimulus illuminators light the stimulus screen above the baby holder so that a baby, lying supine in the holder, only sees the screen and the stimulus spray-painted on it. The TV camera records through the screen. (From Haith, in press, courtesy Springer-Verlag.)

where the baby looked at any moment by measuring the distance between the reflections of the calibration lights and the center of the pupil on the videotape record.

The stimulus in this particular setup is a window screen that is supported by rails just in front of the overhead metal platform. Typically, black and white stimuli are spray-painted on the screen. Because the screen is illuminated by lights located on either side of the baby's head and there is no light behind the screen, the baby sees only the stimulus. Of course, the invisible beams from the lamps pass through the screen, and the camera records the light reflected back through it. To summarize, as the baby looks at the visual stimuli on the screen, his eye is illuminated by invisible lights and recorded by an infrared TV camera onto videotape. Because we record only a 1-inch × 1-inch area, we typically try to stabilize the baby's head by presenting a nipple for the infant to suck. We also cover the unrecorded eye to eliminate the effect of binocular deconvergence. Sucking activity can be recorded with a pressure transducer and polygraph for later analysis and correlation with visual activity. A sketch of a recorded eye is shown in Figure 2.2.

One problem with this technique is that it is difficult to show a baby three-dimensional or projected stimuli; the experimenter is limited to stimuli that can be spray-painted on screens or to flat stimuli that can be placed on the screen outside the paths of the light beams and camera field. Figure 2.3 shows a variation of this basic procedure that solves this problem. A 20-inch × 12-inch mirror tilted at a 45° angle is mounted above the baby and reflects the field above and behind his head. The mirror is special, transmitting about 90° of the infrared light and reflecting about 90° of the visible light so that the baby sees only the light reflected from the mirror's front surface. Real three-dimensional stimuli may be placed in the reflected field, or a rear-projection screen may be used for projected stimuli. If care is taken to position these stimuli on the same virtual plane as the infrared lights and to register the stimulus with the infrared lights in this virtual plane, one can later determine exactly where the infant was looking at each moment.

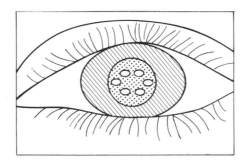

FIG. 2.2.   Photograph of an eye as it appears on the TV screen from the viedotape record. The six bright spots are infrared reflections of illuminators.

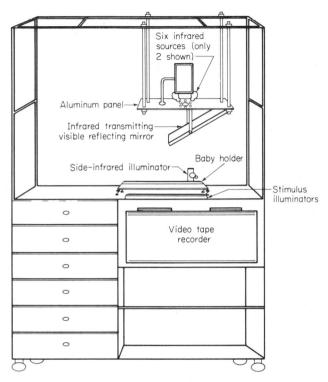

Six infrared
sources (only
2 shown)

Aluminum panel

Infrared transmitting
visible reflecting mirror

Baby holder

Side-infrared illuminator

Stimulus
illuminators

Video tape
recorder

FIG. 2.3.   Illustration of modified apparatus to record visual activity. Mirror reflects field above and behind the infant's head, permitting the presentation of three-dimensional or projected stimuli.

There is still a problem with both of these techniques. One cannot study how the infant inspects a stimulus whose position changes unless the motion is rigidly specified in time. Thus, for example, it is not possible to study how a baby scans his mother's face as she moves naturally while interacting with him. Figure 2.4 shows a further elaboration of the basic corneal-reflection procedure that solves this problem. There are two cameras behind the overhead mirror, both mounted horizontally. The top camera, as in the earlier arrangements, records the infant's eye, which is now reflected from a mirror (Mirror X) in front of the lens. The lower camera records what the baby sees directly through Mirror Y — in this case, the mother's face. The outputs of these two cameras are time synchronized to record alternately ½ sec of the infant's eye and ⅟₃₀ sec of the mother's face onto videotape. Each time a face is recorded, an audio pip is also recorded on the sound track of the videotape for later recovery of each face frame. Thus, the location of the mother's moving face can be measured each half sec and correlated with where the baby is looking on his visual field, permitting a determination of how the baby scans a face that moves in a fairly natural unconstrained manner.

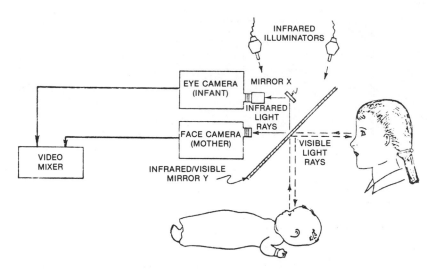

FIG. 2.4.   Illustration of apparatus to record simultaneously the infant's visual activity and the location of an adult's face that moves unpredictably. (From Haith, Bergman, & Moore, ©1977, with the permission of the American Association for the Advancement of Science.)

Other refinements in recording that we have used are as follows. A videomixer and another TV camera can be added either to the single camera or to the dual camera setup to record a videoframe counter that aids later identification of specific portions of the videotape. Of greater experimental interest, we have recorded a digital readout of heart rate on the videoframe. The resulting simultaneous display of physiological and visual activity is invaluable for gaining an intuitive feeling for the interrelation of these variables, an especially important feure in exploratory research.

Measurement

It is important to appreciate that measurement of the video record of visual activity can be carried out on several levels that require different degrees of technical sophistication. Although the recording techniques I described have been possible for at least 7 years, they have not been widely adopted, and I think the key reason is that investigators have assumed a necessary link between the recording technique and the purpose for which it was initially used — to measure the sequence of fixation points. I have used the term *visual activity* to this point rather than *eye movements* advisedly. Specification of fixation sequences capture only one aspect of visual activity, an aspect that may be irrelevant for many purposes. It is important to remember that the recording procedure, a procedure that is fairly easy to implement, simply provides a very accurate and complete record of the original behavior that experimenters can later evaluate in accordance with their own purposes. Although specific determination of fixation sequences is an expensive and technically complicated matter, a number of useful measures may be obtained without special equipment. Basically, we can break down the variables we have used into observational measures and fixation measures.

Kearsley (1973) used an observational measure in a study of newborns' orienting and defensive reactions to various parameters of sound. The videotape was judged each sec for the direction of eyelid opening or closing that, in turn, was correlated with heart-rate responsivity. Kearsley obtained definite evidence of positive orienting (eye opening) to some sounds and an effect of the rate of sound onset on the direction of eyelid opening. For most parameters, the simple eyelid-opening measure was more powerful than the more complicated heart-rate measure that is typically used to measure orienting.

Observational measures have also been used in research I have done on newborns' visual activity in complete darkness and in a situation with light but no pattern (Haith, 1976; Haith, in press). Three- and four-category scales were devised for judgments that were made each 2.5 secs for degree of eyelid opening, sharpness of eye movement, size of eye movement, and degree of control of eye movement. The reliability of these scales usually exceeded 0.90, and all of them discriminated scanning in light from that in darkness. Since continuous scanning activity was observed in darkness, even these relatively crude measures permitted strong disclaimers to the notion that newborns' visual scanning consists only of reflexive responses to available light stimulation.

It is even possible to use observational techniques to judge location of fixation in the visual field if one can be satisfied with an indication of the general region in which the infant is fixating. Essentially, the observer makes regular, time-sampled judgments concerning the relation of the center of the pupil to the reflected infrared light array (Salapatek, 1975). The general region of the visual field fixated can be designated and fixation frequency in each of several regions determined fairly reliably.

Precise determination of fixations requires careful measurement and a much higher level of technical sophistication. Basically, one must measure the distance from the center of the pupil to one of the infrared reflections on the cornea for each videoframe of concern.[1] A measurement is obtained as shown in Figure 2.5. First, the videotape record is played back into a video disc, which records a videoframe from the tape each half sec and

---

[1]The uncorrected corneal reflection procedure assumes that a line drawn through the center of the pupil and lens strikes the retina at the position of the fovea. This assumption is correct only to the first order because of a 5° average divergence (for the adult) between the visual and geometric axes of the eye. A discussion of this problem and our techniques for dealing with it may be found in the *procedure* section of Mendelson and Haith (1976).

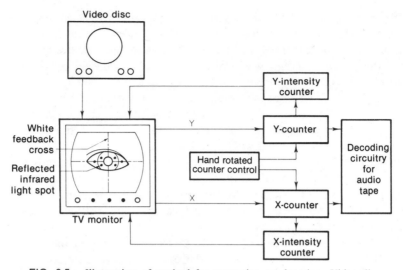

FIG. 2.5. Illustration of method for measuring eye location. Video disc displayed a single videoframe permitting measurement of the Cartesian coordinate of pupil center and one infrared light spot from which fixation position could be determined. Hand-rotated counter controls were adjusted until intersection of white cross was positioned at point of interest. Contents of X and Y counters were recorded onto audiotape. (From Haith, in press, courtesy Springer–Verlag.)

stores up to 500 individual frames. The disc can display any one frame indefinitely to permit the necessary measurements. A scorer rotates knobs to move vertical and horizontal crosshairs across the screen until they intersect at the point of interest—either a reflection of an infrared light or the center of the pupil. Electronic counters keep track of the number of TV lines from the top of the TV screen to the horizontal line and the number of points from the side of the TV screen to the vertical line, which, of course, constitute the Cartesian coordinates of the measured point. The scorer then presses a button that automatically records the contents of these counters onto an audiotape recorder (Lentz & Haith, 1969), along with information about which frame was recorded and which infrared light was measured.

If a moving stimulus field was used as described in the third recording version, then alternating pictures of the stimulus (e.g., a face) and the eye are recorded onto the video disc through circuitry that senses the recorded pip on the audio track of the videotape recorder. In the case where a mother's face is used, we measure the location of her eyes every half sec.[2]

The audiotape containing the numerical measurements is fed into a com-

---

[2]Nine points on the adult's face are measured on 10 separate frames for accurate determination of the position of facial features for data analysis. Thus, by measuring only the position of the eyes on each face frame, the location of all other face features on that frame can be specified.

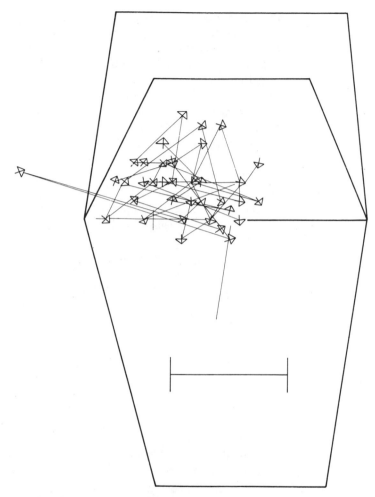

FIG. 2.6. Computer plot that reconstructed the scanning of a 7 week old of his mother's face as she talked.

puter that retrieves the numbers and calculates the subject's fixation point on his visual field. These numbers can be used to recreate the infant's fixation sequence over the field as shown in Figure 2.6, which depicts the scanning of a 2-month old over his mother's face. Each arrow represents a fixation point. The arrow is upright for the first fixation and rotates a few degrees clockwise for each successive fixation. The numbers can also be entered into statistical analyses to obtain various indicators of the infant's scanning activity.

Analysis

Of the recording, measurement, and analysis triad, analysis is by far in the most primitive state. A major frustration in faithfully preserving the original visual behavior is the difficulty of translating that behavior into numbers that do it justice. We have developed in excess of 25 measures that can be separated into measures of fixation and measures of scanning.

The measures of fixation include average location on the vertical and horizontal axes, the range or spread of fixation along these axes, and the frequency of fixation in various regions of interest (e.g., in the eye area of the mother's face). All of these measures have proved informative.

Measures of scanning combine fixations from successive fixation points to derive parameters of eye movement. The possibilities for analysis are endless. We have found average size of eye movement and the frequency of movements that cross particular areas of the stimulus to be most useful. A key concern is to go beyond analysis of successive fixations, two at a time, in order to represent the pattern of scanning. Here is where the frustration lies. Analysis by Markov chains or other techniques of sequential analysis are simply not adequate. Although we have explored a variety of approaches, including Fourier analysis of eye-movement patterns, we still have not arrived at an approach that we feel captures the most interesting aspects of the scanning pattern. One of the problems is that not every eye movement is meaningful for questions that are typically asked about the data; but there is currently no objective way to determine which eye movements are meaningful and which are not. To utilize fully the powerful techniques available to us, we need breakthroughs in both statistical analyses and in theories that can make sense of potential patterns.

Future directions

One of the most difficult aspects of doing eye-movement research is the tedium involved in measuring pupil center and reflected infrared light markers after the data are recorded. This activity alone requires about 4.5 hours for 3 minutes of real-time data, even when with stimulus is stationary and does not itself have to be measured. Ideally, a computer could read the output from the TV camera that records the eye or from a videotape recorder and automatically determine the pupil center and the point of fixation. Such a system would permit faster determination of scan sequences, making it possible to pace presentation of visual stimuli to the subject's level or even to vary stimuli in real time so that what is presented to an infant depends on how he scans the field. This is not a novel idea as systems have been used to do exactly this with adults (e.g., see Young & Sheena, 1975). However, video systems that require no attachment to the head have only recently been developed to the point where they are operable. The basic principle is as follows. As the TV picture is generated by a flying spot that moves from the top of the screen to the bottom and from left to right, a computer keeps track of the particular horizontal TV line and the location of the flying spot on the horizontal axis at each moment. When the flying spot reaches the black area of the pupil, the output voltage from the camera drops below a threshold value. The computer keeps track of the TV lines and points on which threshold was crossed. After each scan (there are 60 scans per sec), a simple division is carried out to find pupil center. Two problems make this technique difficult to use with infants. The first is that poor iris pigmentation, especially in newborns, makes the iris–pupil boundary difficult to detect electronically. The second is that the slightest head movement causes problems, because the computer cannot distinguish between a shift in pupil center caused by a head movement and a shift resulting from eye movement. Thus, severe head constraint is required.

A technique reported by Merchant and Morrissette (1974) overcomes these limitations, and our laboratory and laboratories at Oxford University (Albutt et al., unpublished manuscript) and the University of Paris (Boudonniere et al., 1978) are adapting this technique for work with infants.[3] The basic setup is shown in Figure 2.7. Again, a TV camera records the image of the eye, but instead of six infrared lights illuminating the eye from around the camera, one infrared light collimator is used that, by use of a small mirror (infrared transmitting and visible reflecting), is placed on the same optical axis as the recording camera. With this arrangement, a very bright but small reflection is again produced from the cornea. Additionally, light is reflected from the retina back from the pupil so that the pupil appears milky white instead of black. This white level is electronically discriminated from the darker-appearing iris much more easily than the black level produced by conventional lighting. There is an additional bonus of this arrangement that permits determination of whether shifts in pupil location are produced by head movements or eye movements. When the head moves, the calculated pupil center and the bright corneal reflection move together; however, when the eye rotates (the point of fixation changes), the distance between pupil center and reflected spot changes. Thus, if a second tracking circuit is used, and the threshold is adjusted to detect only the brighter white corneal spot, the difference in location of spot center and pupil center can be calculated, indicating fixation position unaffected by head position. This setup permits determination of eye position 60 times a sec, and we have achieved accuracy over a $12° \times 12°$ visual field of better than $.33°$ of visual angle with 5 year olds and adults.

There are still some problems to be worked out with this approach. For example, in newborns, part of the pupil is often obscured, and large head movements and changes in corneal moisture change light reflectance levels. But both the Oxford lab and our lab have achieved some success with this approach, and its full use seems imminent.

---

[3]The white-pupil procedure described here is a spinoff of a technique developed for research with older children. Ronald Sturm and Dale Steffen designed the electronics, and Gwilm Parry and Owen Barnes implemented the electronics and optics. Karen Cohen developed the necessary computer programs and Bruce Platt, Bennett Bertenthal, and Owen Barnes have adapted the techniques for infant research. Apparatus development was funded principally by the Grant Foundation.

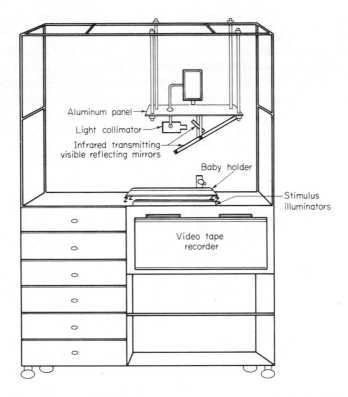

FIG. 2.7.   Illustration of modified apparatus to record visual activity.
Light collimator produces an invisible collimated beam that is reflected by
the small mirror to the eye along the same optical axis as the recording
camera. With this arrangement light reflected from the retina backlights the
pupil, making it appear white.

QUESTIONS ABOUT NEWBORNS

Now that I have described the basic techniques, it seems reasonable to ask
what they are useful for. Rather than present a series of studies we have
done, I will organize this discussion around 5 questions: What can a baby
see? How is visual activity organized? What drives visual activity? How is
visual activity related to the activity of other perceptual systems? What can
visual activity tell us about cognition on the one hand and brain function on
the other? Newborn research and research on older infants are considered
separately. Only the major features of studies are described as they pertain
to the questions under consideration.

What Can Newborns See?

This question typically takes the form: To what aspects of the visual world arc newborns scnsitivc? Our obscrvations (Haith, 1976; Haith, in press) of visual activity in light and in absolute darkness confirm what other techniques have told us: newborns detect light as shown by measures of degree of eye opening, eye control, size of eye movements, and sharpness of eye movements (for reviews of other techniques see Haith, in press; Haith & Campos, 1977). Also, even unaided observation of the eyes indicates that newborns will track a moving object (Barton, Birns, & Ronch, 1971). Studies of eye movements indicate that newborns detect lights presented to their peripheral visual fields at least as far as 25° from center and make directionally appropriate first eye movements toward them (Harris & Mcfarlane, 1974).

Further studies have inquired into the degree to which newborns see patterns by capitalizing on their tendency to look at a patterned surface in preference to an unpatterned one. By successfully reducing the size of elements in a pattern and finding when preference vanishes, one can even estimate visual acuity at this early age (Fantz, Ordy, & Udelf, 1962).

In our own research we have demonstrated that newborns respond fairly enthusiastically to vertical or horizontal bars and edges, as shown in the first two rows of Figure 2.8. Fixation patterns were measured as infants scanned one of these patterns or an unpatterned field. Comparison of scanning in these two situations revealed that newborns fixated the regions of black–white contour and that they tended to make eye movements that

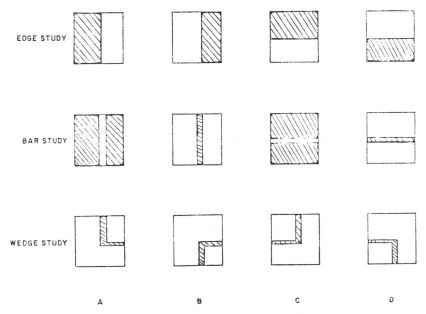

FIG. 2.8.   The edges and bars used are illustrated in the first two rows and the angle stimuli in the third row. Subjects were presented either Stimuli A and C or B and D. (From Haith, in press, courtesy Springer-Verlag.)

crossed back and forth over the contours. We have gone somewhat further in asking whether more than contour, per se, is detected. In an earlier report that newborns scanned near the angles of an equilateral triangle, Salapatek and Kessen (1966) suggested that the babies might be sensitive to at least the element of form represented in an angle. However, the 60° angles of a triangle also provide more contour density than the straight sides. We carried out a study with a 90° angle formed by joining vertical and horizontal bars, as shown in the third row of Figure 2.8. Analyses of fixation distribution in critical regions revealed no special attractiveness of the angle. To this point, then, we are justified in saying that newborns detect light even in the periphery, stimulus movement, sharp contours, and probably the difference between regions of high and low contour density. There is no compelling evidence that contour arrangement is detected.

How is Visual Activity Organized?

As mentioned earlier, questions about the organization of visual activity at birth are virtually foreign to the field of early infancy. Perhaps this is because newborns have been characterized as totally reflexive to light; given this assumption, "organization" lies in the stimulus world, not in the baby. But the lack of concern for this question may also reflect the tendency of investigators not to think about how organismic structure affects behavior. The closest facsimile in the area of infancy are theories of visual preference that are concerned with how much longer a baby will look at Stimulus A as opposed to Stimulus B, depending on the difference in levels along some parameter that distinguishes them. However, this is only a question about stimulus selection, not about the way babies deal with or process the stimuli. For a full understanding of cognitive development, I believe that it is as important to learn how infants deploy their resources as it is to learn what resources they possess. Translated to our work, I think it is as important to study how infants acquire information from their visual world as it is to study what infants can see. Such studies about newborns can tell us interesting things about how biology structures infants and influences their earliest explorations of the visual world.

In our first study, we observed newborns in absolute darkness in order to get the purest indication possible of the organization of newborn visual activity free of visual stimulation. Strict reflex theory would predict the absence of visual activity in the absence of visual input. For comparison, we also observed the same infants as they scanned a homogeneous field. In darkness, newborns opened their eyes widely, frequently to the point of strain, and actively scanned, moving their eyes almost every half sec. In contrast to the unpatterned light situation, they showed wider eye opening, more eye control, and eye movements that were sharper, smaller, and had more clearly defined initial and terminal fixation. Thus, newborns enter the world equipped to seek out visual unput on their own, apart from external stimulation. The impression newborns give in darkness is that they are engaged in an intense visual search, an activity that perhaps maximizes the likelihood of detecting subtle contours and dim stimuli. An unexpected finding was the greater degree of eye control in darkness than in light; temporal and nasal nystagmus were observed in about 20% of the 2.5-sec intervals in the light situation but in less than 1% of the intervals of darkness. I have suggested elsewhere (Haith,1976; Haith, in press) that scanning may be controlled by an endogenous system in darkness, but that control may be given over partially to exogenous stimuli in light; in a homogeneous field, no exogenous stimuli are available around which scanning can be organized. Out of control episodes result.

I have mentioned already the stimuli (Figure 2.8) that we used in studies of pattern scanning. When horizontal or vertical bars or edges are placed in a scannable portion of the newborns' visual field, they tend to fixate near the contours and to make eye movements that cross them. Those eye movements that cross the contours are larger on the average than those that do not, indicating that newborns do not simply happen to cross the edge because they are close to it; if we can talk about intention in newborns, it indeed appears that they intend to cross contours.

From these findings and a logic I have elaborated elsewhere (Haith, in press), I have summarized our observations in terms of the organization that I think newborns bring to their visual world. This can be stated in terms of rules that the newborns obey:

1. if awake and alert, open eyes;
2. if no light, maintain an intense vigilant search;
3. if find light but no edges, continue to search;
4. if locate contour, stay near it and attempt to cross back and forth over it;
5. maintain a relatively narrow scanning range if the located contour is in a region of other contours and a broader range if the contour density is low.

This last rule accounts for constrained scanning reported near 60° angles by Salapatek and Kessen (1966) that was not found when 90° angles were used.

Admittedly, this "rule system" is little more than an empirical generalization of the findings we have obtained. But, because it addresses the organization of visual scanning and does so from the organism's point of view, I think it conveys the general idea of the approach I am arguing for. I have also postulated two scanning routines in newborns that serve these rules: an Ambient Scan Routine (ASR) that serves to find contours and an Inspection Routine (IR) that processes a contour once located. I suggest that the IR suppresses the ASR to the extent that the latter produces firing in cells of the visual cortex; but this discussion is treated under the next question.

Future work will be directed at articulating the characteristics of the ASR and IR and what the newborn's stop rules might be. What terminates inspection? One lead a postdoctoral fellow in my lab, Bruce Platt, is following, is that interesting peripheral stimuli may terminate inspection of a central stimulus.

What Drives or Motivates Visual Scanning?

It is reasonable to ask about the "force" behind visual scanning. One answer is that no such construct need be entertained; visual scanning simply reflects the activity of a biological organism and partially defines the wiring or structure of that organism. This basic question has not been treated adequately in the literature, but motivation has been implicitly assumed in virtually every account of visual attention. "Preference" is a concept that has found broad acceptance in a motivational as well as in a paradigmatic sense. In fact, often unappreciated is the fact that most of the past research on infant vision has been addressed more to the question of infant motivation than to that of visual perception.

I have elaborated elsewhere (Haith, in press) the full logic for assuming that the "force" driving newborns' scanning activity is the desire to maintain visual cortical firing activity at a maximal (up to an asymptote) level. Actually we can state this in a less anthropomorphic form. Newborns behave in a fashion that tends to increase the rate (up to a level) of cortical firing. When the IR is not producing a high firing level, as when a baby scans a low-contour area, the ASR is relatively unsuppressed, resulting in a broad scan and a high probability of detecting other contour regions with higher firing potential.

Maintenance of visual cortical firing rate is postulated as the "force" for organization because this simple assertion accounts for so many phenomena:

1. Why newborns scan in darkness: ambient cortical firing rate is low in the absence of stimulation, especially in an immature organism (Hubel & Wiesel, 1963; Huttenlocher, 1967; Purpura, 1971).

2. Why they continue to scan broadly in unpatterned light: light levels, per se, do not affect cortical firing rate (Huber & Wiesel, 1959), only contrast edges do.

3. Why newborns fixate near a contour: edges falling near the fovea stimulate more receptive fields and, hence, produce more cortical firing than when they fall on peripheral fields.

4. Why newborns cross back and forth over edges: maximal cortical firing for particular cells is produced when edges first fall within their receptive field (Hartline, 1969; Hubel & Wiesel, 1962). Relocation of an edge by eye movement would tend to stimulate unadapted regions.

5. Why newborns stay near contours more as contour density increases: the more edges, the more firing.

What is the Interrelation Between Sensori-Perceptual Modes?

I have already mentioned Kearsley's (1973) use of visual activity to index newborn sensitivity to auditory stimuli. I think we can conclude from Kearsley's study that in addition to indexing (a) what newborns can see, (b) how they are organized to seek visual information, and (c) what information they have gathered, visual activity reflects general system mobilization. Casual interaction with other adults suggests that the eyes serve as general communicators of expression and meaning, and it appears as though the same sort of general system status may be indexed by measures of newborns' visual activity.

Typically, however, newborns' visual activity has been used only in a reflexive manner to measure the integrity of the auditory sense — as in the auropalpebral and oculogyric reflexes. Some work has been done to determine whether newborns move their eyes toward a sound source, presumably an indication of sound localization, but only brief sound pulses have been used (for a review, see Mendelson & Haith, 1976). To my knowledge, no one has attempted to study how extravisual input affects scanning activity. In a series of studies in which long-duration, natural sound stimuli were used, Mendelson and I demonstrated not only that newborns tend, initially, to scan a stimulus more when it is congruent with the spatial location of a sound than when it is not, but also that sound tends to organize visual activity (Mendelson & Haith, 1976). For example, the out-of-control eye movement reported when newborns scan a blank field is sharply reduced when they hear a human voice. These findings suggest interrelations between audition and vision that are much more complicated than the reflexive connections that were thought to be all that exists at birth.

Bennett Bertenthal, Bruce Platt, Morton Mendelson, and I are now beginning to research the question of whether newborns are equipped to detect auditory–visual correspondences other than spatial location as found, for instance, in common rhythms. Is the maintenance or termination of visual scanning of a stimulus determined by the extent to which it corresponds to the rhythm of an auditory stimulus?

QUESTIONS ABOUT INFANTS BETWEEN 3 WEEKS AND 4 MONTHS

What Do Older Infants See?

We concluded in our discussion of the research on newborns that little or no evidence exists that they detect anything more than contours and differences in contour density. One of the more exciting questions in the field of early infancy is how and when infants begin to put together portions of their visual field; i.e., organize the elements of their visual world. There have been several demonstrations that babies beyond 2 months of age do sense differences in arrangements of elements (Cornell, 1975; Fantz, Fagan, Miranda, 1975; Ruff & Birch, 1974), but we have no good conceptualizations of what principles might be involved.

Kathy Lochridge is now carrying out a dissertation to test the idea that at the age of around 2 months, babies begin to obey Gestalt principles of visual organization. She is examining babies' scanning of the forms shown in Figure 2.9 before and after 2 months of age. She expects infants after 2 months of age to look at the location of the changed element more when the nonsymmetric form (top two rows) is presented than when the symmetric form (third row) is shown. If so then it must be the case that the unchanged elements possess a perceptual continuity that is clearly a factor in appreciating configuration. Note that even though the concern here is with

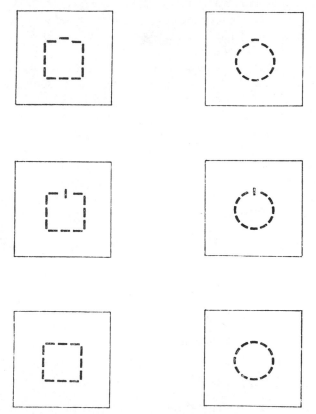

FIG. 2.9.   Stimuli used in configuration study by Kathy Lochridge.

what babies see rather than with how they scan, it would still be next to impossible to do this study without precise measures of scanning.

Another graduate student, Sandy Pipp, has studied when babies perceive visual depth (Pipp & Haith, 1977). She presented raised, recessed, or flat white bars on a black field to 1- and 2-month-old babies. Evidence for sensitivity to depth cues was indicated by different visual measures for the two groups: Number of fixations near the bars was the best indicator for 4 week olds whereas style of scanning was best for the 8 week olds.

How Is Visual Activity Organized
After the Newborn Period?

The organization of visual scanning in infants beyond 2 months of age has not been explored as extensively as in newborns, so we lack a succinct set of principles to account for information seeking and inspection activity. However, the information that has been gathered suggests that the rules of scanning are much more complicated for older infants than for newborns. Perhaps newborns' visual activity is governed by fairly general principles that make adaptive biological sense for virtually any environment into which they are thrust. Older infants' behavior, on the other hand, may be more dependent on experience and the meaning of the situation.

Striking differences between newborns and infants in their first 2 months have been uncovered in visual scanning. For example, whereas newborns will scan a blank white or black field virtually as long as they are awake, older infants will not scan a blank field at all (Donnee, 1972; Pipp, 1975; Salapatek, 1973). Pipp suggested that the cue for termination of the ASR changes after the newborn period; essentially, older infants act as though they do not expect to find information in a blank field after having once taken an inventory of it.

A second shift in the organization of scanning or, more precisely, inspection activity, is the tendency for newborns to scan the external features of a stimulus whereas older infants scan internally. We utilized the third version of the apparatus I described (p. 27), to examine how babies at different ages scan real adult faces when the face remained stationary, moved, or moved and talked (Bergman, Haith, & Mann, 1971; Haith, Bergman, & Moore, 1977). Babies 3 to 5 weeks of age acted like newborns in that they tended to scan the high contrast skin–hair and chin–garment borders of the face. However, at 7 weeks of age babies primarily scanned the internal features of the face. The differences were very substantial, with 3 to 5 week olds devoting only 43% of their face fixations to the internal portions whereas 7 and 9 to 11 week olds gave 66% and 67%, respectively.

Maurer and Salapatek (1976) confirmed these findings, and Salapatek (1973) also reported similar tendencies for younger infants to scan the borders of geometric figures whereas older infants looked more at internal detail. We have not yet determined whether the crucial aspect of this difference is the inability of newborns to process internal features or whether it simply reflects their attraction to long, continuous, high-contrast edges. This latter interpretation fits with Fantz, Fagan, and Miranda's (1975) suggestion that newborns prefer larger stimuli more than do older infants. However, if there is something about borders that obscures internal detail for newborns, then Salapatek's (1975) suggestion that this age shift may imply something about brain function is intriguing. He pointed up a similarity between border scanning in newborns and the inability of monkeys with visual striate lesions to find stimuli surrounded by a border.

The organization of scanning may also be increasingly affected by the meaning of a stimulus based on the infant's past experience. Of course, meaningful associations are only possible if the infant has a durable memory capacity; several studies have demonstrated that feats requiring memory such as habituation, response to novelty, and learning are much more easily demonstrated after 2 months than before (Jeffrey & Cohen, 1971; Sameroff, 1972). An interesting finding in the face study I just described is that 7 and 9 to 11 week olds scanned the eye more than any other internal feature of the face. Although the attractiveness of eyes is probably based partially on physical features alone, eyes may also be attractive because they carry information concerning the intentions and feelings of the caretaker. An additional finding, which I discuss below, cannot be explained in terms of visual physical features alone: when an adult speaks to an infant, fixation density in the eye area increases, and the size of eye movements in that area decreases.

Still another factor affecting scanning may be memory. One would expect that a familiar object would be scanned differently from an unfamiliar one. I am somewhat embarrassed to say that, although we know from a host of studies that familiar objects will be looked at less than novel objects, we have no data on how familiarity affects the style of scanning in infants. Andre Bullinger recently carried out an interesting study in our laboratory to test a suggestion by Bower (1974) that infants at one age treat an old object as new if it changes location, whereas, for older infants, the identity of an object is not vulnerable to spatial relocation. Bullinger constructed a fascinating multicolored "thing-a-majig" out of Lego blocks and presented it in one location for about 30 secs. He then moved it to a different location or returned it to the same location. Visual activity was monitored continuously. Analyses have not been completed, but the data from one subject revealed a clear tendency to look back at the old vacated location when the object was moved to a new spot.

All of us who have studied infant vision have concentrated on how various parameters affect visual exploration of a currently present visual array. As I mentioned previously, these parameters include the physical features of the array, infants' familiarity with that array, and its meaning for them. But we are leaving something out by treating infants as though the here-and-now comprises all the factors affecting visual activity. Certainly, adults not only explore their world based on what is present, but also on what they *expect* to see and where they expect to see it (Neisser, 1976). Visual activity is ideal for studying infants' ability to anticipate future events because eye movements are so fast and mobile, and therefore capable of reflecting the type of rapid continuous brain activity we usually associate with the moment-to-moment changes in the visual world that probably form the substance of early expectations.

We have now carried out a study of eye movements in 2 and 3 month old babies to a two-light pattern that alternates regularly or flashes randomly. An alternating pattern consists of onset of Light 1 for 0.5 secs, followed by nothing for 0.5 secs, then Light 2 for 0.5 secs, nothing for 0.5 secs, and so on. We have seen 3 month olds repeatedly anticipate the next flash in this sequence by an appropriate eye movement in the interflash interval after only 30 secs of experience. Two month olds have not shown much anticipation, only managing to fixate each new location after flash onset; often, in fact, they do not land on the new location until the light has gone off. These data are preliminary, but I cannot think of a more cognitively relevant area to study than the development of expectancies. If our paradigm for studying expectancy can be optimized, we should be able to vary the complexity of the sequence that generated the display and, thereby, learn at what age level various sequences can be mastered. The potential for studying individual differences and the effect of brain trauma should also be obvious.

I should point out that anticipation is not an all-or-none affair; one can see the actual unfolding of an anticipation, sometimes in less than a minute. Infants have been observed to go through the following sequence in less than 1 min with the repeating right-off-left-off light series: (a) general orientation to the lights without regular tracking; (b) regular tracking but fixations lag so far behind light onset that the light is off by the time the baby begins an eye movement; (c) regular tracking and faster response so that the light is fixated before offset; (d) regular tracking and fixation so soon after light onset (within 200 msec) that the command for an eye movement must have been generated before the light came on; (e) anticipation of the light with an eye fixation at the oncoming light position before light onset. Obviously, partial ontogenesis of anticipation could be studied even if full anticipation were not accomplished.

What Drives Visual Scanning in the Older Infant?

We do not have a satisfying answer to this question, certainly nothing as straightforward as for newborns. I have suggested above that the organization of scanning is affected by features of the visual array, its meaning and familiarity, as well as by what the infant expects to happen next. In fact, I am speculating about most of these factors because, even though they satisfy good sense, the hard data are still lacking. Thus, I have little more to suggest about what drives visual scanning in older infants than I do for adults whose inspection and scanning activities are affected both by the visual context and the tasks they have set for themselves. A "task" for an infant might be a search for meaning, for familiarity, for relief from boredom, etc. The question then becomes what determines the task, and I do not know the answer. I can suggest, however, that current formulations for what controls visual activity (such as the amount of contour in the stimulus, the novelty of the stimulus, or, for that matter, any stimulus dimension) put emphasis on the organization of the visual world and do not begin to address the important questions about what lies behind the organization of visual activity.

How Do the Auditory and Visual Interrelations Develop?

When discussing auditory–visual relations in newborns, I made the point that the question is not only how auditory stimuli affect the reception of visual stimuli, but how the activity of listening affects the activity of look-ing. In newborns, we learned that the location of a sound affects the direc-tion of scanning activity and that when babies listen to a voice, their visual scanning is more controlled than when they are not listening.

We have evidence that the auditory–visual relations may become more specified, even by the age of 7 weeks. In the face study I described earlier, a condition of theoretical interest was that in which the adult talked. By most predictions, the increased lip movement and lip–tooth contrast that accom-pany talking should have produced greater fixation on the mouth area than was obtained in the nontalking conditions. However, 7 and 9 to 11 week olds looked relatively less at the mouth area and more at the eye area during talking, which suggests a natural tie between what babies are listening to and what they look at. But not only does sound affect where they look, it affects how they look. Eye movements were smaller and the range of fixa-tions more constricted in the talking condition; these measures indicate a more intensified scan of the eye area. Future work will determine whether the effect of voice on scanning of a real face is unique to the voice or a general property of sound.

APPLICATION

I stated earlier that we have not been concerned principally with the real-world application of our techniques. But you may be interested to hear about an adaptation of our procedures that was carried out by Perry Butterfield in collaboration with Robert Emde and Bruce Platt (Butterfield

& Platt, in press). Emde has been interested in the mother–infant interaction in the first few hours after birth and feels that visual interaction may be an important component. A factor that may decrease the possibility of interaction, however, is the silver nitrate prophylaxis required for protection against gonorrhea, because it causes swelling and irritation to many newborns' eyes. As far as is known, the silver nitrate application can be delayed for several hours after birth with equal prophylactic effect. Thus it is reasonable to ask if it restricts visual activity to the possible detriment of mother–infant interaction. If so, consideration of delayed treatment might be reasonable. It was found that silver-nitrate treatment did impede visual tracking and eye-opening in neonates. These investigators are currently attempting to replicate this finding and to determine whether, in fact, there is also an effect on mother–infant interaction.

COGNITION AND BRAIN FUNCTION

I started this chapter by considering briefly whether it is reasonable to treat early infant activity as though it were cognitive. I hope by now it is apparent that the issue is not worth arguing. Visual scanning in newborns may be closely bound by the strictures of biology and current visual context, but soon afterwards visual activity reflects processes we can all agree form, at least, the basis for cognitive activity. And we will not understand even 8 week olds without knowing the principles governing their earlier activity.

Although I have not yet addressed the inferences we can draw from visual activity to brain function, several speculations have been put forward and are relevant to the goals of this conference. Bronson (1974), for example, suggested that the shifts in visual activity of infants around 2 months of age that I have talked about, as well as other behavioral changes, may reflect a change from subcorticl to cortical control of visual behavior. Specifically, he argued that the phylogenetically older collicular system might control visual activity prior to 2 months and the phylogenetically more recent primary cortical pathways control it later. My counterarguments to this idea have been presented elsewhere (Haith & Campos, 1977). However, I do not disagree that the associative cortical areas probably begin to play a role only after 2 months of age, the time when memory and meaning begin to play a role in visual activity. If so, then we may be able to tell something about the development of brain function from the techniques we have developed.

Although it may never be possible to test fully the interrelation between brain function and visual activity, it may be possible to explore such relations in an animal model. Morton Mendelson and Patricia Goldman at the National Institute of Mental Health and myself are exploring this possibility in the rhesus monkey. First, Mendelson is gathering data on normal visual development from birth in intact rhesus monkeys, using the techniques of eye recording I described earlier. If the normal sequence in rhesus monkeys parallels that found in humans, then studies of the effects of specific surgical interventions will be indicated. If selected behavioral functions are affected by such intervention, we will have a basis for conjecture about what visual accomplishments or lack of them mean in terms of brain development in human infants. This project itself is in its infancy but has exciting potential.

SUMMARY

Let me reiterate the major points of this paper. The eyes are a goldmine of information for the researcher of infancy. The facial and extraocular musculature is remarkably well developed at birth. Significant information can be gained at several levels of analysis starting from the most general observational level using parameters such as degree of eye opening to the level of precision required for exact determination of fixation position. Careful observation of visual activity serves as a source of inference about the infants' states (arousal and emotional), what they can see and have seen of the presented array, how their exploratory and inspection activities are organized, and what factors motivate their looking behavior. Under the proper conditions, further inferences can be made concerning their ability to process, remember, and expect visual information as well as inferences concerning its meaning for them. Finally, visual activity can indicate some aspects of infants' whole-system, multimodal organization as in the effect of sound on visual search. From this list, I hope that it is clear that much more can be learned about babies from their visual activity than simply what they can see. In fact, the important aspect of cognitive ability is not the receptive capabilities or even the stored knowledge organisms possess: it is how these resources are deployed that matters.

Unfortunately, our conceptual and statistical tools for analyzing patterned behavior over time are still severely limited. We need better theories to guide the search for meaning in the patterned data and better quantitative procedures for uncovering patterns that, in turn, can suggest theories. It is a bootstrapping operation, but one that is well worth the effort.

ACKNOWLEDGMENTS

It is the result of the cooperation and help of many people. I am grateful to the staff and administration of the Cambridge (Massachusetts) Hospital, and the Swedish Hospital (Denver, Colorado) for providing space and facilities for this work. Phil Porter, Chief of Pediatrics and Mildred Howard, head nurse, of the Cambridge Hospital, and Childress of the Swedish Hospital have been especially supportive of our work. Robert Lentz made invaluable contributions to technological development. Henry Gerbrands and Fred Morrison helped in the early stages of setting up laboratories, and Gwilym Parry and Owen Barnes have kept our laboratories functioning. Tina Turner, Gail Brent, Diane Lusk, Joy Corsi, Terry Bergman, Leah Mann, Morton Mendelson, Karen Cohen, Bennett Bertenthal, Debby Porter, and Cathy Purcell all helped in the running of subjects and/or the reduction of data. Many of these people have also helped in the development of the conceptualizations, as have Kathy Lochridge and Sandy Pipp, and I owe special thanks to Jerome Kagan, William Kessen, Phil Salapatek, and Arnold Sameroff for their counsel over the years as this research developed. Morton Mendelson and Michael Moore commented on an earlier version of this paper. Finally, I am grateful to Celeste Newman and Betty Richardson for help in preparing the paper.

This research was supported by NIMH Grant No. MH22020, by NICHHD Grant No. MH23412 and by a University of Denver Biomedical grant.

REFERENCES

Albutt, M. G. V., Bamborough, P., Churcher, J., Heywood, S. P., Rice, P. D., & Salter, S. H. *Eye movement recording by on-line analysis of television.* Unpublished manuscript, Oxford University.

Barton, S., Birns, B., & Ronch, J. Individual differences in the visual pursuit behavior of neonates. *Child Development,* 1971, **42**, 313–319.

Baudonniere, P. M., Pecheux, M. G., & Taranne, P. Un novel apparcil d'enregistrement automatique de l'activité occulomotrice du jeune enfant. *L'Annee psychologique,* 1978 (in press)

Bergman, T., Haith, M. M., & Mann, L. *Development of eye contact and facial scanning in infants.* Paper presented at the meetings of the Society for Research in Child Development, Minneapolis, 1971.

Bower, T. *Development in infancy.* San Francisco: W. H. Freeman Co., 1974.

Bronson, G. The postnatal growth of visual capacity. *Child Development,* 1974, **45**, 873–890.

Butterfield, P. M., Emde, R. N., & Platt, B. D. Effects of silver nitrate on initial visual behavior. *Amer. J. of diseases in children.* In press.

Cornell, E. H. Infants' visual attention to pattern arrangement and orientation. *Child Development,* 1975, **46**, 229–232.

Donnee, L. *The development of infants' scanning patterns to face and face-like stimuli under various auditory conditions.* Unpublished doctoral dissertation, Harvard University, 1972.

Fantz, R. L., Fagan, J. F., III., & Miranda, S. B. Early visual selectivity. In L. B. Cohen & P. Salapatek (Eds.), *Infant perception: From sensation to cognition* (Vol. 1). New York: Academic Press, 1975.

Fantz, R. L., Ordy, J. M., & Udelf, M. S. Maturation of pattern vision in infants during the first six months. *Journal of Comparative Physiological Psychology,* 1962, **55**, 907–917.

Haith, M. M. Infrared television recording and measurement of ocular behavior in the human infant. *American Psychologist,* 1969, **24**, 279–283.

Haith, M. M. *Organization of visual behavior at birth.* Paper presented at the twenty-first International Congress of Psychology Meetings, Paris, July 1976.

Haith, M. M. Visual competence in early infancy. In R. Held, H. Leibowitz, & H. L. Teuber (Eds.), *Handbook of sensory physiology* (Vol. VIII). Berlin: Springer-Verlag, in press.

Haith, M. M., Bergman, T., & Moore, M. Eye contact and facial scanning in early infancy. *Science,* 1977, **198**, 853–855.

Haith, M. M., & Campos, J. Human infancy. *Annual Review of Psychology,* 1977.

Harris, P., & Macfarlane, A. The growth of the effective visual field from birth to seven weeks. *Journal of Experimental Child Psychology,* 1974, **18**, 340–348.

Hartline, H. K. Visual receptors and retinal interaction. *Science,* 1969, **164**, 270–278.

Hubel, D. H., & Wiesel, T. N. Receptive fields of single neurons in the cat's striate cortex. *Journal of Physiology,* 1959, **148,** 574–591.

Hubel, D. H., & Wiesel, T. N. Receptive fields, binocular interaction and functional architecture in the cat's visual cortex. *Journal of Physiology,* 1962, **160,** 106–154.

Hubel, D. H., & Wiesel, T. N. Receptive fields of cells in striate cortex of very young visually inexperienced kittens. *Journal of Neurophysiology,* 1963, **26,** 944–1002.

Huttenlocher, P. R. Development of cortical neuronal activity in the neonatal cat. *Experimental Neurology,* 1967, **17,** 247–262.

Jeffrey, W. E., & Cohen, L. B. Habituation in the human infant. In H. Reese (Ed.), *Advances in child development and behavior* (Vol. 6), New York: Academic Press.

Kearsley, R. The newborn's response to auditory stimulation: A demonstration of orienting and defensive behavior. *Child Development,* 1973, **44,** 582–590.

Lentz, R., & Haith, M. M. Audio tape storage of experimental data: An application to tachiscopic research with children. *Behavior Research Methods & Instrumentation,* 1969, **1,** 273–275.

Maurer, D., & Salapatek, P. Developmental changes in the scanning of faces by infants. *Child Development,* 1976, **47,** 523–527.

Mendelson, M. J., & Haith, M. M. The relation between audition and vision in the human newborn. *Monographs of the Society for Research in Child Development,* 1976, **41**(Whole No. 4).

Merchant, J., & Morrissette, R. Remote measurement of eye direction allowing subject motion over one cubic foot of space. *IEEE Transactions on Biomedical Engineering,* 1974, **21,** 309.

Neisser, U. *Cognition and reality. San Francisco: W. H. Freeman Co., 1976.*

Piaget, J. *La naissance de l'intelligence chez l'enfant.* Neuchatel: Delachaux et Niestlé, 1936. [*The origins of intelligence in children.* New York: International Universities Press, 1952.]

Pipp, S. L. *Infant visual scanning patterns to depth and contrast.* Paper presented at the meetings of the Society for Research in Child Development, Denver, 1975.

Pipp, S., & Haith, M. M. Infant visual scanning of two- and three-dimensional forms. *Child development,* 1977, **48,** 1640–1644.

Purpura, D. P. Synaptogenesis in mammalian cortex: Problems and perspectives. In M. B. Sterman, D. J. McGinty, & A. M. Adinolfi (Eds.), *Brain development and behavior.* New York: Academic Press, 1971.

Ruff, H. A., & Birch, H. G. Infant visual fixation: The effects of concentricity, curvilinearity, and number of directions. *Journal of Experimental Child Psychology,* 1974, **17,** 460–473.

Salapatek, P. *Visual investigation of geometric pattern by the human infant.* Paper presented at the meeting of the Society for Research in Child Development, Philadephia, 1973.

Salapatek, P. Pattern perception in early infancy. In L. B. Cohen & P. Salapatek (Eds.), *Infant perception: From sensation to cognition* (Vol. 1). New York: Academic Press, 1975.

Salapatek, P., & Kessen, W. Visual scanning of triangles by the human newborn. *Journal of Experimental Child Psychology,* 1966, **3,** 155–167.

Sameroff, A. Learning and adaptation in infancy: A comparison of models. In H. Reese (Ed.), *Advances in child development and behavior* (Vol. 7). New York: Academic Press, 1972.

Young, L. R., & Sheena, D. Eye-movement measurement techniques. *American Psychologist,* 1975, **30,** 315–330.

3 Reactivity to Perceptual–Cognitive Events: Application for Infant Assessment

Philip R. Zelazo
Center for Behavioral Pediatrics and Infant Development
Tufts-New England Medical Center

A rebirth of infant research has occurred during the past 20 years. Major advances in methodology and technology have allowed basic research on infancy to flourish in a manner reminiscent of the early 1930s. Clearly, the infant has reignited the imagination of research psychologists. Insights and findings about infant development are occurring at an exponential rate, and there is a new, large, and respectable corpus of knowledge about infancy that has not yet influenced the daily life of infants or their parents. It is proper and reasonable to encourage the application of this knowledge to a vulnerable and sorely needed area of development, namely, the assessment of infant abilities.

It is widely accepted that tests of infant development have not fared well. It has been over a decade since Stott and Ball (1965) and Bayley (1966) have demonstrated that overall performance on tests of infant development among a normal sample does not predict later IQ. More recently, Willerman and Fiedler (1974) have shown that a retrospective examination of children with IQs of 140 or more at 4 years of age were not distinguishable from normal children at 8 months of age. They concluded that scores on the Bayley Scales of Mental and Motor Development did not distinguish the intellectually precocious children from the total sample of infants at 8 months with any useful reliability. What are the reasons for the predictive difficulties of infant tests? Many explanations have been offered (cf, Zelazo, 1976a) but it has generally not been considered that the measures of motor performance that play such a dominant role in existing tests may be invalid indices of cognitive development. For example, Bayley (1969) reported that the mental portion of the widely used Scales of Infant Development bears a sizable correlation ($r = .55$) with the motor scale.

The fallibility of existing infant tests, if not their lack of validity, appears clear. There are numerous reported instances of children who have suffered thalidomide poisoning and who have gone on to display normal cognitive and intellectual development (Decarie, 1969; Kopp & Shaperman, 1973). For example, in a sample of 22 infants predominantly between the ages of 1.5 and 2.7 years, Decarie found that 44 % of the sample scored from normal average to superior on the Griffiths Mental Development Scale (Griffiths, 1954). The majority of these children had severe malformations associated with thalidomide. It is particularly revealing that there was no relation between severity of malformation and IQ but a marked negative correlation between test performance and percentage of time spent in an institution (Pearson product-moment coefficient, .76): the longer children spent in an institution, the lower their score. Moreover, approximately one-third of the children who display varying manifestations of cerebral palsy during the early period of their development eventually display normal intelligence as adults (Crothers & Paine, 1957; Holman & Freedheim, 1959).

These observations of acknowledged limitations with traditional tests bear implication. At least 3 points merit explicit articulation. First, it appears to be clear that "brain damage" can be severe and extensive without necessarily impairing cognitive capacity. Second, as demonstrated in Décarie's (1969) sample, environmental factors are often more destructive of intellectual development than are the neurological insults per se. Third, it should also be recognized that the specific infant responses upon which inferences about intellect are made have not been systematically researched and are also of questionable validity. For example, Zelazo, Zelazo, and Kolb (1972) recently demonstrated that newborn infants who receive exercise in eliciting the stepping reflex retained that response beyond the period when it typically disappears. If a response such as stepping can be maintained with only brief periods of daily stimulation, what is its significance on an infant examination at 6 months of age? If infants learn to stand with support or take steps or walk alone sooner, does that mean they are brighter than the next child? Can it still be assumed that there is a general level of intelligence (called "g") that is reflected equally in motor, language, sensory, perceptual, and cognitive behavior? None of these challenges to prevailing procedures for infant assessment has been dealt with sufficiently, and serious doubt about the validity of current tests remains.

An examination of specific items on the traditional tests reflects three main categories: measures of gross- and fine-motor performance; imitative behavior that implies the capacity for gross- and fine-motor performance; and both comprehensive and productive language (cf, Bayley, 1969; Gesell, 1925; McCall, Hogarty, & Hurlburt, 1972). It should be emphasized that speech requires a specific motor facility. Even a cursory review of the scales reveals that the preponderance of items are bound to motor facility. The observation of the child with thalidomide poisoning or cerebral palsy who grows to maturity with intact intellect, the known poor predictive validity of the traditional tests of infant development and the questions raised by specific motor items that improve with practice, all imply that cognitive and neuromotor development may progress independently. However, the independence between cognitive and neuromotor growth is neither acknowledged in existing measures of assessment nor in their underlying theory.

Of course, traditional measures have been valuable. Clinical observations indicate that age-appropriate motor and language production on traditional tests of infant development may indeed reflect age-appropriate cognitive development. The problem is that inappropriate performance need not announce delayed intellect. The primary source of error appears to be in identifying children with delayed motor development and intact cognitive capacities as children with general developmental delays. What are the consequences of labeling a cognitively intact 20-month-old child as developmentally delayed or retarded simply because the child does not walk alone, lacks speech, and/or fails to comply with the examiner's demands? There is overwhelming evidence that labels can influence expectations, often with pernicious effects (Hobbs, 1975). Less ambiguous situations occur with cerebral palsied children who have spastic quadriplegia, and children with multiple congenital anamolies who may have missing limbs. At best, these children are untestable using measures of gross-motor performance, imitation, or speech.

There is a sense of urgency about the early detection of the cognitively intact children with cerebral palsy. The detection should be made before the weight of our negative expectations fulfills the prophecy conveyed by the physical inability of these children to perform appropriately on our traditional tests. The most humane and intelligent application of existing assessment procedures renders cerebral palsied children untestable; the most pernicous application relegates then to the status of cognitively retarded, a judgment based on tests that are severely biased against them. In the case of neuromotor damaged children, the promise of procedures designed to detect subtle reactivity to perceptual-cognitive events is indisputable—indeed, long overdue. It is not intended to place blame. On the contrary, it appears to be an unfortunate accident of psychological and medical history that cognitively intact children with marked neuromotor damage are shortchanged by prevailing assessment procedures. The guiding theories of early intellectual development have been unanimous in assuming that intellect is first reflected through motor actions.

LIMITATIONS OF CURRENT APPROACHES TO INFANT COGNITIVE ASSESSMENT AND NEW POSSIBILITIES

Our knowledge of infant development and technology for studying infant behavior has matured to the point where we can take a fresh look at past procedures for assessing infant maturation. Most of the existing procedures can be traced back to the late 1920s and early 1930s and the work of Gesell (1925). Some, like Gesell's test of infant mental development, are based on an explicit theory of neuromotor development. Others have a more pragmatic atheoretical orientation that include a potpourri of items that are tried and proven to capture children's attention. More recent procedures influenced by Piaget's theorizing tend to be more explicitly cognitive in orientation but are nevertheless committed to a view of sensorimotor intelligence. In practice, these tests rely heavily on gross-motor performance. Few of the existing procedures deliberately exploit children's capacity to attend to and process visual and auditory events. In general, the theories underlying traditional tests of infant development are less sophisticated than is our current research knowledge about infant behavior. For example, most tests of infant development do not consciously use our new found knowledge of the infant's response repertoire. In fact, little independent research was undertaken to study the meanings of infant behaviors observed in most existing tests of child development, e.g., only recently have we explored the determinants and implications of visual fixations, smiling, and vocalizing. Indeed, only recently was it possible technologically and methodologically to explore the correlates of infant heart-rate decelerations and accelerations. Yet, conclusions about cognitive status have been drawn in the absence of this knowledge.

These limitations are, in part, the product of our historical development as a scientific discipline. Research on infancy flourished during the early 1930s, and it was primarily during this creative period that the foundations for the tests of infant development were laid. This fertile era was followed by practically 30 years of relative research inactivity. During the early 1960s through the 1970s, there was a tremendous resurgence of infant research. The data from this most recent research explosion have not been integrated into procedures for assessing infant development; however, the promise they hold for improving our capability to assess intact cognitive functioning among infants is great.

The discrepancy between recent research in infancy and the status of infant assessment is also, in part, a question of domain. Much of the initial assessment and examination of infants is the purview of pediatricians. They are the ones who give the children routine examinations, innoculations, and sick care on a reasonably regular basis and who are in the best position to detect problems of development. However, pediatricians and developmental psychologists generally do not communicate, and many pediatricians appear unaware of developments in infant behavioral research. In fact, when in need of assistance, pediatricians usually consult neurologists, specialists who explicitly hold neuromotor development as a principal criterion for evaluating cognitive development. Pediatricians who seek neurologists' advice about infant cognitive development are usually guided back to procedures that assess and emphasize the child's neuromotor status.

Often developmental psychologists who have participated in the recent resurgence of basic research in infancy are in a frustrating position; they have knowledge of what can be done and a realization of what is. To paraphrase George Bernard Shaw, they dream of things that never were and ask why not? The knowledge that infants can process visual and auditory information centrally almost from birth remains to be translated into a valid instrument for assessing cognitive status free from reliance on traditional neuromotor measures. The truth of an information-processing approach is almost self-evident, yet neuromotor indices will continue to be used until the basic research is translated into a usable assessment instrument.

THE MEANINGS OF INFANT RESPONSES

Kagan (1971) has suggested that each of the infant's responses — smiling, vocalizing, looking time, heart-rate increases and decreases — are analogous to windows on a house, each with different refractory errors. Each window provides a partial view of the contents and activity in the house; each opens a different room with different players. In order to provide a coherent and complete picture within the house, it is necessary to solve the refractory problem at each porthole. In many ways, our past efforts at cognitive assessment in infancy have ignored the refractory problems. Recent research allows us at least a partial view; we have approximated the refractory indices on some of the windows. There is good evidence that smiling occurs following assimilation of a moderately difficult event and is accompanied by a release in tension (Sroufe & Waters, 1976; Zelazo, 1972). There is sound data to imply that vocalization also accompanies assimilation, especially toward the end of the first year of life, although it is also clear that vocalization to redundant events may indicate boredom, particulary with infants under a year of age (Kagan, 1971; Zelazo, Kagan, & Hartmann, 1975). There are numerous studies indicating that infants show longer sustained fixations to stimuli that are moderately discrepant from what they already know (e.g., Kinney & Kagan, 1976; McCall & Melson, 1969; Super, Kagan, Morrison, Haith, & Weiffenbach, 1972; Zelazo, Hopkins, Jacobson, & Kagan, 1974). It has been shown that heart-rate deceleration often accompanies orientation and initial attention to a new event (Lewis & Goldberg, 1969) and dishabituates most to stimuli moderately discrepant from the experimental standard (McCall & Melson, 1969). Recent research, some of which will be discussed in this chapter indicates that heart-rate acceleration accompanies situations involving active thought or stimulus-related fear (Campos, 1976; Kagan, 1972; Kahneman, Tursky, Shapiro, & Crider, 1969; Lacey, 1967). We are beginning to learn the language of infants; we partially understand their response repertoire.

In *Change and Continuity in Infancy,* Kagan (1971) proposed a theory of perceptual–cognitive development that is heavily grounded on the infant research that has taken place over the last 18 years. He argued that the primary determinants of attention become increasingly more experiential over the first year of life. Relying heavily on research by Haith (1968), Kagan reported that stimuli containing sharp contrast and motion are the most effective determinants of attention during the first 2 months of life. Stimuli, moderately different from those that the infant already knows (i.e., from the experimental standards repeated in most of these studies), are postulated to play an increasingly greater role from about the second month of life. Findings from a number of laboratories support the suggestion that a moderate degree of discrepancy relative to childrens' existing knowledge elicits the greatest degree of sustained attention and positive affect (Kinney & Kagan, 1976; McCall & Kagan, 1967; McCall & Melson, 1969; Super et al., 1972; Zelazo et al., 1974). In other words, moderately discrepant stimuli become increasingly more effective in engaging and sustaining children's attention, and presumably their cognitive processing, during the early years.

However, more recent research summarized by Kagan (1972) and Zelazo (1975) implies that still another fundamental cognitive capacity emerges towards the end of the first year. A reexamination of old data and the results of new experiments imply that year-old infants enter a cognitive metamorphosis that enables them to activate specific associations to specific situations. This capacity is akin to active thought and appears to be the underlying capacity that permits the many new behaviors that year-old infants display. The onset of speech, separation distress, conservation of weight, and functional play are a few of the major new developments that require the ability to retrieve and activate specific ideas and associations, an ability that younger infants do not readily display, not even with brief practice.

The elucidation of the research supporting this perceptual–cognitive view forms the central core of this paper. However, there are several important premises in this approach that contradict widely held assumptions underlying traditional tests of infant development. These should be made explicit. The first assumption, supported by recent research, is that infants have the capacity to form a memory for a perceptual event without the necessity for gross-motor involvement. The assumed relation between motor performance and memory formation is either explicit or implicit in most traditional tests (Bayley, 1969; Cattell, 1960; Frankenburg, Dodds, & Fandal, 1970; Gesell, 1925; Griffiths, 1954) and even among Piagetian tests of sensorimotor development (Escalona & Corman, 1967; Uzgiris & Hunt, 1975). In the case of the sensorimotor tests if it is argued that subtle motor reactions, such as eye movements or muscle contractions, will suffice to meet the assumption of motor involvement, as a liberal interpretation of Piaget might state, then the issue becomes a moot point. The question of gross vs. subtle motor involvement for the acquisition of information is a distinction reminiscent of the stimulus–response vs. stimulus–stimulus debate carried out by the learning theorists of the past. The debate is unproductive, and the distinction is blurred by practical considerations. In the end, both views lead to the conclusion that the simple presentation of an event is sufficient to allow children to extract information regarding the event.

A second assumption that merits explicit discussion is that the capacity to form a memory for a perceptual experience begins almost from birth. For example, Ungerer, Brody, and Zelazo (1978) have shown differential reactivity among 1-month-old infants to speech phrases spoken consistently from the second week of life. Half of the mothers in the experimental group repeated the word *beguile* and the other half repeated the word *tinder* daily until criterion responding was achieved—usually about 13 days. Infants in the experimental groups were tested with the familiar training words and novel words. A control group of mothers and infants did not receive training, but were tested with the same words. Widening of the eyes and orienting occurred to the training words, but not to the novel words, implying formation of schemata to familiar spoken words. Further documentation is essential because the implication is profound: the infants' brain appears ready to form and store memories for auditory and visual information from birth. The methodologically rigorous research by Haith (see Chapter 2 of this volume) is consistent with this interpretation. These data imply that our current assessment approaches should be modified, however, they also imply that our current view regarding the psychological care of the infant, particularly the institutionalized and neuromotor impaired infant, must be more cognitively structured.

A third assumption is that infants form schemata for events in both visual and auditory modalities and presumably code information on a central level. Support for this assumption comes from research on the smiling response in infants (Zelazo, 1972; Zelazo & Komer, 1971) and from research using discrepant auditory stimuli (Kinney & Kagan, 1976). One intrinsic difference between the two modalities is the sequential nature of auditory stimuli. The smiling research indicates that if visual stimuli are presented sequentially, the patterns of reactivity to repeated visual and auditory events are similar, implying central integration of the information.

These three premises derive their support from a reasonably solid data base that exploits the methodological, technical, and statistical advances of recent years. These new data provide a radical view of the infant as an organism that is capable of receiving sensory information from many modalities and transducing that input into a common electrical–chemical language. The information appears to be integrated and stored at a central level, and, more importantly, the memory process occurs with or without gross motor involvement. Thus, the recent methodolgically rigorous body of research in infancy challenges the conventional interpretation of the widely held assumption of sensorimotor intelligence.

These recent data raise a related issue. Not only must we relinquish our ties to old assumptions, but we must develop new statistical procedures for analysis. The use of both visual and auditory modalities for assessment, use of sequential rather than stationary or simultaneous stimuli, and repeated presentations of the same stimuli to examine the dynamic qualities of information processing rather than a static assessment of stored knowledge raise unique statistical challenges. In each instance, a prototypical pattern of reactivity for multiple response systems is generated. The object is to assess an infant's ability to process actively a dynamic event, but the subject is hopelessly noncompliant. Each of the stimulus characteristics that contributes to the maintenance of attention raises difficulty with statistical analyses. As urged in other chapters in this volume, there is a recurring need for further development of the capacity to analyze statistically patterns of responsiveness. The limitations of correlational procedures have long been known, and we have stretched the application of the analysis of variance procedures beyond their intended purpose.

RESEARCH ON PERCEPTUAL-COGNITIVE DEVELOPMENT

Past research is obviously too extensive to report in any detail; however, a sketchy summary is sufficient to convey the general thrust of this work. In the late 1950s and early 1960s, Fantz (1958) demonstrated that infants would attend differentially to various stimulus patterns. His research led to the finding that looking time (or differential fixation) was a reliable and valid index of children's attention to visual events. This study of visual fixation also led to the development of the habituation–dishabituation paradigm that has figured so prominently in the study of infant attention. An experimental technique was adapted by Lewis and Goldberg (1969) from procedures used to study habituation of physiological responses (Sokolov, 1963). In this paradigm, a stimulus is repeated so that the child can form an expectancy. The expectancy is inferred from a decrement in responding called *habituation*. For example, a child shown several presentations of a checkerboard pattern will eventually show less and less looking. Further evidence that an expectancy or memory has been formed can be found by presenting a different stimulus, e.g., a bullseye. In the example given, looking time increases to the bullseye, thus ruling out the possibility that the decrement in fixation was attributable to fatigue.

Much of the subsequent research was devoted to determining the optimal properties of the dishabituating stimuli. Obviously, stimuli that are near identical to the standard produce minimal recovery of responding. One question posed by researchers was whether the optimal stimulus for recapturing the infant's interest is a linear or curvilinear function relative to the standard. In other words, is the dishabituation following repeated exposure to a standard greater for stimuli that are similar, moderately different, or maximally different from the original? There have been limitations to past efforts. Frequently, only simple, static two-dimensional stimuli are used, and presentations of dishabituating stimuli are not repeated. For example, in one experiment, eight presentations of a vertical array of Xs and Ys served as the standard. One dishabituation trial of the same array in a 45° orientation immediately followed for one experimental group. A sequence of two originals, one dishabituation, two original, one dishabituation, and one original stimuli finished out the presentation (cf, McCall & Melson, 1969). Rarely have the dishabituation and return stimuli been repeated for three or more trials in experiments on perceptual–cognitive development in infancy, and, generally, complex sequential visual stimuli have not been studied. One problem with the use of simple stimuli presented only once or twice is that the paradigm does not provide an optimal view of children's reaction. Infants' processing of information appears to occur too rapidly.

Developing a paradigm that would reveal infants' reactions to the stimuli to allow inferences about the development of "cognitive schemata" is central to the question of whether moderately different or maximally different dishabituating stimuli are most compelling. A paradigm that accomplishes the gradual unfolding of the schema-formation process will also allow a distinction between initial orienting reactions and sustained attention. Both data from a recent experiment (Zelazo et al., 1974) and reflection upon one's own phenomenological experiences imply that moderately discrepant stimuli elicit the greatest sustained attention. This view argues that stimuli that are slightly discrepant from what we already know are too easy to assimilate and do not engage us for long periods of time. Stimuli that are too discrepant, i.e., novel, are initially unassimilatable and, similarly, do not engage us for a great length of time. However, unlike familiar or slightly different stimuli, novel stimuli elicit marked initial attention. We appear to be attracted to the very unusual but often cannot relate extremely discrepant events to our own experiences. It is the moderately different stimulus that elicits both a high degree of initial attention and the greatest amount of sustained involvement. It is as though moderately different events can be integrated into many facets of our existing knowledge.

A college senior majoring in U. S. history may find an introductory textbook of U. S. history boring. The same history major may find a textbook on the fundamentals of electrical engineering utterly incomprehensible. However, an overview of Chinese history, or a more specific and detailed treatise of a particular segment of U. S. history, e.g., the *Ideological Origins of the American Revolution* or Mrs. Frances Trollope's *Domestic Manners of the Americans,* may be approached with delight.

Zelazo et al. (1974) showed that the curvilinear relation between discrepant information and infant reactivity holds when a priori ordered stimuli and an operant response, lever pressing, are used. One hundred-and-forty boys and girls, 7.5 months of age, showed the greatest recovery of looking time, positive vocalization, and operant responding and the least amount of fretting to geometrical forms that were moderately different form the habituated standards. A three-dimensional object was exposed for 1.5 secs each time the infant pressed the lever. The reduced exposure time allowed for the gradual increase in interest followed by habituation to the standard and less rapid, more elaborate reactivity to one of four levels of discrepant stimuli. The results, displayed in Figure 3.1 provide strong support for the argument that moderate discrepancy is an important determinant of sustained infant attention and affect. Moreover, in an extension of this study

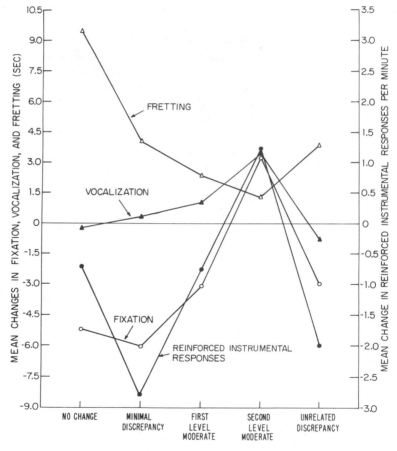

FIG. 3.1.   Change scores for mean differences in instrumental responses, fixation time, vocalization, and fretting between the last two mins of the standard and the first two mins of the transformation for five discrepancy groups. (From Zelazo, P., Hopkins, J., Jacobson, S., & Kagan, J. Psychological reactivity to discrepant events: Support for the curvilinear hypothesis. *Cognition,* 1974, *2,* 385–393.)

(Hopkins, Zelazo, Jacobson, & Kagan, 1976), a detailed analysis of the transformation period, displayed in Figure 3.2, revealed that initial lever pressing was greatest for moderately discrepant and very discrepant stimuli. However, as the transformation period progressed, reactivity declined markedly to the very discrepant stimulus but remained high and relatively stable to the moderately discrepant objects.

Two important procedural points make this demonstration possible.

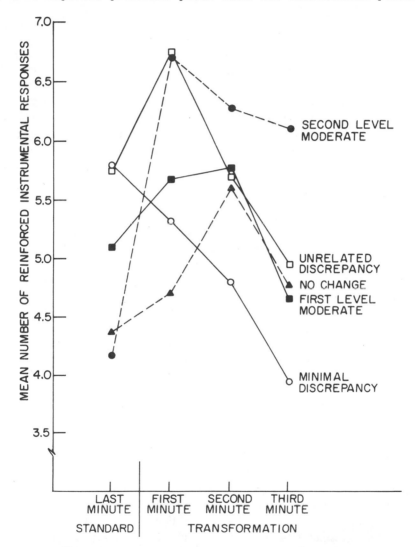

FIG. 3.2.   Number of reinforced instrumental responses for standard and transformation periods for each discrepancy group. (From Hopkins, J., Zelazo, P., Jacobson, S., & Kagan, J. Infant reactivity to stimulus–schema discrepancy. *Genetic Psychology Monographs*, 1976, **93**, 27–62.)

First, each lever press provided a 1.5 sec exposure of the stimulus. Simple stimuli, such as the geometric forms used in this experiment, are assimiliated so rapidly that longer exposure times would yield little or no data. Second, sufficiently long standard and transformation periods allow for a detailed analysis of the patterns of responding.

An Alternative Paradigm

This research using brief exposures of the stimuli led to the development of a slightly different expectancy paradigm. The standard was repeated often enough to allow a firm expectation to develop, the discrepancy itself was repeated to allow for the possibility of assimilation of the new event, and the original event reappeared and was repeated so that assimilation of the return sequence could also occur. In this paradigm, each stimulus event contained three repeated segments varying in degree of difficulty: the standard, the return, and transformation. However, the critical distinction between this paradigm and previous work was that sequential visual stimuli rather than static stimuli were used. It has been argued elsewhere (Zelazo & Komer, 1971) that presenting visual stimuli sequentially is an important factor in making comparisons to auditory stimuli that normally occur sequentially. The principal purpose for using sequential visual stimuli is to reduce the speed with which schemata can be formed and assimilated in a natural situation. The effect is analogous to that accomplished in the lever press study in which visual stimuli were presented for very brief durations. When visual stimuli are presented sequentially, the speed with which assimilation occurs is slowed down because the event itself takes time to unfold. This procedural change cannot be overemphasized because the sequential nature allows for the gradual elicitation of reactions reflecting the development of memory and assimilation of the information.

A series of visual and auditory sequences was designed in which the standard–transformation–return paradigm was used (cf. Zelazo, 1972; Zelazo et al., 1975). A given event was repeated often enough for an expectancy to be formed. Without warning, a moderate variation of this standard was presented and repeated for either three or five trials, depending upon the child's age. Again, without warning, the standard reappeared and was presented for three trials. In one highly successful visual event, shown in Figure 3.3 (cf. Zelazo, 1972), the presenter lifts the rod attached to an 18-inch rectangular box and moves it through a 240° arc to make contact and light three brightly colored bulbs. The lights remain on for 4 secs, after which the presenter returns the rod to its original position. The event is clearly sequential: the experimenter's hand appears from behind the curtain, takes 3 secs to lift the rod, 4 secs to make contact with the bulbs, which remains on for 4 secs, and takes a total of 4 secs to return behind the curtain. An 11.5-month-old child is shown eight presentations of the standard. On

FIG. 3.3. Sequential light stimulus.

the ninth trial, and without warning, the discrepant variation occurs. In one of the most successful transformations, the experimenter's hand appears, touches the rod but does not move it through the arc, 4 seconds elapse, and the bulbs light. All conditions remain the same in this presentation, except that the rod does not move.

An example of one of the auditory sequences involves the repetition of a simple meaningful phrase followed by a change to a different meaningful phrase. The transformation is repeated and followed by the return of the original phrase. In one instance, the phrase "Give me a big smile" is repeated for 10 standards. On the 11th trial, without warning, the child hears "Throw me the red ball" with the same rhythm and intonation. After five presentations of the changed sequence, the original event returns for three more trials. A number of visual and auditory sequences have been developed, and usually two visual and three auditory sequences are presented in a given testing.

Both visual and auditory events are typically presented in a setting resembling a puppet theater with large black wings. It can be seen in Figure 3.4 that the most salient feature in the setting is a stage upon which the visual events are presented. Four 100 watt bulbs and the activity on the stage are the attractive features in the otherwise darkened room.

On either side of the stage, small plexiglass windows embedded in the curtains permit coders to record on button boxes the occurrence and duration of certain targeted behaviors. One coder observes visual fixation to the stage, smiling, vocalization, and fretting. A second coder records pointing toward the stage or speaker, clapping, waving and twisting. The latter usually occurs prior to fretting. Twisting accompanied by searching is coded when the infant turns toward the mother to share the event. Turning to mother, clapping and pointing are mature reactions. If the event is visual, the coder also records anticipatory looking, which involves glancing ahead in the sequence of events. Anticipatory looking is more reliably observed on the car–doll sequence, an event not described here. Because the car–doll sequence involves a greater distance than does the light, looking ahead is unambiguous. Anticipatory fixation, as we call it, is an index of an expec-

FIG. 3.4.   Laboratory setting.

tancy that has high face validity. If an auditory stimulus is presented, the observer codes searching rather than anticipatory fixation. Searching, defined as maintaining eyes widened and at a plane parallel to the ground or above, may be accompanied by head movement and often occurs with motoric quieting. Searching has proved to be the auditory analog of visual fixation, implying attention and processing of the event.

In addition to the behavioral measures, the child has small electrodes attached to the sternum to permit recording an electrocardiogram (EKG). The EKG signal is converted to a beat-by-beat recording of heart rate through a cardiotachometer. The stimulus event itself is also recorded throughout the sequence for all trials. For example, in the light sequence, a press on a foot pedal signals the appearance of the presenter's hand; a second press indicates the lift of the rod, and a circuit is closed providing another automatic signal when the rod makes contact with the bulbs. When the experimenter's hand retreats behind the curtain, another press on the foot pedal is made. All of the measures are integrated on a polygraph recorder, providing for a time-locked picture of the stimulus event and measurement of behavioral and physiological responses. The visual sequences and their appropriate intervals are kept constant by carefully timed recordings that instruct the presenter.

Four comments should be made about the procedure. First, the use of sequential stimuli represents an important departure from existing research and, as such, carries some element of risk. However, it is clear to us that many of the responses displayed and the lawfulness of reactivity among infants to the different stimuli would be sharply reduced if sequential stimuli were not used. The difficulties using static visual stimuli to elicit sustained attention become particularly acute when attempted with children beyond about 6 months of age. In contrast, the sequential stimuli elicit attention and yield useful information up to about 3 years of age. Second, the procedures are passive, do not require the production of speech or gross-motor responses and make few demands for infant compliance. This approach relies on the compelling quality of the stimuli in a systematically prepared context to sustain attention and on the lawfulness of elicited responses believed to reflect children's cognitive processing to assess their level of cognitive development. Thus, if a child has functional vision and hearing and has experienced a reasonably "normal" visual and auditory environment, the child is inclined to look at visual events, search to auditory events, and when assimiliation occurs, smile, vocalize, and display heart-rate deceleration (cf., Lewis & Goldberg, 1969). If the child is more able physically, he/she may also applaud or point at the moment of assimilation and or turn to his/her mother to share the event. The use of multiple elicited responses is a shot-gun approach. No one measure can be guaranteed in an eliciting situation, not even heart rate: A child's heart rate may not be labile and may not provide a sufficient degree of information. Fortunately, when assimilation occurs, a cluster of responses are usually observed. Thus, in an appropriate situation, such as the fifth presentation of the light sequence, the infant may display marked heart-rate deceleration, smiling, vocalization, and point, and if mature enough, may even say "light".

Third, one strength of the procedures is that they are compelling. Those of us who have worked with infants are fully aware that it is nearly impossible to command them to comply. The situation itself must be designed to seduce the child to attend long enough to allow the monitoring of capacity to process information. Indeed, the situation is so reliable that the child's capacity to attend is itself an index of cognitive development. It appears that up to some point, the more associations the child can relate to the stimulus, the longer the child will attend. Finally, the procedures are dynamic and measure the child's ability to actively process visual and auditory information, rather than assess the child's storehouse of specific past experiences. It is less important to have seen lights before than to indicate an understanding of the unique configuration of lights and the discrepant variation of this sequence following repetition, for example. In addition to the child's capacity for sustained attention, the perceptual-cognitive procedures attempt to measure the child's ability to form a memory, assimilate changes in the sequence within a reasonable brief period, and to assimilate the re-appearance of the standard following a period of distracting discrepant information. In other words, each of the visual and auditory events with its repeated standard, presentation of a discrepancy, and return of the original event attempts to assess the child's capacity to solve simple perceptual-cognitive problems.

The original data were collected with the collaboration of Jerome Kagan and Richard Kearsley at Harvard University. Initially, over 250 children were observed in a cross-sectional sample. At least 8 boys and 8 girls were tested at 5.5, 7.5, 9.5, and 11.5 months of age with all 20 of the visual and auditory events that were originally tried. Stimuli that were subsequently selected were tested on 12 infants per cell and included no change control groups. These refined procedures were tested on over 100 children observed longitudinally at 3.5, 5.5, 7.5, 9.5, 11.5, 13.5, 20 and 29 months of age (Kagan, Kearsley, & Zelazo, 1978). Thus, children in the longitudinal sample were observed for eight testings during the first 2.5 years of life. A third sample, numbering about 100 children between the ages of 5 and 36 months was observed in a clinical setting at Tufts-New England Medical Center. These latter children represent an attempt by Kearsley and myself to apply the procedures developed in a carefully controlled laboratory situation to a clinical sample. Children seen at the Center for Behavioral Pediatrics and Infant Development have a variety of presenting problems; However, the majority of infants fit two general categories: those with developmental delays in speech and motor performance and those with severe multiple, congenital handicaps, including cerebral palsy. Obviously, there is too much data to present here, but an attempt will be made to summarize the laboratory findings for one visual event, provide supporting data from other sources and illustrate the utility of these perceptual–cognitive procedures in a clinical setting by providing two case studies.

RESULTS OF THE LIGHT SEQUENCE

There are many lawful reactions to perceptual cognitive events that occur during the first 3 years of life and that reflect the infant's maturing cognitive abilities; however, the data emphasized in this presentation concentrate on the suggestion that a major cognitive change occurs between about 7 and 12 months of life. For example, both the mean duration of vocalization and the percentage of children to vocalize during a trial block are consistent in showing overall decreases in vocalization at 9.5 months of age. The percentage of children vocalizing at 5.5, 7.5, 9.5 and 11.5 months of age is shown in Figure 3.5. These data, based on a total of 203 children who were tested in the first cross-sectional experiment using four variations of the light discrepancy, indicate relative quieting at 9.5 months. Examination of vocalization over trial blocks to the "no-rotor"light sequence for the four ages clarifies this effect and reveals that, although the range of mean variation is modest, babbling is low at 5.5 months and high but indiscriminate at 7.5 months. At 9.5 months, vocalization is generally lower, and there is quieting to the discrepancy and return trial blocks. Vocalization increases to the return trial blocks at 11.5 months, especially for girls.

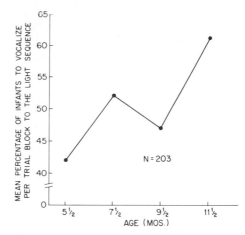

FIG. 3.5. Percentage of infants vocalizing to the light sequences at four ages during the first year.

Ninety-two percent of the infant girls vocalized to the reappearance of the standard following the "no-rotor" discrepancy, whereas only 33% of the 9.5 months girls did. Vocalization for girls in particular appears as a diffuse and indiscriminate response at 7.5 months, quiets at 9.5 months (perhaps as a result of a maturing capacity for inhibition), and reappears in the service of assimilation at 11.5 months.

A more detailed examination of the changes occurring between 9.5 and 11.5 months was undertaken in a second experiment with the light sequence. A "no-change" control and an additional "disordered" discrepancy group, in which all the components were presented in a scrambled order, were compared with the "no-rotor" discrepancy. One objective was to determine whether vocalization occurred following redundant or moderately discrepant stimuli. Sample sizes were also increased to 12 infants of each sex at each age.

Analyses of the results using the additional groups and including trial blocks as a repeated measure support the previous findings. Older girls display increased vocalization to the reappearance of the standard following the moderate discrepancies, apparently as a concommitant of the excitement accompanying assimilation. Boys display increased vocalization to the repetitive control stimulus presumably indicating boredom. These results appear in the near-significant Series × Sex × Block interaction displayed in Figure 3.6. Examination of the mean duration of vocalization during each trial block indicates that vocalization increased primarily for older girls following the no-rotor and disordered discrepancies, but did not increase for girls in the control group. Examination of the percentage of children to vocalize during a trial block reveals the same result. Ninety-two percent of the older girls in the "no-rotor" group and 79% in the "disordered" group vocalized on the last trial block, whereas only 58% of repetition-control infants vocalized.

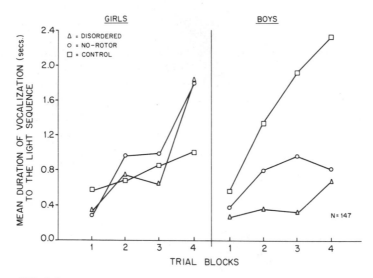

FIG. 3.6. Mean duration of vocalization to three variations of the light sequence at 9.5 and 11.5 months.

To briefly summarize, it appears that vocalization to the light sequence is high but indiscriminate at 7.5 months, declines at 9.5 months, and is followed by increased vocalization at 11.5 months. The results from the second experiment using additional discrepancy and control groups imply that vocalization among girls accompanies assimilation. The vocalization data are consistent with the results from another visual sequence in which a 2-inch wooden cube is changed to a 1.5 inch cube (cf. Zelazo et al., 1975). Eleven-and-one-half month-old girls vocalized to the return of the 2-inch cube following the moderate discrepancy. There was no comparable increase in vocalization in the novel (1.5-inch yellow rippled cylinder) or no-change control groups. Consistency between the simple cube sequence and the light sequence indicates that the pattern of vocalization is generalizable to a complex nonsocial stimulus.

A similar dip in vocalization at 9 months of age was recently reported for first-born infant boys in response to social stimulation (Roe, 1975), reflecting impressive generality of the phenomenon. The percentage of positive vocalization (babbling and cooing) to occur during a 3-min session of mother's verbal interaction repeated at 3, 5, 7, 9, 11, 13, and 15 months of age is shown in Figure 3.7. In Roe's own words, the average vocal responsiveness "to stimulation was high at 3 and 5 months, decreased appreciably around 9 months, and increased again around 11 months of age [p. 939]." Lewis (1959) suggested that vocalization increases to spoken speech at around 10 months of age, just prior to the onset of the first spoken words. It should be pointed out that the onset of speech, set at 12 months in the Bayley Scales (1969), requires the capacity to activate a specific sound for a specific object.

Also it is interesting that 3 minutes of structured verbal interaction produced consistent and lawful results, but two 60-min recordings of "natural" vocalizations made over 1-week intervals did not produce statistically significant or psychologically meaningful changes over age in Roe's study. These results starkly accent the advantage of a structured context in which research conditions and objectives are specified. This contrast in quality of data within the same study strongly supports the suggestion that measures of development must be more specific than is generally assumed.

An examination of looking time to the light stimulus revealed a linear increase from 5.5 through 11.5 months. The highly significant main effect for age, displayed in Figure 3.8, was observed in a sample of 203 infants and reflects increased interest with maturity. A critical question posed by this result is why looking time to the same stimulus should increase with greater cognitive maturity? The weight of experience with infants observing simple visual stimuli indicates that looking time declines more rapidly with greater-cognitive sophistication (cf. Lewis, 1970). One possible explanation is that children bring more associations to the simulus situation when they are more mature; they look more because they can ask more questions of the stimulus information.

The heart-rate results help to explain both the dips in reactivity (particularly vocalization) that occur toward the end of the first year and the increase in looking time. The means of the two highest and the two lowest values were obtained for four periods of the light sequence: base (a 3-sec period prior to the appearance of the hand), hand (a 3-sec period from the

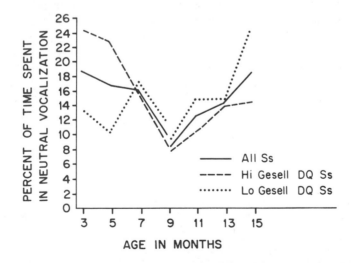

FIG. 3.7.   Percentage of neutral vocalization to verbal interactions during the first 15 months of age. (From Roe, K. V., Amount of infant vocalization as a function of age: Some cognitive implications. *Child Development*, 1975, **46**, 936–941.)

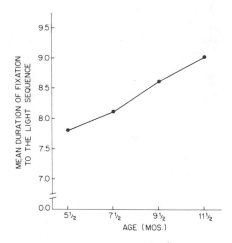

FIG. 3.8.   Fixation to the light sequence at four ages during the first year.

appearance of the hand to the lifting of the rod), rotor-light (an 8-sec segment including the movement of the rod and lasting to the offset of the bulbs), and post-light (a 5-sec segment lasting to the disappearance of the experimenter's hand).

The results of the mean highest heart-rate values during the base, hand, rotor-light, and post-light segments of the light sequence for the four trial blocks in the no-rotor and control groups ($p < .005$) are presented in Figure 3.9. The highest heart-rate values, scored only if accompanied by visual fixation, show a distinct acceleration to the discrepancy (third trial block - B3) during the rotor-light period in the no-rotor group, but not in the control group. A greater increase to the onset of the light without movement of the rotor (B3) can also be seen in the mean lowest values ($p < .005$) displayed in Figure 3.10. Both the highest and lowest heart-rate values accelerated to the discrepancy, in this case, the deletion of the moving rotor, whereas no corresponding increase occurred in the no-change control group. The heart-rate acceleration appears to be a correlate, although not necessarily a cause, of mental effort implying the onset of active thought in these infants.

An association between heart-rate acceleration and mental effort was established by Kahneman et al. (1969) in a carefully controlled experiment with adults. They demonstrated that heart rate increased as a function of task difficulty on a series of digit problems. It is possible that the heart-rate acceleration accompanying the perceptual cognitive event in the experiment with infants also marks the occurrence of mental effort. Cardiac acceleration may be due to tensing of the body and the quiet attention that appears to accompany the infant's attempts to understand the discrepancy. Individual records in this and subsequent experiments often show 5 to 10 beat heart-rate accelerations during a single trial accompanied by uninterrupted quiet attention. Moreover, increased looking following the deletion of movement in the discrepancy sequence strongly implies that cognitive changes are occurring within the infant. The increased fixation with age to the same stimulus sequence and heart-rate acceleration to the discrepency, especially when a compelling action component is deleted, implies that the 11.5-month-old infant processes the discrepant experience differently than does the younger child. It appears that although the 5.5- and 7.5-month-old children have many responses to perceptual–cognitive events at their disposal, these responses are more stereotyped and carry different meanings than those of the 11.5-month-old children.

The patterns for fixation and vocalization to the light and cube sequences reported previously are consistent in showing a progression from nonspecific responding at 7.5 months, inhibition of vocalization at 9.5 months, and vocalization in the service of assimilation to the reappearance of the standard at 11.5 months. The similarity of response patterns to such different nonsocial stimulus sequences and the adult verbal stimulation reported by Roe (1975) imply a common determinant. One compelling possibility implied by the overall increase in looking time that occurs with age and heart-rate acceleration to the discrepant light sequence at the older ages is that infants' emerging capacity to generate their own thoughts may orchestrate the discharge of these responses. The decline in reactivity around 9.5 months may announce the child's emerging capacity to inhibit indiscriminate reactions to perceptual–cognitive stimuli and to choose among responses. It is as though inhibition of reactivity (or wariness) allows other associations to occur. By about 11.5 months, the infant appears capable of

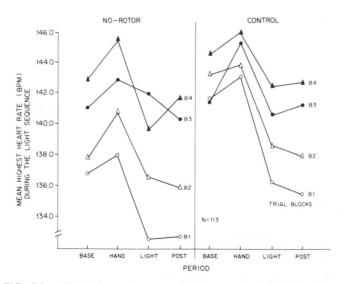

FIG. 3.9.   Highest heart-rate scores during four periods of the light sequence for the no-rotor and control groups.

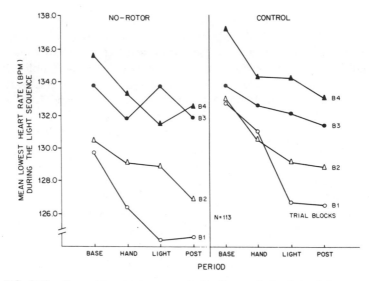

FIG. 3.10. Lowest heart-rate scores during four periods of the light sequence for the no-rotor and control groups.

activating specific associations as implied by increased visual fixation and heart-rate acceleration, and it appears that vocalization, in particular, is used more exclusively to announce a cognitive success. Each of these results, particularly the first indication of assimilation of the return portion of the sequences at 11.5 months, implies a major cognitive transition.

A Cognitive Metamorphosis?: Additional Data

Conservation of weight.   The suggestion that a cognitive metamorphosis occurs toward the end of the first year of life gains support from the intriguing research on the conservation of weight in infants reported by Mounoud and Bower (1974). The pattern describing the development of the conservation of weight closely parallels the patterns of reactivity to the light and cube sequences and to the verbal social stimulation. Each instance culminates in the infant's capacity to apply specific hypotheses to specific complex situations. Mounoud and Bower examined infants' capacity to conserve weight by presenting babies small brass rods and measuring their arm drop and force of grasp. They found that 6- to 7-month-old infants show no capacity for conservation of weight, despite short-term practice. There is no correction for arm drop or force of grasp on successive presentations. Seven-month-old-infants neither understand the relation between weight and size nor that the same object weighs the same at each presentation. In Bower's (1974) own terms, these infants "apply the same response to all objects regardless of their past experience with either the specific object or similar objects [p. 312]."

At about 9 months of age a change occurs. A second and third presentation of an identical weight produced corrections in both arm movements and force of grasp, indicating an emergent comprehension of the relation between stimulus and instrumental response in accordance with immediate prior experience. However, these infants are not capable of predicting weight from size until 12 months of age. By 1 year of age, infants, according to Bower (1974) "know that the same object weighs the same on each presentation and that the longer an object is, the heavier it will be [p. 312]." This latter capacity—the prediction of a relation between size and weight—is still another clear example of the year-old infant's newly emergent cognitive capacity to activate a specific thought for a specific situation. The conservation of weight in infants develops from indiscriminate reactivity at 7 months, to an emerging capacity for correct responding on the basis of prior experience at 9 months, to intentional reactivity in the service of specific hypotheses at 12 months. At 12 months infants have the capacity to generate a response (implying a specific thought) appropriate to a new situation; they know specifically that the longer rod will weigh more.

Separation anxiety.   Zelazo (1975) re-examined the research on separation anxiety and argued that if statistical criteria are used and methodologically sound data are emphasized, separation anxiety is not reliably found until about 12 months of age. For example, Kotelchuck and his associates (Kotelchuck, 1972; Kotelchuck, Zelazo, Kagan & Spelke, 1975) observed a cross-sectional sample of 144 first born infants of both sexes. Twelve infants of each sex were observed at 6, 9, 12, 15, 18, and 21 months of age for their responses to departures by their mothers, fathers, and an unfamiliar woman. In addition, childrens' behaviors were recorded and analyzed in response to the presence of each adult alone. It can be seen in Figure 3.11 that little change occurs for each of the measures of separation distress at either 6 or 9 months, whether a comparison is made across ages or to the unfamiliar person. Crying and proximity to the door did not increase, nor did play decrease following parental departure until 12 months of age. Moreover, children did not touch their parents more frequently upon their return from the separation until 12 months. Of course, it is possible that statistically significant changes in the measures could have occurred at 10 or 11 months, but they did not occur at or before 9 months. The results displayed in Figure 3.11 indicate that differential reactivity begins at one year, increases at 15, peaks at 18 and begins to recede by 21 months of age. Thus, these data are remarkably consistent with the non-social data in implicating the last quarter of the first year as a period of major cognitive and behavioral change culminating in a statistically significant and reliable expression of these changes by 12 months.

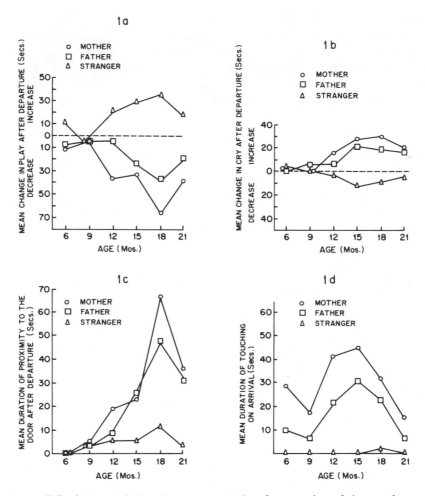

FIG. 3.11. (a–d) Reactions to separation from mother, father, and stranger at six ages between 6 and 21 months. Mean changes in duration of play (a) and crying (b) and duration of proximity to the door following adult departure (c). Mean duration of touching (d) occurs upon the return of the adult. (From Kotelchuck, M., Zelazo, P., Kagan, J., & Spelke, E. Infant reaction to parental separations when left with familiar and unfamiliar adults. *Journal of Genetic Psychology,* 1975, **126**, 255–262.

An important finding in this study is that protest was elicited only when the infant was left alone with the stranger and did not occur to mother or father separations per se. Moreover, using a comparable paradigm, Ross, Kotelchuck, Kagan, and Zelazo (1975) found that 12-, 15-, and 18-month-old children protested three times as much when left alone with a stranger in an unfamiliar laboratory than in their own homes. Context plays an important role in the elicitation of separation distress and implies that children assess the consequences of the entire situation. An unfamiliar laboratory bears greater uncertainty than the children's home and, therefore, is more likely to elicit distress. Separation protest appears to occur to unfamiliarity and correlates highly with infants' emergent cognitive ability to activate specific associations to specific situations. The year-old infant not only detects a discrepant experience. but appears to have the capacity to question and anticipate the consequence of an event. The infant's capacity for thought may create the conditions for uncertainty and distress; a stranger in a strange place is an uncertain situation that the child may not understand and may elicit protest. Presumably, as a child comes to understand through experience that separation is regularly followed by reunion and that with exposure, strange people become familiar (or do not produce harm), the distress disappears. Mothers of children close to 2 years of age frequently report that their children will not cry if they tell them that they will be right back. The explanation reduces uncertainty. Indeed, Weinraub and Lewis (1977) found that mothers of 24-month-old-children who explained both their departure and return and suggested a response during their absence (e.g., to play with the tinker toys) had children who protested least. Thus, it may be that separation protest is also an interpretable manifestation of infants' newly emergent capacity for active thought.

Functional play. A recent experiment by Zelazo and Kearsley (1977) strengthens the suggestion that the maturational change reflected in vocalization, fixation, and heart-rate patterns towards the end of the first year involves the emergent cognitive capacity to generate specific ideas. Functional play defined as the manipulation of one or more objects according to an arbitrary, but specific set of adult-determined purposes, unambiguously reveals the infant's capacity to activate ideas. Play with a carefully chosen set of toys (including a tea set; telephone; large doll with clothes; small doll with furniture; truck with blocks and garage; and a baseball bat, glove, and hat) were scored for the appearance of several conservatively chosen behaviors reflecting appropriate purposeful actions. For example, stirring a spoon in a tea cup, pouring imaginary tea from a pot, placing a telephone to one's ear, babbling into the mouthpiece, cuddling a doll, and pushing a truck (wheels down) along the floor are considered functional play. The specific appropriate actions representing different functional acts or ideas were coded for 10-sec blocks during a 15-min episode of free play at 9.5, 11.5, 13.5 and 15.5 months of age.

A clear change in the qualitative nature of the children's play occurred with the appearance of functional play in 75% of 11.5 and 100% of 13.5 month-old infants in the sample. It appears that 9.5 month-old infants are very likely to mouth, bang, wave, or finger the receiver of the telephone; 11.5 and 13.5-month-old children are more inclined to put the receiver to their ear, babble, and even attempt to dial the phone. Younger children

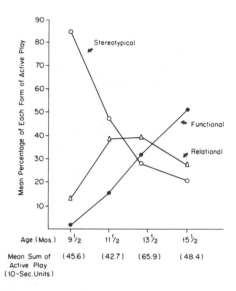

FIG. 3.12   Percentage of stereotypical, relational, and functional play at four ages between 9.5 and 15.5 months.

bang the toy spoon against the tea cup or tea pot, whereas the older children stir imaginary tea, bring the spoon to their mouth, or drink from the cup. The use of a set of toys with functionally distinct applications permitted an unambiguous view of the year-old-infant's capacity for active thought. The results displayed in Figure 3.12 reveal the infant's progression from indiscriminate stereotypical actions at 9.5 months to stimulus specific and functionally appropriate actions that first appear reliably at 1 year and continue to increase through 15.5. months. The mean number of different ideas expressed in play increased from .32 at 9.5 months, to 2.62 at 11.5, 7.88 at 13.5, and 10.38 at 15.5 months indicating that the breadth of specific associations, not just the frequency of a single association expands over this period. A transitory response in which two objects are associated in a nonfunctional manner called *relational play* appears to bridge the development from stereotypical to functional behavior.

Examination of the content of children's play for the expression of cognitive changes was suggested by Piaget (1962). Moreover, the appearance of functionally appropriate actions reported in this study were observed, in part, by McCall (1974) and Fenson, Kagan, Kearsley and Zelazo,(1976), although their results only implied changes that were clearly verified in this study. The concordance with their suggestions and the high face validity inherent in the functionally appropriate use of toys strongly support the postulation of a cognitive metamorphosis. The change occurring toward the end of the first year — like the change from caterpillar to butterfly — is completed over a relatively short period. There are precursors to functional play (apparently stereotypical and relational play serve this purpose to some extent) and there is a qualitatively different product at the end of this transition. The cognitive metamorphosis, possibly beginning as young as 8 months and complete by about 13 months, produces the capacity for a host of new behaviors. The term metamorphosis does not in itself imply a stepfunction, only a relatively rapid qualitative change. Unlike many of the behaviors discussed here, functional play permits relatively easy and direct access to the cognitive abilities emerging toward the end of the first year of life.

ADDITIONAL INDICES OF COGNITIVE DEVELOPMENT

The documented cognitive change that occurs at about 1 year of age is precisely defined relative to other cognitive changes that occur in development. The hypothesized cognitive metamorphosis appears to occur over a period of less than six months. Moreover, the evidence for active thought seen in the form of assimilation of the perceptual–cognitive procedures can be verified with most children by immediately testing for functional play. A teaching session can be used in which mother demonstrates functional play to her child. This teaching procedure serves as a check against environmental deficits in which the chosen toys are either not available or their use has not been encouraged. Thus, if a child reveals assimilation on the perceptual–cognitive procedures implying the capacity for generating specific associations, but does not display functional play during the free play sequence, he/she should, nevertheless, acquire functional uses during very brief periods of instruction lasting only a few minutes. On the other hand, children who do not assimilate the perceptual–cognitive events, may not acquire specific functional associations despite short-term practice. The emergent capacity for active thought observed in the perceptual–cognitive procedures can and should be verified immediately when possible using other procedures. It has been argued in this paper that numerous additional behaviors are implied by this emergent ability. Indeed, much of the second year of life appears to be consumed by the realization of the potential inherent in the ability to activate specific associations or ideas.

It should not be surprising that there are additional behaviors and indices of cognitive development observed with the perceptual–cognitive procedures. For example, fixation of the sequential stimuli increases with maturity on the fixed numbers of trials used in these procedures. Paradoxically, assimilation occurs more rapidly with age. That is, it appears that children both look longer and assimilate more quickly with maturity. To contribute to the difficulty, Lewis (1970) compiled an impressive array of evidence to show that habituation to static visual stimuli occurs more rapidly with age. The resolution of the apparent contradiction between these results and the perceptual–cognitive procedures reported here appears to rest with the nature of the stimuli employed. In the vast majority of previous studies, relatively simple static visual stimuli were used and habituation occurred more rapidly for older children than for younger children. When complex sequential visual stimuli are presented, attention is elicited at the earlier ages, but assimilation does not occur and fixation wanes. As children get older, they bring greater cognitive sophistication to the task, are a better cognitive match for the stimuli, attend longer, and assimilate the events.

An additional discriminating feature of the perceptual cognitive procedures is the particular segment of the sequence that is assimilated. The data clearly reveal that assimilation of standards is followed by assimilation of the return sequence and only last by assimilation of the transformation itself. Moreover, even after children possess the capacity for active thought, speed of assimilation discriminates cognitive maturity. For example, an 11.5-month-old child may give evidence of assimilation on the third presentation of the return sequence whereas a 20-month-old child may react immediately to the first reappearance of the standard. During the second and third years, assimilation occurs with increasing rapidity and ease. The data derived from the perceptual–cognitive procedures consistently and stongly imply that speed of processing is a central indicator of cognitive maturity during the first three years of life.

Finally, there are additional highly discriminating responses that appear among more mature infants who watch the perceptual–cognitive sequences. These responses, in themselves, index cognitive sophistication. For example, pointing and clapping often occur in concert with fixation, heart-rate deceleration, smiling, and vocalizing to the visual events, especially during the second and third years. Lewis and Goldberg (1969) observed this cluster of behaviors among 20, 3.5-year-old children who were shown four sets of colored slides. The perceptual–cognitive procedures can be refined further, but the approach can also be used to develop new procedures, especially between the ages of 2 and 4.

THE THERAPEUTIC TRIAL

Obviously, these procedures are new, unorthodox to many who have not been involved in infant research, challenge long established and widely held assumptions, and require validation. I believe that the logic involved in the development of the perceptual–cognitive procedures and the foundation of research upon which they rest is sound. Long-term validation using appropriate control groups, independent assessment, and follow-up procedures is underway. This form of validation will require about 3 years to complete and will provide an evaluation for which there is no substitute. Nevertheless, preliminary and partial validation is needed in the mean time.

One strategy for validation is to use each child as his own control, to employ the concept of a therapeutic trial. If an assessment using the perceptual–cognitive procedures implies that a child processes information age-appropriately, then delays in speech or motor performance can be viewed independently of cognitive performance. In some instances, the delays observed in speech and/or motor development in a child whose physical and neurological structure is grossly intact may be due to environmental factors. Contrary to an extreme view still held by some researchers, clinical experience has convinced Kearsley and me that the child's development will not simply unfold according to schedule without appropriate environmental stimulation. This hypothesis can often be verified by a sound case history, parental interview, and a structured parent–child interaction session in which the parent is asked to teach the child several activities. In these instances, an appropriate change in the child's environment should lead to the elimination of the delays. A child who is not walking can be encouraged to walk with appropriate daily stimulation from the parents or caretaker (cf. Zelazo, 1976b).

An equally common, but somewhat more complex problem is the child who does not speak. One such child, P., not only did not speak or walk at 20 months of age, but was beneath the 3rd percentile in height, weight, and head circumference, and had a serious feeding problem associated with an ulcerated tongue. P. was diagnosed as 8-months-delayed using conventional procedures. The extent of the parents' acceptance of the assessment was displayed in their instructions to their 8-year old daughter who was told, "Do not push P. She is retarded and cannot do everything that a normal child can."

P. responded age appropriately on the perceptual–cognitive procedures when tested at 20 months. After the feeding problem was corrected with behavioral intervention, a program to encourage walking and talking was designed. The child's ability to speak was demonstrated to the parents during an office visit in which P. was rewarded with a small cookie for each spoken word. It can be seen in Figure 3.13 that speech increased exponentially over the 30-min session, with six different words produced. Moreover, crying, which was accompanied by beads of perspiration indicating impending projectile vomiting (an additional problem experienced by the child), occurred through most of the first 10 mins, diminished sharply during the second 10-min block, and was replaced by smiling and laughter during the final 10 mins.

P. is now using speech communicatively and has been judged by her teachers upon entry to a Montessori School to be a normal 3-year-old child. Both the delays in speech and motor development improved with appropriate therapeutic intervention. Every available indication supports the initial assessment of intact cognitive ability in this child.

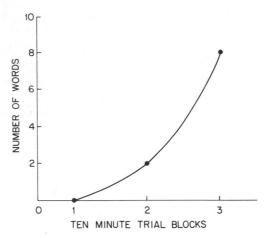

FIG. 3.13. Number of words spoken during a 30-min shaping session with a 26-month-old "developmentally delayed" child.

How can the child with severe spastic quadriplegia validate the procedures through a therapeutic trial? M., a 6-year-old with cerebral palsy, severe incoordination of all limbs, and extreme difficulty chewing and swallowing represents the limiting case of neuromotor dysfunction. At the time of testing with the perceptual–cognitive procedures, M. did not speak or communicate with her parents or teachers in any reliable manner. She was able to look, smile, vocalize, and cry, but was unable to speak, play functionally, walk, sit, crawl, or otherwise control her limbs. She was untestable using conventional procedures; however, the conventional procedures had been used previously, and her performance was set at 6 months.

M.'s performance on the perceptual–cognitive tasks was consistently high, indicating assimilation of the standards, returns, and transformations. Sustained looking to the visual events and searching to the auditory events were accompanied by heart-rate deceleration, smiling, and vocalizing on the fourth and fifth standards, first returns, and second and third discrepancy trials. This cluster of responses observed at points in the sequence that imply assimilation and comprehension of the perceptual–cognitive problems was displayed consistently across the various visual and auditory sequences. This performance was appropriate for a 30- to 36-month-old child and represents the upper limit of the procedures. Indeed, M. may be cognitively more mature than 36 months.

M.'s cognitive performance implies that she has a resonably intact mind locked in a broken body. For many reasons, we elected to attempt to unlock her ability by teaching her a simple binary system of communication. Our objective was to provide a yes–no means of communication to allow for additional assessment and, of course, further cognitive growth. Only three operant-training sessions spaced about 1-week apart have been possible to date. A button-pressing device was designed for her most promising response: a right hand and arm movement. The task set for M. was a green–yes vs. red–no discrimination problem with facility shaped using operant-conditioning procedures. In this paradigm, a correct press with her right hand was immediately rewarded. It should also be emphasized that M. has poor control of her arms and an all or none extensor thrust. Also, it was necessary to support her head and body in a Mulholland chair. Music was initially used as a reward because M. had an uncontrollable biting reflex and extreme difficulty swallowing. Nevertheless, mashed bananas were introduced as a reward during the third 30-min conditioning session when music lost its appeal.

The latency to press from the onset of a signal light is plotted over trial blocks in Figure 3.14. It is clear that M. responded very quickly to training and reduced her average latency from about 50 secs on the first two trial blocks to about 10 secs during the last two trial blocks in Session 2. This rapid learning supports the overall impression of maturity conveyed by the perceptual cognitive testing, but is not an adequate test in itself. The speed with which M. began to press the button, a latency of about 10 secs, also demonstrates the tremendous force with which the mind can pull the body— even when the body is disabled.

The third session was even more remarkable. During the first nine trials, it became clear, from the high latency to responding, that M. was not in the mood for music. Despite her severe feeding problem, we chose to offer her bananas contingent upon correct pressing of the yes button. The mean la-

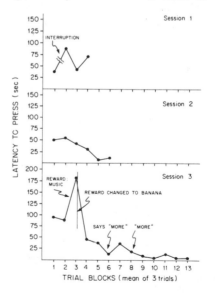

FIG. 3.14. Latency to press a button upon command during three training sessions with a child with severe quadriplegia.

tency of 175 secs on Trial Block 3 dropped abruptly to a mean of about 45 secs on Trial Block 4 and down to a mean latency of less than 3 secs on Trial Blocks 10, 12, and 13. The most astounding result occurred during Trial Block 6. In response to the question, "Do you want more bananas, "M, a child who never spoke previously, answered, "more." Fortunately, to eliminate any doubt in our minds, M. repeated the word *more* during Trial Block 8 when asked, "Do you want more? Press the button to say yes."

Clearly, much remains to be done before M. fully acquires the ability to communicate her needs and express her abilities either through button pressing or speech. However, the gratifying fact is that M. responded rapidly and at such variance from previous expectations to suggest that her level of competence far exceeds that inferred from conventional testings. Her behavior convinced us that not only does she possess the potential to validate the procedures but that gaining the ability to communicate will provide her an avenue to facilitate development of her greatest remaining asset — her mind.

CONCLUDING COMMENTS

Our success with the perceptual–cognitive procedures indicates that new approaches to infant assessment are not only needed, but possible. The results from this huge array of data were remarkably consistent. The findings from the original cross-sectional normative sample have been confirmed with the large longitudinal sample. The results across stimulus sequences were consistent, as illustrated by the similarity for vocalization to the cube and light sequences. The findings for the perceptual–cognitive procedures were confirmed with the functional play procedure in which face validity was particularly clear. Finally, the therapeutic interventions applied with the clinical sample have repeatedly led to developmental progress where little hope was present. We have learned that it was necessary to relinquish long-held assumptions; the developing infant had to be viewed through different lenses. Clearly, the ultimate test of this perceptual–cognitive assessment approach rests with the infant's improvement following intervention. Fortunately, for most practitioners, whether physicians or psychologists, the child is more sacred than the theory; improving the infant's lot is uniformly more desirable than adherence to an overly taxed sensorimotor theory. In the last analysis, the perceptual–cognitive procedures will gain acceptance if they work.

REFERENCES

Bailyn, B. *The idealogical origins of the American Revolution.* Cambridge, Mass.: Belknap Press, 1967.

Bayley, N. Psychological development of the child, Part III: Mental measurement. In F. Faulkner (Ed.), *Human development.* Philadelphia: Saunders, 1966.

Bayley, N. *Bayley Scales of Infant Development.* New York: The Psychological Corporation, 1969.

Bower, T. G. R. Repetition in human development. *Merrill–Palmer Quarterly,* 1974, **20,** 303-318.

Campos, J. Heart rate: A sensitive tool for the study of emotional development. In L. Lipsitt (Ed.), *Developmental psychobiology: The significance of infancy.* Hillsdale, N. J.: Lawrence Erlbaum Associates, 1976.

Cattell, P. The measurement of intelligence of infants and young children. New York: The Psychological Corporation, 1960.

Crothers, B., & Paine, R. S. *The natural history of cerebral palsy.* Cambridge, Mass.: Harvard University Press, 1957.

Decarie, T. G. A study of the mental and emotional development of the thalidomide child. In B. M. Foss (Ed.), *Determinants of infant behavior* (Vol. IV). London: Methuen & Co., 1969.

Escalona, S., & Corman, H. *The validation of Piaget's hypothesis concerning the development of sensori-motor intelligence: Methodological issues.* Paper presented at the bienniel meetings of the Society for Research in Child Development, New York, March 1967.

Fantz, R. L., Pattern vision in young infants. *The Psychological Record,* 1958, **8,** 43-47.

Fenson, L., Kagan, J., Kearsley, R. B., & Zelazo, P. R. The developmental progression of manipulative play in the first two years. *Child Development,* 1976, **47,** 232-6.

Frankenburg, W. K., Dodds, J. B., & Fandal, A. *The revised Denver Developmental Screening Test manual.* Denver: University of Colorado Press, 1970.

Gesell, A. *The mental growth of the pre-school child,* New York: MacMillan, 1925.

Griffiths, R. *The abilities of babies.* London: University of London Press, 1954.

Haith, M. M. *Visual scanning in infants.* Paper presented at the regional meetings of the Society for Research in Child Development, Clark University, 1968.

Hobbs, N. *The futures of children.* Washington, D. C.: Jossey-Bass, 1975.

Holman, L. B., & Freedheim, D. K. A study of I.Q. retest evaluation on 370 cases of cerebral palsy. *American Journal of Physical Medicine,* 1959, **38,** 180-187.

Hopkins, J. R., Zelazo, P. R., Jacobson, S. M., & Kagan, J. Infant reactivity to stimulus-schema discrepancy. *Genetic Psychology Monographs,* 1976, **93,** 27-62.

Kagan, J. *Change and continuity in infancy,* New York: Wiley, 1971.

Kagan, J. Do infants think? *Scientific American,* 1972, **226,** 74-82.

Kagan, J., Kearsley, R., & Zelazo, P. *Infancy: Its place in human development.* Cambridge, Mass: Harvard University Press, 1978.

Kahneman, D., Tursky, B., Shapiro, D., & Crider, A. Pupillary, heart rate and skin resistance changes during a mental task. *Journal of Experimental Pschology,* 1969, **79,** 164-167.

Kinney, D. K., & Kagan, J. Infant attention to auditory discrepancy. *Child Development,* 1976, **47,** 155-164.

Kopp, C. B., & Shaperman, J. Cognitive development in the absence of object manipulation during infancy. *Developmental Psychology,* 1973, **9,** 430.

Kotelchuck, M. A child's tie to his father. Unpublished doctoral dissertatin, Harvard University, 1972.

Kotelchuck, M., Zelazo, P. R., Kagan, J., & Spelke, E. Infant reactions to parental separations when left with familiar and unfamiliar adults. *Journal of Genetic Psychology,* 1975, **126,** 255-262.

Lacey, J. I. Somatic response patterning in stress: Some revision of activation theory. In M. H. Appley & R. Trumball (Eds.), *Psychological stress: Issues in research.* New York: Appleton-Century-Crofts, 1967.

Lewis, M. M. *How children learn to speak.* New York: Basic Books, 1959.

Lewis, M. Individual differences in the measurement of early cognitive growth. In J. Hellmuth (Ed.), *Exceptional infant* (Vol. 2) Bainbridge Island, Wash.: Brunner, Mazel, 1970.

Lewis, M., & Goldberg, S. The acquisition and violation of expectancy: An experimental paradigm. *Journal of Experimental Child Psychology,* 1969, **7,** 70-80.

McCall, R. B. Exploratory manipulation and play in the human infant. *Monographs of the Society for Research in Child Development,* 1974, **39,** Serial No. 155.

McCall, R. B., & Kagan, J. Stimulus–schema discrepancy and attention in the infant. *Journal of Experimental Child Psychology,* 1967, **5,** 381-390.

McCall, R. B., & Melson, W. H. Attention in infants as a function of magnitude of discrepancy and habituation rate. *Psychonomic Science,* 1969, **17,** 317-319.

McCall, R. B., Hogarty, P. S., & Hurlburt, N. Transitions in infant sensory-motor development and the prediction of childhood I. Q. *American Psychologist,* 1972, **27,** 728-748.

Mounoud, P., & Bower, T. G. R. Conservation of weight in infants. *Cognition,* 1974, **3,** 29-40.

Piaget, J. *The origins of intelligence in children.* New York: International University Press, 1952. (Originally Published, 1936.)

Piaget, J. *Play, dreams, and imitation in childhood.* New York: Norton, 1962.

Roe, K. V. Amount of infant vocalization as a function of age: Some cognitive implications. *Child Development,* 1975, **46,** 936-941.

Ross, G., Kotelchuck, M., Kagan, J., & Zelazo, P. Separation protest in infants in home and laboratory. *Developmental Psychology,* 1975, **11,** 256-257.

Sokolov, E. N. *Perception and the conditioned reflex.* (S. W. Wadenfeld, trans.) New York: Macmillan, 1963.

Sroufe, L. A., & Waters, E. The ontogenesis of smiling and laughter: A perspective on the organization of development in infancy. *Psychological Review.* 1976, **83,** 173-189.

Stott, L. H., & Ball, R. S. Infant and preschool mental tests: Review and evaluation. *Monographs of the Society for Research in Child Development,* 1965, **30,** (Serial No. 101).

Super, C., Kagan, J., Morrison, F., Haith, M., & Weiffenbach, J. Discrepancy and attention in the five-month infant. *Genetic Psychology Monographs,* 1972, **85,** 305-331.

Trollope, F. *Domestic manner of the Americans* (D. Smalley, Ed.). New York: Alfred Knopf, 1949.

Ungerer, J., Brody, L., & Zelazo, P. Long-term memory for speech in the newborn. *Infant behavior and development,* 1978, **1,** 177-186.

Uzgiris, I., & Hunt, J. *Assessment in infancy: Ordinal scales of psychological development.* Urbana: University of Illinois Press, 1975.

Weinraub, M., & Lewis, M. The determinants of children's responses to separation. *Monographs of the Society for Research in Child Development,* 1977, **42,** Serial No. 172.

Willerman, L., & Fiedler, M. F. Infant performance and intellectual precocity. *Child Development,* 1974, **45,** 483-486.

Zelazo, P. R. Smiling and vocalizing: A cognitive emphasis. *Merrill–Palmer Quarterly,* 1972, **18,** 349-365.

Zelazo, P. R. *The year old infant: A point of major cognitive change.* Paper presented at the conference on "Dips" in Learning and Developmental Curves: Organization for Economic Cooperation and Development, St. Paul-de-Vence, France, March 1975.

Zelazo, P. R. Comments on "Genetic determinants of infant development: An overstated case." In L. Lipsitt (Ed.), *Developmental psychobiology: The significance of infancy.* Hillsdale, N. J.: Lawrence Erlbaum Associates, 1976 (a)

Zelazo, P. R. Fom reflexive to instrumental behavior. In L. Lipsitt, (Ed.), *Developmental psychobiology: The significance of infancy.* Hillsdale, N. J.: Lawrence Erlbaum Associates, 1976.(b)

Zelazo, P. R., Hopkins, J. R., Jacobson, S. M., & Kagan, J. Psychological reactivity to discrepant events: Support for the curvilinear hypothesis. *Cognition,* 1974, **2,** 385–393.

Zelazo, P. R., Kagan, J., & Hartmann, R. Excitement and boredom as determinants of vocalization of infants. *The Journal of Genetic Psychology,* 1975, **126,** 107–117.

Zelazo, P. R., & Kearsley, R. B. *Functional play: Evidence for a cognitive metamorphosis in the year-old-infant.* Paper presented at the biennial meeting of the Society for Research in Child Development, New Orleans, March 1977.

Zelazo, P. R., & Komer, M. J. Infant smiling to non-social stimuli and the recognition hypothesis. *Child Development,* 1971, **42,** 1327–1339.

Zelazo, P. R., Zelazo, N. A., & Kolb, S. Walking in the newborn. *Science,* 1972, **176,** 314–315.

4

Methods Used to Measure Linguistic Competence During the First Five Years of Life

Paula Menyuk
Boston University

Linguistic competence is a concept that is difficult to define in terms of specific behavioral measures. The notion, as first described by Chomsky (1966), was the speaker–listener's knowledge of the rules of the language: meanings of words and the relations between them (semantics), the forms used to expressed relations in sentences (syntax), the rules for composition of words (morphology), and the rules for generating the speech signal (phonology). This knowledge is tacit, that is, it does not play a role in the comprehension and production of language. Knowledge of linguistic competence can only be inferred from the language behavior that is manifested, derived primarily from the "intuitions" of the speaker–listener about the structure of the language. The speaker–listener's actual use of language was termed *performance.*

Since Chomsky's initial description of language competence, several additions and alterations have been made to this notion. The principal one, the one most germane to the topic of this paper, is the inclusion of "rules of use" in the repertoire of the speaker–listener's knowledge of the structure of language (Hymes, 1971) to carry out specific communicative acts (Searle, 1972). Thus, both the selection of what speech signal to generate and the circumstances that surround its production is what the speaker–listener has knowledge of, and both form what has been termed *linguistic competence.*

There are two basic problems that these descriptions create in any attempt to measure linguistic competence over the first 5 years of life. The first is the complexity of the behavior to be measured. That is, semantic, syntactic, morphological, phonological, and pragmatic (rules of use) knowledge(s) are involved simultaneously in any communicative act. Therefore, both the specific aspects of each of these components and the act as a whole should be measured. Second, because it has been assumed, thus far, that competence does not play a direct role in the comprehension and production of language but can only be inferred from the behavior, any attempt to measure competence per se is presumably doomed to failure. This is obviously an untenable position for those who are concerned with developing assessments of language behavior that will indicate whether a child has or *will* have a language problem as well as the nature of the problem itself. Therefore, for the purposes of this discussion, it is necessary to assume the position that we can make valid inferences about language competence from measures of language behavior (performance) and can predict from these measures how a child will function over time in a variety of communicative situations.

However, a cautionary note is needed with regard to both the selection of stimuli to assess linguistic competence and exemplar situations in which to test it. The selection of stimuli, for example, can, during later periods of development within the first 5 years, seriously affect the results of assessments, because different dialects of a language, as well as different languages, realize so-called universal linguistic categories and relations (Greenberg, 1966) in somewhat different ways. A number of researchers have examined the linguistic competence of children from varying sociolinguistic backgrounds and have concluded that these children are language deficient (Menyuk, 1971). It is, however, important to distinguish between those children who have a problem in language development and those children who have not acquired some aspects of a language different from their own.

In addition, in order to generalize about the level of structural and pragmatic linguistic competence of children, it is important to select, control, and manipulate those processing and situational factors that have been found to have the greatest effect on the particular language behaviors. For example, spontaneous language production in a particular communicative situation (i.e., describing objects for selection) does not tell us anything about this behavior in other communicative situations nor does it provide any information about how language will be used in an academic task, such as learning to read, where conscious awareness of linguistic categorization is required (Menyuk, 1976b). Similarly, assessment of communicative competence in the situation described above can be affected by whether the child is talking about familiar or unfamiliar objects and events (Krauss & Glucksberg, 1967). These problems are discussed at greater length in the section *Measures Used to Assess Linguistic Competence.*

There is still another problem that needs to be addressed in measuring linguistic competence over the first 5 years of life and using these measures to predict or to plan programs of intervention. Compensatory developmental changes may occur, but too late. That is, there may be critical periods for language development. Because of the plasticity of the human infant, it has been suggested that lesions suffered at birth might lead to changes in the functional neurological substrates of language behavior. These changes, despite the lesion, might yet result in a "normal" pattern of language development (Lenneberg, 1967). Thus, the linguistic consequences of some birth defects may be compensated for during later stages of the child's development. Other research findings suggest that there can be long-lasting effects of lesions sustained before or at the time of birth (Kinsbourne, 1975) and that language development may be "different" under those circumstances. Whether compensations do or do not occur presumably depends on the nature of the lesion (Geschwind, 1967). These possibilities create problems in assessment. That is, it is not clear that the data of early assessments can provide us with appropriate predictive information nor tell us when or how to intervene. Indeed, the state of the art indicates that a question that needs to be carefully researched is: What linguistic behaviors at an early age are good predictors of either normal or nonnormal language development?

In summary, adequate assessment of linguistic competence over the first 5 years of life is beset with the general problems of what to measure, how to measure it, and when (or how often).

The remainder of this paper is a discussion of what is known about language development during this period, the explanations provided for these developments, and the techniques used to acquire these data. Some suggestions are made for the development of techniques that might overcome some of the problems outlined above.

MANIFESTATIONS OF LINGUISTIC COMPETENCE

The following is a brief summary of the developmental changes that occur in language behavior over the first 5 years of life. There has been a rapid expansion of literature in this area because there appears to be increased recognition that language development is crucial to the social, emotional, and cognitive development of the child. It is for this reason that those who are concerned with the development of handicapped children have directed attention to their language development. Studies of premature infants indicate that a sizable percentage are retarded in all aspects of language development in addition to behavior and level of educational achievement (e.g., deHirsch, Jansky, & Langford, 1964; Dreyfus–Brisac, Lézine, & Berges, 1964). The effect of retardation of language development on social and intellectual development has not been seriously explored with a premature population. There is a possibility that negative effects occur from the earliest stages. The details become clear as linguistic behavior is described during this period.

To facilitate the discussion, I have divided the 0 to 5 year period into separate subperiods that are based on distinctive changes in language production. These subperiods are: vocalization and babbling (ages 0 to 12 months), acquisition of lexical items and basic relations (12 to 18 months), expression of basic relations (18 to 24 months), expansion of basic relations (24 to 36 months), and acquisition of the specific rules of the language (30 to 50 months). Despite this segmentation, there is a great deal of overlapping of behaviors between the periods that indicates a continuity or dependency of later development on earlier stages.

The aspects of language behavior that have been examined, with varying degrees of detail over these developmental subperiods, are the production of language, the perception of language, the use of language in varying cognitive tasks, and the use of language in communicative interaction. Over the entire period obvious changes occur in the structure of language that is perceived and produced. Changes also occur in the degree to which children use language to remember, plan actions, and solve problems, and the degree to which they take into account the situation in which they are communicating and the person they are addressing. This latter behavior has been described as *communicative competence.* The developments described below are discussed in much greater detail elsewhere. Some of these sources are: vocalization and babbling (Eimas, 1974; Menyuk, 1972, 1974; Morse, 1974); lexical acquisition (Bloom, 1973; Greenfield & Smith, 1976; Nelson, 1973); basic relations (Bloom, 1970; Bowerman, 1973; Brown, 1973); expansion of basic relations (Brown, 1973; McNeill, 1970; Menyuk, 1971); acquisition of specific rules (Bever, 1970a; Brown, Cazden & Bellugi–Klima, 1968; McNeill, 1970; Mehler, 1971; Menyuk, 1969, 1971); use of language (cognitive: Wozniak, 1972; communicative: Menyuk, 1977).

During the vocalization and babbling period, systematic changes occur in infants' production of the speech signal, but apparently not in their discrimination of differences between speech signals. Research to date indicates that infants are capable of making these discriminations as early as 1 month of age. Non-cry as well as cry vocalizations occur from birth, and these vocalizations are indicative of the physiological, comfort, or discomfort state of the child. Initial non-cry sounds are primarily vocalic; i.e., modification of the air stream occurs by random manipulations of the articulators, but no deliberate closure along the vocal tract, necessary for consonants (Cs), occurs. The vocalic repertoire changes toward the end of this early period in terms of the proportional use of certain vowels (Vs). As the infant achieves greater control of the vocal mechanism and spends longer periods of time in a sitting position, true babblings (CVs or VCs) are produced as a string of vocal utterances. Over the babbling period, the infants' consonantal repertoire changes in terms of the proportional use of types of consonants. Changes also occur in the CV composition of babbled strings. These changes in proportional usage of different types of vowels, consonants, and syllables may indicate deliberate attempts on the infants' part to match auditory categorizations to articulatory productions rather than simply being a product of greater control of the vocal mechanism. In addition to segmental (speech sound) changes occurring over this period, the suprasegmental (intonation and stress) aspects of the utterances change. Initially, the fundamental frequency patterns of these utterances are either a gradual rise and fall or a sharp rise and fall (unmarked and marked breath groups). Later, modifications of these basic patterns are observed as infants use non-cry vocalizations more frequently to communicate needs, feelings, or simply to socialize. Finally, patterns of rising, falling, and then rising again (the request pattern) are observed towards the close of the babbling period.

Studies of the speech sound and suprasegmental discrimination of infants indicate that at about 1 to 4 months of life, infants discriminate between acoustic signal changes that mark speech sound and suprasegmental pattern differences over a syllable. It is not clear that they can hold in memory more than a syllable-length utterance at this early age. They do not respond differentially to acoustic signal changes that are *within* a segmental or suprasegmental category but only to those which cross categories. These behaviors, plus data that indicate that there are hemispheric differences in the processing of acoustic information (speech vs. nonspeech) at 1 month of age (Molfese, 1973), have led to the hypothesis that human infants have, as part of their biological repertoire, acoustic-feature detectors. The features that infants are sensitive to are those that do, indeed, mark speech-sound categories (Eimas, 1974). Observational data also indicate that infants are sensitive to those speech-sound signal characteristics that distinguish friendly and unfriendly voices, male and female voices, and female stranger vs. mother voices. Thus, infants are capable of discriminating the difference between the acoustic characteristics of intonational patterns that mark rising vs. falling contours, as well as some features of communicative intent and speaker identification. At a very early age, between 2 and 3 months of life, turn-taking in vocalization interactions has been observed between infant and caretaker. These have been termed *proto-conversations.* The intent of these vocalization interactions does not appear to be manipulation of the environment to bring about some desired change, but, rather, to socialize. Vocalizations, then, over this period serve to express needs and feelings, indicate desired objects and events, and simply communicate with caretakers.

At about 13 to 14 months, the infants' vocalizations become reduced in length from strings of syllables to word-length utterances. Before this occurs, researchers have observed that infants respond by attention to and search for familiar people, objects, and actions that have been named. Assuming that perception precedes production, and there is ample evidence to indicate that this is the case, it can be concluded that before the period of word approximations begins, children have achieved not only an understanding of the communicative intent of utterances (conveyed by suprasegmental features of the utterance, facial expression, and gesture) but also comprehension of the fact that particular phonological sequences (words) are being used to *predicate* (to refer specifically) about objects and events in the environment. Children, then, begin to map the articulatory gestures that they have previously generated during the babbling period onto particular sequences that are understood. These articulatory "realizations" are, in turn, used by children to predicate about objects and events in the environment as well as to communicate needs and feelings and to socialize. Thus, the word approximations or standard lexical items that are produced reflect a minimal level of the children's semantic knowledge (word meaning) and phonological knowledge. In like fashion, it is reasonable to suggest, and there is experimental evidence to support the suggestion, that over the so-called holophrastic (one word) period, children acquire knowledge not only of the semantics and phonology of words, but also, an understanding of some semantic relations (e.g., action–object) and of some syntactic rules of word order to express the semantic relation. The rules of word order that are acquired reflect those of the particular language to which the child is exposed (Menyuk, 1976a).

The sequence of development over this period and into the lexical production period is shown in Table 4.1, which outlines what the infant perceives and produces linguistically and the communicative intent of the utterances produced. There is obviously continuity (in the comprehension and use of intonation, facial expression, and gesture to communicate intent) and dependency (in the mapping of speech-sound articulatory gestures onto a new domain—the word). There is also new knowledge required during this period as reflected in the use of phonological sequences to predicate about objects and events in the environment. It is important to observe that by the time children reach the word-acquisition period, they have *already* acquired a great deal of knowledge about both the structure and use of language.

This period is followed by sequential word utterances, which in turn is followed by the two-word utterance period. During the sequential one-word period, the basic relations of actor + object, action + object (drink juice), actor + action (Mommy go) and attributes of objects and actions, adjective + noun (big truck), possessor + possessed (baby eye), demonstrative + noun (that ball), object + location (boy down), and action + location (go out) are expressed in utterances produced and, for the most part, in the correct order in terms of the language of the environment (Horgan, 1976). There is evidence that when the child is primarily producing one-word utterances, there is good understanding of action + object and actor + action relations (Sachs & Truswell, 1976) and that when sequential one-word utterances are produced, there is an understanding of the range of relations described above plus some three-part relations (actor + action + object) (Horgan, 1976). Two-word utterances presumably describe the *same* relations as those found in sequential one-word utterances. What happens over this period is that changes occur in the proportional usage of certain relations, not in the acquisition of new relations. This latter accomplishment seems to take place over the holophrastic period. The term *sequential single-word utterances* is used to describe utterances of two related words with a marked pause between them, but *not* a falling to base level of the fundamental frequency characteristics of each word (Branigan, 1976). Thus, what one is observing during this period is the coding of already acquired knowledge into more and more skilled motor movements. The problem the child has is to code semantic–syntactic knowledge into phonological representations that must then be realized in terms of articulatory gestures. This is quite a different task than that of understanding how basic relations are encoded in the language.

TABLE 4.1
Perception and Production of Structural Properties of Speech
and Use of Properties: From Vocalization to Words

Production	Perception	Use
Vocalization-change in proportional use of vowels	Speech sound and intonation Differences of syllable length Segments Affective intent Speaker identification	Express needs and feelings, and socialize
Babbling-change in proportional use of speech sound, syllabic, and intonation patterns	Relation between speech signal and some Objects and Events Communicative intent (State, demand, request	Indicate desired objects and events
Word approximations and words (integration of perception and production)	Observations of semantic syntactic relations	Represent relation between objects and events

In terms of the communicative functions of language, changes occur both over the one-word and two-word utterance periods. This has been described as a shift in function from the purely performative (used to demand or indicate) to the reportative (Gruber, 1967). Performatives are verbalizations of what one does by means of the utterance at the time of the utterance and serve as label to the act. Reportatives attribute characteristics to the topic of the sentence and, during the two-word period, refer to events that have occurred or will occur, ("Donnie out," "Kathleen coming"). During the one-word period, a shift also occurs from performative to reportative utterances, but in utterances of both types produced during this period, reference is made only to states or actions that are present. Again, there is continuity and dependency between the periods of development from one-word to two-word utterances and also in the acquisition of new knowledge. What is newly acquired during the two-word utterance period is the use of language to refer to events that have or will take place. The

TABLE 4.2
Function and Structure of Two-Word Utterances

Function	Structure
Performatives	Wanting: me, my, more + object or action[a] Negating: no + object or action Affirming: yes, do + object or action Requesting: (please) + object or action Question: wh[b] object or action
Reportatives	Action + object Actor + object Actor + action Location + object Location + action Attribution + object Possessor + possessed

[a]Appropriate intonational patterns are applied to indicate communicative intent, i.e., to state, demand, request, or question.
[b]Wh words are what, where, etc.

developmental changes that occur in the functional use of language and the structural content of utterances over this period are indicated in Table 4.2.

The following two periods have been labeled the "expansion of basic relations" and "acquisitions of the specific rules of the language" periods. At the beginning of the first period, three-part relations of subject, verb, and object become the rule rather than the exception. That is, in terms of mean word length of sampled utterances, we are now in the 3+ word period. Simultaneously, each of the above main constituents of the sentence and the sentence itself begins to be expanded. Subjects become article + adjective + noun (the big boy), verbs become verb + tense (going), or auxiliary + verb (is go) and modal + verb (can go), verb + adverb (want drink now), and objects become object + prepositional phrase (the book on floor). Sentences become expanded by conjunction (I see boy and girl) and by embedding (I want to go). By the time children are 3, 4, or 5 years of age, depending upon their rate of development, the basic syntactic, morphological, and phonological rules of the language have been acquired. The specific rules of the language for generating simple sentence types, marking time and number, and generating conjoined and embedded sentences occurs over this period. In addition, developmental changes occur in the relations between actors, actions and objects that will be encoded. Thus, "place" relations are encoded before "manner" relations, which are encoded before "time" relations.

As new lexical items are acquired, the child must determine the relation implied by the lexical item and how to realize it syntactically. For example, certain verbs are transitive (hit) whereas others are stative (know). These distinctions are marked in the syntax of the utterance by the use of differing tense markers ("I am hitting the boy," but not "I am knowing the boy."). Still other verbs require an embedded sentence, ("He realized that she was sick," but not "He realized the apple."). Other types of lexical items such as causal, conditional, and disjunctive connectives (because, if, but) impose different logical constraints on the predications that follow from them (semantic relations) and, therefore, on how they are realized (syntactic relations). Because lexical acquisition continues to occur, and additional or changing properties of lexical items are also added (Anglin, 1970), language continues to develop after age 5. Table 4.3 presents some examples of the developmental changes that occur in the expansion of main sentence constituents (subject and verb) and the development of simple sentence types, the expansion of sentence by embedded constructions, and the encoding of different semantic relations over time during the periods of expansion of relations' and acquisition of specific rules. It should be kept in mind that further developments occur after these periods but that the basic rules of all components of the grammar have been acquired by around age 5.

TABLE 4.3
Development of Sentence Types,
Embedding, and Semantic Relations

Sentence Types	Embedding	Semantic Relations
Negative	Complements	Within sentences
No go	I want to go	Place: in, on, under
He no go	I want *him* to go	Manner: slowly, in a hurry
He no *can* go	I see him *going*	Time: now, later, first
He *can't* go	Relatives	Across sentences
Question	I know what *is* he doing	Causal: because
Where go	I know what *he's* doing	Conditional: if, so
Where *he* go	I see the boy *who* fell	Temporal: when, before, after
Where he *did* go	The boy *who* fell is hurt	
Where *did* he go		

Two other aspects of the development of linguistic competence over this developmental period need to be considered. The first is the use of language in various cognitive tasks. Language begins to be used to plan and organize action at approximately age 3 and continues to function for these purposes into adulthood (Wozniak, 1972). In addition, there appears to be a shift from visual imagery to verbal imagery in certain memory tasks toward the close of this period, which also continues into adulthood (Conrad, 1972; Stevenson, 1970). Thus, by the time children enter school, language is being used in certain cognitive tasks that are very similar to the tasks that they will be asked to undertake in the school situation. It is also during this period that children begin to exercise their metalinguistic abilities, the ability to use language to think about and talk about language (Menyuk, 1976c). Again, these abilities are crucial to success in the academic tasks that will confront children in the school situation

The second aspect that needs to be considered in this discussion of the development of linguistic competence over this period is what has been termed *communicative competence*. It was long held that children were egocentric in their language use until the middle childhood years. What egocentrism implied to many interpreters of Piaget was that at a young age children engaged primarily in monologues and, at an older age, were unable to take their addressee's point of view. Some recent data indicate that very young middle-class American children are sensitive to the implications of such situational and linguistic subtleties as polite requests ("could you put your sweater on?") (Shatz, 1974) and also produce these subtleties by the use of intonation and mitigators (please) at an early age. In a group situation, they begin engaging in verbal communicative interaction with their peers at age 2 and by 4 years are directing most of their communication to their peers (Honig, Caldwell, & Tannenbaum, 1970). By 3.5 years of age, most of their communications are attended to and responded to by their peers (Mueller, 1972). Preschoolers engage in a variety of communicative acts. They know how to invite, request, insult, and excuse (Garvey & Hogan, 1973). These data all indicate that young children do not engage primarily in monologues.

The question of whether young children are sensitive to the communicative needs of their addressees has also been studied. Four year olds simplify and use attention-getting verbalizations when talking to 2 year olds (Shatz & Gelman, 1973) and take into account whether their listeners can see the situation they are describing (Maratsos, 1973). Given the data on turn-taking in infancy and these other data, it is clear that very young children have the desire to communicate with others, and learn fairly rapidly how to do so effectively. What develops in time is both the ability to take into account *all* the aspects of the situation that need to be considered in a communicative act (amount of information), the ability to observe abstract aspects of the situation (type of information), and the ability to express a range of communicative intents (available linguistic repertoire) (Menyuk, 1977). The degree to which children can communicate effectively with others in the linguistic community seriously affects the course of their emotional and social development.

The above descriptions of the development of linguistic competence have been derived primarily from studies of white middle-class American English-speaking children. As stated previously, different communities can have somewhat different structural rules and rules of communication. They may also have somewhat different expectations concerning the acquisition of these rules by the children in the community. These possible differences need to be taken into account when attempting to assess the development of linguistic competence.

THE BASES FOR DEVELOPMENT OF
LINGUISTIC COMPETENCE

Bever (1970b) has suggested that multiple factors affect language behavior and its development and that no one factor is logically prior to another. These factors are: social urge, common properties of human communication systems, psychological mechanisms, semantic structures, biological universals of human communication systems, and common properties of human cognition systems. These factors interact and modify each other. Although the above position is eminently reasonable, in order to understand normal and nonnormal language development, it is necessary to attempt to specify what these factors mean in terms of the physiological structures and psychological mechanisms available to the human and to examine how they interact with one another at different periods of development. Although at the present time we are far from achieving this goal, the following discussion is an attempt to provide the level of specification that is currently possible based on data that have been obtained from the language development of normal children as well as those whose development deviates from the norm.

To begin with, the factors mentioned above need to be explicated and expanded. These are my own interpretations and not necessarily Bever's. "Social urge" can best be translated into motivation on the part of the infant and child to interact communicatively with other humans in the environment. Bell and Ainsworth (1972) have suggested that this is an innate mechanism. Common properties of human communication systems are those structures and the relations of structures (e.g. semantics, syntax) that make up any language. Thus, the problems confronting any child in acquiring any language are those involved in determining the underlying meaning of utterances from a set of arbitrary symbols represented in the speech signal. An example of this kind of problem is the fact that the acoustic signal for any word varies from speaker to speaker and from context to context. The child must learn what features distinguish a particular word from any other despite this variation. Psychological mechanisms refer to the processing strategies used by the listener to derive meaning from the signal. An example of this would be to search for the main verb in an utterance, determine its subject, chunk the main predication, and then chunk the subordinate predication (for example, "The boy who hit the ball hid under the table." "The boy hid under the table." "The boy hit the ball."). This is in contradistinction to processing one word at a time. These same strategies are reflected in production in that pauses occur at boundaries of clauses.

Semantic structures refer to the ability to relate language to objects and events in the environment. An example of this is the ability to relate spatial terms to location relations of objects. Knowledge of categories and relations of objects and events in the environment will obviously affect whether such a relation is made.

Biological universals of human communication systems can be defined as those aspects of the system that, through evolution, have developed to fit the capacity of the human in processing temporal auditory information (Hockett, 1966) and reproducing it (Lieberman, Crelin, & Klatt, 1972). An example of this is the fact that every language has a consistent ordering typology for constituents of a sentence (Greenberg, 1966). Therefore, processing strategies can be developed that will, in most instances, lead to successful interpretation.

The final factor mentioned by Bever (1970b), common properties of human cognition systems, is more difficult to define because the nature of these properties is not clear. It may be that the special nature of human memory, how information is stored and retrieved, and how it develops in the young child, is the common property of human cognition systems. However, the nature of human memory is still a matter of some controversy (e.g., Russell, 1971; Woodburne, 1967). In addition, there is also the question of the role of language in contributing to the uniqueness of man's memory. A factor not mentioned by Bever, but obviously an important one, is an appropriate response from the environment. A distinction is made in the following discussion between modeling and the appropriate response that, I believe, is important in terms of possible interventions.

During the period of vocalization and babbling, three factors can be identified as affecting language development: biological readiness to acquire language, biological readiness to interact with the environment, appropriate responses from the environment. As has already been mentioned, there are data indicating that at 1 month of age, there are hemispheric differences in response to speech and nonspeech stimuli (Molfese, 1973) that may be related to individual differences in the relative size of the hemispheres in the human neonate (Geschwind, 1972). There is also the suggestion that in the human infant, there is particular sensitivity to *certain* acoustic-signal differences. These differences are those that mark speech-sound boundaries (Eimas, 1974). Presumably, this special sensitivity to certain parameters can be found not ony in the auditory domain but also the visual (Karmel, 1972). In addition to these possible acoustic–visual feature detectors, the human infant's vocal track is unique in its capacity to phonate and articulate speech sounds (Menyuk, 1971). The behavioral repertoire of infants' respones to speech is different from that observed with other acoustic stimuli, and their motoric responses appear to be synchronous with adult speech (Condon & Sander, 1974). These sensitivities and responses may together lead to that behavior described as conversational turn-taking at 3 months of life. There is evidence, however, that this "readiness" can either be enhanced by appropriate responses from the environment or somewhat diminished. Those infants whose cries are responded to promptly are those whose crying behavior diminishes more rapidly in frequency and urgency over the first year of life and who more quickly and frequently replace cry vocalizations with non-cry vocalizations as a means of interaction (Bell & Ainsworth, 1972).

The chances that appropriate responses will come from the environment are much diminished for those infants who do not display the response to adult speech described above. A dramatic example is the case of autistic infants who respond with startle to speech as well as other sounds, do not establish eye contact with their caretakers, and withdraw from touch. Under these conditions, it is difficult for caretakers to respond appropriately. Conversational turn-taking usually takes place when the infant is content and face to face with the mother, at a certain minimal distance (Bateson, 1969). If the infant is highly irritable, which is often the case with premature infants, then the opportunities for conversational turn-taking may be much reduced. It should be emphasized that prompt response to cry and engaging in conversational turn-taking is not directly tutorial in terms of establishing speech-sound categories and sequences, and their relation to objects and events. Menyuk (1974) has observed that some mothers spend a great deal of time attempting to elicit imitations, whereas others tend to name objects for their infants, and still others do both. However, no direct effect of these varying types of input or amount of input on the child's vocalization and babbling behavior has been found (Tulkin & Kagan, 1972). Perhaps only extremes of input behavior have an effect on the rate of acquisition or the quality of linguistic behaviors during this period.

Given normal development over the previous period, three factors play a role in further development during the lexical item and basic relations acquisition period: cognitive factors, psychological mechanisms, and types of input. Recent discussions regarding the relation between cognitive factors and language acquisition have emphasized what is termed *cognitive prerequisites to language behavior*. The cognitive prerequisites for lexical acquisitions and acquisitions of basic relations are said to be object permanence and logical ordering of objects and events (Sinclair de Zwart, 1971). This position is quite different from the one previously suggested. *That* position did not imply dependency of language achievements on particular cognitive achievements. Rather, it implied that during the vocalization–babbling period (or sensorimotor period), the child's ability to categorize all sensorimotor experiences, to sort, and retrieve these experiences changes over time (Menyuk, 1975a). The exact nature of these changes is a matter of speculation, but the behavioral products, in both the linguistic and nonlinguistic domain, suggest that changes in information storage occur in both amount and type. Acquisition of linguistic and nonlinguistic structures may initially be independent (behaviorally and neurologically) of each other but are subsequently recruited together in the acquisition of lexical items and basic relations. This proposed integration of linguistic and nonlinguistic processing as a prerequisite to comprehension and production of single word and sequential utterances, and to categorization of objects and relations between objects and events, is certainly not new. Vygotsky (1962) spoke of this integration as a coming together of thought and word. The only alteration that I would make to Vygotsky's suggestion is that it is not simply thought and word that come together but, rather, sensorimotor "schema" and a *predication*. The word is not representative of a single entity but of a relation between entities. Further, as was stated previously, by the time the child is well into the holophrastic period, there is evidence indicating that such relations are understood in the utterances heard. Motor-planning constraints, when the amount of information to be encoded increases, are those that appear to limit utterances to holophrases or sequential single words rather than limits in comprehension of relations.

Two aspects of the "psychological mechanism' factor play a role in further development, and these are perceptual strategies and productive strategies. Retrieval of information for generating language may be the factor that is particularly germane to the language problems of premature infants who have been observed to have both articulation problems and problems of stammering or stuttering. Although there appears to be a close relation between what is linguistically perceived and what is produced throughout the course of development, how closely and faithfully these facets of development are related seems to vary depending on the processing factors involved in the generation of particular phonological and syntactic structures (Menyuk, 1969, 1972). For example, although perceptual distinction between strident sounds (/s/, /f/, /sh/) are made at an early age in a minimal triad task, they cause difficulty in a reproductive task. These differences between the requirements of a perceptual task vs. a reproductive task are particularly evident in some studies of children with suspected neurological abnormalities. *Some* of these children who are still only able to produce or reproduce subject–verb–object sentences or some simple expansions of these sentences at a fairly advanced age (4 to 9 years) are able to perceive syntactic and phonological distinctions that are far beyond this level of development. There are others for whom both aspects of processing are involved (Menyuk & Looney, 1972a). Difficulties in the generation of language may affect the use of language in various cognitive tasks and, therefore, not only affect communicative competence but other functions as well. There is the question of whether actual production, or subvocal articulation of utterances, or acoustic imagery plays an important role in memory tasks and reading (Menyuk, 1976b).

The general productive strategy seems to be to encode somewhat less than you perceive. Thus, during the holophrastic stage, there is perception of two-part relations; during the two-word utterances period, there is perception of three-part relations, etc. However, at later stages of development, there is evidence that some structures are spontaneously produced or reproduced (e.g., center embedded relatives) that are not understood. In general, the relations between perception, reproduction (imitation), and production in the acquisition of linguistic competence has not been carefully examined over the entire developmental period of 0 to 5 years. For example, evidence exists that there is large individual variation in the amount of spontaneous imitation a particular child will engage in (Nelson, 1973) but no follow-up data to indicate whether this makes a difference in the level of linguistic competence achieved at age 5. These data, if obtained, could have obvious importance in furthering our understanding of the language development and educational achievements of children whose primary problem appears to be one of output.

The perceptual–psychological mechanisms that are employed during this period are used to determine how the language encodes actor–action, action–object, possession, location, and attribution, i.e., the syntactic forms that encode semantic relations. The strategy used appears to be to ignore any of the noise before, between, and after these basic relations (Bever, 1970a). The question that arises is: How does the child manage to do this? It has been suggested that the language data presented to the child, at the beginning periods of language development, are in a form that allows the child to make these generalizations about the language. Caretakers are highly repetitive and speak in simpler forms during this period than at later periods (Snow, 1972). It is possible that particular patterns of intonation, stress, and gesture are used by caretakers to get the child to attend initially to the topic of conversation and then a topic + comment relation (Donahue & Watson, 1976). The relations may be isolated and stressed for the child. Here too, an interactive situation exists. There is evidence indicating that over a communication interlude (the same topic being discussed), mothers use the cues provided by the child's responses to continue using the same device or to modify it in some way. The important factor in input is that it be attuned stylistically (Nelson, 1973) and structurally (Phillips, 1973) to the child's level of language competence in general and to specific responses in communicative interactions in particular. This appears to be a matter of appropriate response from the environment rather than a modeling of language behavior.

In sum, the factors presented to account for further developments (expansion of basic relations and acquisition of the specific rules of the language) and for the *pattern* of these developments (the sequence in which structural knowledge is acquired) are: cognitive, psychological mechanisms, and the properties of the communication system to which the child is exposed. This last factor can account for differences among children who are acquiring different languages in the sequence or pattern of development of subsystems of the language (semantics, syntax, morphology, and phonology). The reason for this difference is because each language presents a somewhat different problem to be solved by the child (Slobin, 1973). Nevertheless, because of the common factors described at the beginning of this section, there is, presumably, universality in the sequence of development if not the *rate* of development. Mean length of utterance (MLU) has been used as a measure of development rate. The ages at which different MLUs are achieved by normally developing children vary. In one small sample population (Brown, 1973), the age range for achieving MLU 2.5 was 25 to 30 months; for MLU 3.5, 24 to 35 months; for MLU 4.5, 32 to 48 months. There are, however, distinct differences between the ranges of ages that would be considered normal for acquisition of these levels and those considered nonnormal (Menyuk, 1978). This is discussed in the section *Methods Used to Assess Linguistic Competence.*

One cognitive factor, presumed to play a role in further linguistic development, is general level of intelligence (as measured by standard intelligence tests). However, this is a tautology because methods of determining general intelligence emphasize verbal behavior. Thus, it is virtually impossible to disentangle linguistic competence from general intelligence.

Another cognitive factor cited is the ability of the child to engage in concrete operations. During this period, the child modifies the subject–verb–object sentence structure (negatives, questions, passives, conjunction, and embedding). Analogies have been drawn between this behavior and the ability of the child to solve such intellectual problems as conservation or reversibility (e.g., Beilin & Spontak, 1969). It may be stretching the argument to hold that the linguistic and nonlinguistic operations are analogous. It may, however, be the case that changes in both linguistic and cognitive performance during this period may be due to changes in information processing. The changes in structure and amount of linguistic information that can be processed during this period appear to be a product of the interaction of changing psychological mechanisms, and the structure of the communication system. By segmenting and chunking utterances (e.g., "The/boy/s/play/ed/in/the/yard"), the child can identify the rules for generating simple sentence types (noun phrase + verb phrase + prepositional phrase) along with markers of tense and number. Some utterances pose more difficult problems in segmentation and chunking because the main predication is interrupted ("The boy who kissed the girl ran away."). In still others the usual subject–verb–object order expected is not present in the main or subordinate clause. ("The boy was kissed by the girl." "The girl is easy to please." "The girl promised the boy to go.").

One proposed model of sentence processing is analysis by synthesis. In this model, the utterance is chunked into main predications with transformational tags, and then phrases segmented into parts, and so on, until, if necessary, a match is made between phonological representations and speech-sound segments (e.g., in sentences where minimal pairs might fit: "I gave him the pill/bill."). Although this process has been questioned in terms of its feasibility for on-line processing of a rapidly fading acoustic signal, and some alternative suggestions have been made, parts of it seem to be reflected in the sequence of development. That is, it provides an explanation of why both amount and structure of information play a role in the sequence. Thus, in language production, expansions of basic structures follow use of basic structures, and addition of elements in sentence types occurs before permutation of elements, first within, and then across sentences. In perception, there is correct interpretation of active sentences before passives, and passives before embedded relatives (Menyuk, 1971).

In studies of the reproduction abilities of children with suspected central nervous system abnormalities, Menyuk (1978) found that these children, again, at an advanced age, reproduce without expansions of main constituents or permutation of items in a string but preserve the main relations of subject–verb–object plus sentence markers of negation and question. When given conjoined and right-embedded sentences that preserve one predication, and when given center-embedded sentences, only last words are preserved. These data suggest that the amount of information and structure of information affect retrieval, reflecting the children's continuing greater difficulty in short-term memory-processing strategies as compared to normally developing children (Menyuk, 1975b).

The factor of the effect of communication experiences on further development during this period has been investigated primarily by studies of the linguistic and communicative competence of children from varying socio-linguistic environments. As stated previously, the data obtained may refer to assessments of linguistic and communicative competence in a language that is somewhat different from the child's native language. Therefore, many of these data should be viewed as reflecting a child's competence in Standard English. Some classic examples that may be referred to as deviancies are: tense markers ("I be playing."), double negation ("He don't never do that."), and reduction of final clusters ("Sen him a letter."). Because these forms may be a part of the linguistic system of the child's community, it seems reasonable that these should be the forms used. Because of this confusion, much of the research on the effect of input on the development of linguistic competence during this period has led to questionable results. The same can be said of studies of communicative competence. Because domain of discourse has a crucial impact on the ability of the child to communicate effectively, the results of such studies are also questionable. It seems necessary to review this whole developmental period with children in varying sociolinguistic environments from a different point of view and with different techniques. Given data on pre- and postnatal care in low socioeconomic status communities, as compared to middle-class communities, it is probable that these children are at greater risk, but the appropriate tools to determine whether they have a language problem need to be applied.

White (1970) referred to the 5- to 7-year age period as the one during which sensitivity is terminated. Presumably, this means that the plasticity observed previously, in the development of learning strategies, is much diminished at the end of this time. During this period, said White, the child has achieved the ability to reason like an adult. Language is used to store and recall information and to integrate information from several modalities. The neurological manifestation of this change, according to White, is that by about age 6 there is substantial completion of cortical maturation and, therefore, low-order cognitive mechanisms become inhibited and supplemented by high-order mechanisms. The 5- to 7-year period is also the age at which children throughout the world, who have the opportunity to do so, begin to attend school. It is the school experience that forces many children for the first time to bring to conscious awareness what they have learned about the structure of language if not the use of language. The process of learning to read, for example, requires bringing to conscious awareness first phonological categories and relations and then semantic categories and relations. If White is correct in his statements, much of the foundation has been laid for either success or failure by the time the child enters school. A large proportion of this success or failure is based on the level of linguistic competence achieved by the child at the time of school entry. As I have tried to indicate, biological, cognitive, and social factors have played specific roles during different periods from 0 to 5 years in the achievement of this competence.

MEASURES USED TO ASSESS
LINGUISTIC COMPETENCE

Both standardized tests and different experimental techniques have been used to assess linguistic competence during different periods over the age range of 0 to 5 years. Again, in this section I discuss each period separately and indicate what experimental techniques or tests have been used to assess linguistic competence during that period. I also comment on the validity and replicability of the techniques and tests used. Because there have been very few follow-up studies of the relation between particular early language behaviors and later language behaviors, the efficacy of these techniques in predicting later development cannot be discussed. I have some suggestions to make concerning this issue. The use of available techniques to sift out abnormal from normal language behavior at certain periods of development has been addressed and will be discussed. Finally, I indicate where I believe there are sizable gaps in the availability of assessment procedures and some possible ways of filling these gaps.

Most of the techniques described have been used by researchers to determine what infants and children know about language during various periods of development. These procedures, for the most part, have not been used to detect children who have or might have language problems, to identify the nature of these problems, or to plan interventions based on specific diagnoses. There are very few tests of linguistic competence that have been developed for children under age 3, and most of these are check lists or inventories that provide little information about young children's language-processing abilities. They do provide one means for determining whether the child *may* have a language problem and, therefore, should be referred for further intensive testing. One such test is The Physician's Developmental Quick Screen for Speech Disorders (Kulig & Baker, 1975). The test manual provides normative data for the accomplishment of certain linguistic behaviors from age 6 months to 6 years and contains information about the age norms for these behaviors that are also part of other frequently used scales. However, such items as "enjoys sound making," "combines sounds," "statements using no real words," which are typical of the 6 to 19 month inventory, are difficult to quantify with any accuracy. It is just these types of questionnaire items that need to be examined accurately to determine whether the child has a language problem as well a the nature of the disorder. The majority of the techniques used to examine, in any depth, linguistic competence before age 3 are either experimental or observational.

During the vocalization–babbling period, three aspects of linguistic competence have been examined: speech-sound discrimination and discrimination of suprasegmental patterns, production of speech-sound categories and of suprasegmental patterns, and communicative interaction. The techniques used to examine discrimination are changes in cardiac rate, haptic-sucking response, and auditory evoked potentials (Morse, 1974). The technique used to examine the production of language is to sample production for a varying amount of time (e.g., a full day's sample to a half-hour sample). The analytic procedures used for these kinds of data vary from phonetic transcription, spectographic analysis, and recently, computer modeling of the speech-sound products (Speech Communication, 1975). This latter technique has been used in an attempt to simulate the infant's cry and could potentially provide information about the source of generation of speech sounds and, thus, about the dimensions and functions of the vocal tract.

If obvious controls for the state of the infant are maintained, presumably replicable and quantifiable results can be obtained using the haptic sucking response as an indication of speech-sound discrimination in infants. Less replicable or quantifiable results are obtained using cardiac-rate change as a measure and still less using the average evoked response as a measure of *discrimination,* although auditory-threshold data can be obtained using this technique. The analytic procedures used with infants' speech-sound productions also vary in their replicability and quantifiability. Phonetic analyses of productions during this period, and later, are prone to listener bias. There is a tendency for adult listeners to categorize the vocalizations heard in terms of their own speech-sounds categories rather than the actual sounds being produced. However, pretraining of listeners can reduce interscorer variability so that at least the same data is being treated in the same way. Spectrographic analyses (a picture of the sounds produced) are much more accurate but difficult to interpret because the sampling procedure of the instrument is not ideally suited to the speech-sound range of infants. Such features as fundamental frequency, amplitude, and timing can be reliably measured, whereas, formant frequencies of speech sounds cannot (Menyuk & Klatt, 1975). Computer modeling of the end products of infant vocalization is potentially promising, but the programs developed have been based on adult vocal tracts, and a great deal of work is needed to modify the software before consistent and reliable data can be obtained.

Despite these difficulties, there is some evidence that the techniques employed to test discrimination and to analyze production can be useful not only in detecting children with difficulty, but also in distinguishing children with various types of difficulty (Menyuk, 1972). Efforts to distinguish among distressed infants on the basis of pain cry (e.g., Vuorenkoski, Wasz-Hockert, Lind, Koivisto, & Partinen, 1972) have met with varying degrees of success. There have been distinct differences found between distressed and nondistressed infants in habituation to acoustic patterns (Eisenberg, Coursin, & Rapp, 1966) and in the amount and quality of the vocalizations of normal hearing, hearing impaired, and at-risk infants (Cairns, Karchmer, & Smith, 1975).

Although it is clear that the differences in the discrimination and production of speech by severely hearing-impaired infants, those with Down's syndrome, and other obviously handicapped infants will lead to language problems at a later age, it is not clear that this is necessarily true for all infants or for those suffering from other types of developmental anomalies. That is, there is a possibility that these initial difficulties might be compensated for in those infants whose initial deficits may not impair the subsequent course of development. The availability of a sufficient degree of methodological sophistication offers the opportunity to run comparative, short-term longitudinal studies (from 6 to 18 months) in normally developing and premature infants in an attempt to identify indices of early language development useful in discriminating normal infants from a "linguistically at-risk" population.

Studies of communicative interaction patterns between infants and caretakers have just begun to be intensively studied (See *Developmental Psycholinguistics, Annals of the New York Academy of Science,* 1975, **263,** for a number of such papers.) The techniques used to examine these interactions are periodic samplings over varying lengths of time using videotape, acoustic tape recordings, and observational check lists to record the interactions. Both micro (sec intervals) and macro analyses of these recordings have been carried out. The parameters examined varied from study to study (e.g., amount of smiling, eye contact, touching, vocalization, type of the previous behaviors, or the conditions that lead to these behaviors within and across interactions). There is one study that has follow-up data at 2 years (Lewis & Freedle, 1972). In examining the language behavior of 3 of 50 infants at 12 weeks and at 2 years, Lewis and Freedle found that certain communicative interaction behaviors on the part of these infants at 12 weeks was predictive of some later language behaviors.

A hypothesis that early communicative interaction behavior is predictive of later linguistic competence is, at present, based on very little data. However, it is important to examine this question carefully for the purpose of planning intervention. For example, it might be the case that categories of interactional patterns for groups of high-risk infants can be determined. Some members of each group might develop language in a near normal pattern whereas others do not. Patterns of interaction may be found to be the critical factor in determining the outcome.

During the lexical acquisition and acquisition of basic relations period the most frequent technique used has been to collect samples of language periodically in the child's home. There have been few studies of language comprehension (Sachs & Truswell, 1976; Shipley, Smith & Gleitman, 1969). The techniques used to examine language comprehension are to ask children to either point to objects or pictures (i.e., comprehension of words) or to carry out actions on objects (i.e., comprehension of relations), or to imitate words or sentences. These techniques have not been standardized, but they are replicable and quantifiable. What is interesting is that children will carry out unfamiliar actions on objects (tickle car) as well as familiar (push car), which indicates that they comprehend both the words and the relations and not simply the context of the situation. In similar fashion, imitative behavior can be a good indication of what children comprehend as well as their ability to retrieve prior information (Menyuk, 1969). There are positive relations between age, number of words used, and number of relations comprehended. These techniques (imitation and comprehension) could be standardized and used to generate important data about normal and abnormal language development during this period.

Nelson (1973) examined the relationships among various indices of language behavior at early (10 to 15 months) and later (24 to 30 months) ages as well as the relation between language behavior and measures of cognitive development (Bayley Developmental Test for Mental and Motor Development, Concept Familiarity Index, and the Peabody Picture Vocabulary Test [PPVT]). In general, there were significant relations between certain language indices measured at the earlier stages and those measured at 24 months. However, by 30 months, most of these correlations, although still positive, were no longer significant. The age at which 10 words were acquired, the age at which 50 words were acquired, the age at which phrases were used, the rate of acquisition of vocabulary, MLU, and type/token ratio of vocabulary were all significantly intercorrelated at age 2 years. The ability to imitate and comprehend items was also significantly correlated with MLU and type/token ratio of vocabulary at age 2 years. The so-called cognitive measures (which were in fact measures of comprehension and/or production of varying syntactic classes: nouns, verbs, prepositions, determiners) were significantly intercorrelated. Moreover, these measures were also significantly correlated with age-appropriate language-behavior indices. Thus, PPVT scores were only significantly correlated with vocabulary at 24 and 30 months and MLU at 30 months. The comprehension tasks given at an earlier age were most predictive of language comprehension and production at 30 months.

These findings indicate that (a) the earlier the onset of productive language, the more rapidly will various aspects of language (lexical acquisition, two-word phrase, and MLU) increase up to 2 years; and (b) these early indications of the level of language development are not significant predictors of language sophistication at age 30 months. The problem, of course, is in the *selection* of appropriate language-behavior indices. Perhaps the techniques discussed previously (elicited imitation and comprehension of relations) would be better predictors than were the measures used. There is some indication in Nelson's (1973) study that comprehension at an early age is related to comprehension at a later age. However, follow-up studies are needed to determine the validity of this observation. During the next period of development, the sequential one-word utterance period, one would need to assess the comprehension of three-part relations, which are different not only in length from two-part relations, but also in structure. Thus, different aspects of comprehension and/or production competence need to be measured during different periods, not simply *more* of the same behaviors. Again, experimental techniques are available, but these techniques need to be standardized.

We turn now to evaluating what are normal ages for the acquisition of certain language behaviors and the relationship between language and cognitive development. Understanding of this relationship is vital in determining when and how to intervene among disabled preschoolers. In a previous section, some data were presented regarding the range of ages at which MLU increases in a normally developing population. Nelson (1973) reported mean ages and age ranges for the acquisition of certain language behavior indices. These data also indicate wide variability. However, when one uses the gross measure of MLU to compare the mean ages at which sentence length increases among a population of normally developing children and those diagnosed as developmentally dysphasic, the results are markedly different for the two populations. The age at which MLU is 2 + words was 60 months for the dysphasic group and 20 months in the normal population. This discrepancy in age of "acquisition" of increasingly longer utterances increases over time so that the age difference between normal and dysphasic groups, when MLU is 5.5 is 71 months. Further, and more importantly, the structures used in the same sentence lengths become increasingly varied for the normal speaking population but are much more limited in the dysphasic popuation (Menyuk, 1978).

The question arises as to what marks the difference, both in length and structure, between normal and abnormal language development at these early periods of development. Is it a 1- or 2-year difference in achieving the same MLU or is it a 10- or 30-structure difference? Although it is clear that the answer to the question is at present unavailable, we have the developmental data and the appropriate techniques to initiate efforts to obtain the answer during these early periods.

As I have said, the data on the relation between cognitive measures and linguistic measures describe a tautology. That is, in many instances cognitive measures simply measure limited aspects of linguistic competence. During these periods of development and later, cognitive tests (or intelligence tests) do not reveal what the processing difficulties of children with language problems are, but only that they have language problems. Researchers have often noted that the depression of overall scores of children described as learning disabled, developmentally dysphasic, mentally retarded, and autistic can be accounted for by comparatively lower scores on verbal scales. A 2-year discrepancy between verbal and performance scales has been found in populations of children with reading problems. Indeed, one group of children, the developmentally dysphasic, are described as being of normal intelligence (as measured by performance scales on intelligence tests), but as having a "special" language difficulty. However, recent data indicate that these children have processing difficulties in nonlinguistic as well as linguistic recall tasks that raise the possibility that performance scales on standard tests are not measuring appropriate behaviors (Menyuk, 1978). These data lead to the conclusion that measures of nonlinguistic processing, other than that currently available on standard tests need to be developed and standardized to examine the proposed relation between cognitive factors and language development.

The purpose of later assessments, from 2.5 years on are twofold. The first is to screen populations for detection of possible language disability. The second is to diagnose the nature of the language difficulty and to plan appropriate interventions. For this latter purpose, there are many tests available to examine varying aspects of children's language behavior. Some of these have been standardized, using a restricted population, whereas others have been standardized on children from varying sociolinguistic backgrounds. Other language versions (primarily Spanish) of some of these tests have been developed. In addition, varying techniques for sampling and analyzing the language production of children are available that do provide age norms for the appearance of certain language behaviors (e.g., Lee, 1974). Some of these tests are significantly correlated with intelligence test scores (e.g., PPVT scores are significantly correlated with Stanford-Binet scores). This is not surprising because, again, the same types of linguistic behavior are being examined. What is surprising are the instances in which apparently related behaviors do not yield significantly correlated test scores (e.g., auditory discrimination and articulation test scores). In other instances, the data are simply not available. Experimental data, however, indicate that there should be a high degree of correlation among certain aspects of the language tested (Menyuk & Looney, 1972b). There is also a question of how adequately these tests assess linguistic competence. For example, Menyuk and Looney (1972a) compared the sentence-repetition ability of a group of language-disordered children with those who were developing language normally, matched in terms of PPVT scores. They found that there were significant differences between the populations in the language task despite this supposed matching on language abilities.

The following are the aspects of language behavior that are examined in available tests and speech sampling techniques: speech sound—discrimination and articulation; vocabulary—comprehension and production; sentence—comprehension and reproduction; and connected discourse—production of speech samples. In addition, audiometric testing and testing of the peripheral speech mechanism are usually a part of any language assessment.

If one carefully analyzes the linguistic-processing requirements of these several classes of tests, a possible reason for lack of intercorrelations between them becomes more apparent. Because none of the tests currently available assess communicative competence (language sampling is not a completely adequate measure of communicative competence because of the possible constraints of the interview situation), there are no data available on the relation between language-processing abilities and communicative competence. Table 4.4 presents a partial analysis of the linguistic requirements in types of tests and/or experimental techniques that are currently available as well as the varying responses required among the different tests. Most of these tests required attending, discriminating, storing, and retrieving information (i.e., a comparison with internalized structures); in addition, some require motor planning (reproduction and production). Some tests require simultaneous auditory and visual or auditory and motor planning whereas others do not. It should be noted that the particular linguistic stimuli used in each task can vary in terms of amount (length) or structure (complexity) and, thus, make different demands on memory.

The fact that the processing requirements of *particular* tasks can affect correctness or incorrectness of response became evident in a recent study (Menyuk & Fraser, 1975). In this study, language-disordered children, who had normal IQ scores on performance scales of standard intelligence tests, were asked to process the *same* linguistic structures in sentences in differing ways: comprehension by pointing to a picture and by manipulating objects, comprehension–reproduction by imitation and by correction of ungram-

TABLE 4.4
Aspects of Assessment in Varying Tests

Linguistic Domain	Categorizations	Task Types
Speech sound in word or nonsense syllable	Semantics, morphology, phonology	Discrimination: judge same or different (minimal pairs, trials, etc.); relate word to object or picture (minimal pairs, trials, etc.) Comprehension/Production Segment Reintegrate Name Imitiate
Word	Semantics, syntax, morphology, phonology	Comprehension: relate word to object or picture Comprehension/Production Associate Recall Name Imitate
Sentence	Semantics, syntax, morphology, phonology	Comprehension: object manipulation, picture identification; judgment of correct identification; Comprehension/Production Complete structure Correct structure Imitate

matical versions of the same forms, production by talking about pictures that expressed the same relations, and by spontaneous speech samplings. Menyuk and Fraser found that although there was consistency of behavior within tasks (those who did well on some items within a task tended to do well across items and inversely), there was inconsistency across tasks, with individual children doing well on some tasks and very poorly on others. These results indicate that for diagnostic purposes it is necessary to devise tests that very carefully control for the linguistic dimensions of the stimulus materials. For intervention purposes, it is necessary to vary the processing requirements across the same linguistic dimensions to determine where the problem/s lie.

In summary, a number of techniques for assessing the linguistic competence of children aged 0 to 5 years are now available. These procedures have led to the development of some good hypotheses concerning the varying contributions of physiological, cognitive, and input factors during different periods of development. What has not been accomplished is the establishment of age-related norms for the development of these competences nor standardized methods for determining in children under 2.5 years of age if a language problem exists, the nature of the problem, and whether the problem will persist. Standardized methods for obtaining a measure of structural linguistic and communicative competence under varying processing conditions have not been developed for children older than 2.5 years. In addition, despite the "good" hypotheses about factors affecting language development, independent measures of physiological, cognitive, and social development and their relation to the development of linguistic competence have not been established. However, the fact that these tasks have not been carried out does not imply that they cannot be accomplished.

REFERENCES

Anglin, J. *The growth of word meaning.* Cambridge, Mass.: M.I.T. Press; 1970.

Bateson, M. The interpersonal context of infant vocalization. *Quarterly Progress Reports,* M.I.T. Research Laboratory of Electronics, 1969, **100**, 170–176.

Beilin, H., & Spontak, G. *Active–passive transformation and operational reversibility.* Paper presented at the biennial meeting of the Society for Research in Child Development, Santa Monica, 1969.

Bell, S., & Ainsworth, M. Infant crying and maternal responsiveness. *Child Development,* 1972, **43**, 1171–1190.

Bever, T. Cognitive basis for linguistic structure. In J. R. Hayes (Ed.), *Cognition and language.* New York: Wiley, 1970.(a)

Bever, T. The integrated study of language behavior. In J. Morton (Ed.), *Biological and social factors in Psycholinguistics.* Urbana: University of Illinois Press, 1970.(b)

Bloom, L. Language development: *Form and function in emerging grammars.* Cambridge, Mass.: M.I.T. Press, 1970.

Bloom, L. *One word at a time.* The Hague: Mouton, 1973.

Bowerman, M. Early syntactic development: *A Cross-linguistic study with special reference to Finnish.* Cambridge, England: Cambridge University Press, 1973.

Branigan, G. *Sequences of single words as structured units.* Paper presented at the Child Language Forum, Stanford University, 1976.

Brown, R. *A first language: The early stages.* Cambridge, Mass.: Harvard University Press, 1973.

Brown, R., Cazden, C., & Bellugi-Klima, U. The child's grammar from I to III. In J. Hill (Ed.) *Minnesota symposium on child psychology.* Minneapolis, Minn.: University of Minnesota Press, 1968.

Cairns, G., Karchmer, M., & Smith, R. *Assessment of infants at risk for language dysfunction through the use of speech production.* Paper presented at the annual meeting of the Council for Exceptional Children. Los Angeles, 1975.

Chomsky, N. *Aspects of the theory of syntax,* Cambridge: M.I.T. Press, 1966.

Condon, W., & Sander, L. Neonate movement is synchronized with adult speech. *Science,* 1974, **183**, 99–101.

Conrad, R. The developmental role of vocalizing in short-term memory. *Journal of Verbal Learning and Verbal Behavior,* 1972, **11**, 521–533.

de Hirsch, K., Jansky, J., & Langford, W. The oral language performances of premature children and controls, *Journal of Speech and Hearing Disorders,* 1964, **29**, 60–69.

Donahue, M., & Watson, L. *How to get some action.* Paper presented at the first annual Boston University Conference on Language Development, Boston: October, 1976.

Dreyfus-Brisac, C., Lezine, I., & Berges, J. Development du premature a partir de deux ans interractions psychologiques, neurologiques et electroencephalographiques. *Revue de Neuropsychiatrie Infantile,* 1964, **12**, (no. 4-5).

Eimas, P. Linguistic processing of speech by young infants. In R. Schiefelbusch & L. Lloyd (Eds.), *Language perspectives: Acquisition, retardation and intervention.* Baltimore: University Park Press, 1974.

Eisenberg, R., Coursin, D., & Rapp, N. Habituation to an acoustic pattern as an index of difference among human neonates.*Journal of Auditory Research,* 1966, **6**, 239–248.

Garvey, C., & Hogan, R. Social speech and social interaction: Egocentrism revisited. *Child Development,* 1973, **44**, 562–568.

Geschwind, N. Neurological foundations of language. In H. Myklebust (Ed.), *Progress in learning disabilities* (Vol. I). New York: Grune & Stratton, 1967.

Geschwind, N. Language and the brain. *American Scientist,* April, 1972, 76–83.

Greenberg, J. *Universals of language.* Cambridge, Mass.: M.I.T. Press, 1966.

Greenfield, P., & Smith, J. *The structure of communication in early language development.* New York: Academic Press, 1976.

Gruber, J. *Correlations between the syntactic constructions of the child and the adult.* Paper presented at the biennial meeting of the Society for Research in Child Development, New York, 1967.

Hockett, C. The problem of universals in language. In J. Greenberg (Ed.), *Universals of Language,* Cambridge, Mass.: M.I.T. Press, 1966.

Honig, A., Caldwell, B., & Tannenbaum, J. Patterns of information processing used by and with young children in a nursery school setting. *Child Development,* 1970, **41**, 1045–1065.

Horgan, D. *Linguistic knowledge at stage I: Evidence from successive single word utterances.* Paper presented at the Child Language Forum, Stanford University, 1976.

Hymes, D. Sociolinguistics and ethnography of speaking. In E. Ardener (Ed.), *Social anthropology of language,* London: Tavistock, 1971.

Karmel, B. *Brain and behavior processing information by human infants: Spatial and temporal changes.* Paper presented at the annual meeting of the American Psychological Association, Honolulu, 1972.

Kinsbourne, M. The ontogeny of cerebral dominance. *Annals of the New York Academy of Sciences,* 1975, **263**, 244–250.

Krauss, R., & Glucksberg, S. The development of communication competence as a function of age. *Child Development,* 1967, **40**, 255–260.

Kulig, S., & Baker, K. *Physicians developmental quickscreen for speech disorders.* University of Texas Medical Branch at Galveston, Dept. of Pediatrics, Galveston, Texas, 1975.

Lee, L. *Developmental sentence analysis.* Evanston, Ill.: Northwestern University Press, 1974.

Lennenberg, E. *Biological foundations of language.* New York: Wiley, 1967.

Lewis, M., & Freedle, R. *Mother–infant dyad: The cradle of meaning.* Princeton, N.J.: Educational Testing Services, 1972.

Lieberman, P., Crelin, E., & Klatt, D. Phonetic ability and related anatomy of the newborn and adult human, Neanderthal man and the chimpanzee. *American Anthropologist,* 1972, **74**, 287–307.

Maratsos, M. Non-egocentric communication abilities in pre-school children. *Child Development,* 1973, **44**, 697–700.

McNeill, D. The development of language. In P. Mussen (Ed.), *Carmichael's Manual of Child Psychology* (Vol. I). New York: Wiley, 1970.

Mehler, J. Studies in language and thought development. In R. Huxley & E. Ingram (Eds.), *Language acquisition: Models and methods.* New York: Academic Press, 1971.

Menyuk, P. *Sentences children use.* Cambridge, Mass.: M.I.T. Press, 1969.

Menyuk, P. *The acquisition and development of language.* Englewood Cliffs, N.J.: Prentice-Hall, 1971.

Menyuk, P. *Speech development.* Indianapolis: Bobbs Merrill, 1972.

Menyuk, P. Early development of receptive language. In R. Schiefelbusch & L. Lloyd,

(Eds.), Language perspectives: Acquisition, retardation and intervention. Baltimore: University Park Press, 1974.

Menyuk, P. The language impaired child: Cognitive or linguistic impairment? *Annals of the New York Academy of Sciences,* 1975, **263**, 59–69.(a)

Menyuk, P. Children with language problems: What's the problem? *Georgetown University Roundtable on Linguistics.* Georgetown, Va.: Georgetown University Press, 1975.(b)

Menyuk, P. *Development of syntax: The bridge between sound and meaning.* Paper presented at the International Symposium on Child Language Acquisition, Acapulco, 1976. (a) (Published in proceedings)

Menyuk, P. Relations between acquisition of phonology and reading. In J. Guthrie (Ed.), *Aspects of reading acquisition.* Baltimore: Johns Hopkins University Press, 1976.(b)

Menyuk, P. That's the "same," "another," "funny," "awful," way of saying it: The development of meta-linguistic abilities. *Journal of Education,* 1976, **158**, 25–38.(c)

Menyuk, P. *Language and maturation.* Cambridge, Mass.: M.I.T. Press, 1977.

Menyuk, P. Linguistic problems in children with developmental dysphasia. In M. Wyke (Ed.), *Developmental dysphasia.* London, Academic Press, 1978.

Menyuk, P., & Fraser, B. *Assessment of language training for pre-school handicapped children.* (Final report, Grant No. OEC-0-74-9186). Washington, D.C.: Bureau of Education for the Handicapped, 1975.

Menyuk, P., & Klatt, M. Voice onset time in consonant cluster production by children and adults. *Journal of Child Language,* 1975, **2**, 223–231.

Menyuk, P., & Looney, P. A problem of language disorder: Length versus structure. *Journal of Speech and Hearing Research,* 1972, **15**, 264–279.(a)

Menyuk, P., & Looney, P. Relationships among components of the grammar. *Journal of Speech and Hearing Research,* 1972, **15**, 395–406.(b)

Molfese, D. Cerebral Assymetry in infants, children and adults: Auditory evoked response to speech and musical stimuli. *Journal of the Acoustical Society of America,* 1973, **53**, 363.

Morse, P. Infant speech perception: A model and review of the literature. In R. Schiefelbusch & L. Lloyd (Eds.), *Language perspectives: Acquisition, retardation and intervention.* Baltimore: University Park Press, 1974.

Mueller, E. Maintenance of verbal exchanges among children. *Child Development,* 1972, **43**, 930–938.

Nelson, K. Structure and strategy in learning to talk. *Society for Research in Child Development Monograph,* 1973, **38**, (No. 1 & 2)

Phillips, J. Syntax and vocabulary of mother's speech to young children. *Child Development,* 1973, **44**, 182–185.

Russell, S. Neurological basis of complex learning. *British Medical Bulletin,* 1971, **27**,278–285.

Sachs, J., & Truswell, L. *Comprehension of two word instructions by children in the one word stage.* Paper presented at the Child Language Research Forum, Stanford University, 1976.

Searle, J. Chomsky's revolution in linguistics. *The New York Review of Books,* June 29, 1972, 16–24.

Shatz, M. *The comprehension of indirect directions: Can two-year-olds shut the door?* Paper presented at the summer meeting of the Linguistic Society of america, Amherst, Mass., 1974.

Shatz, M., & Gelman, R. The development of communicative skills: Modifications in the speech of young children as a function of listener. *Society for Research in Child Development Monograph,* 1973, **38** (No. 5).

Shipley, E., Smith, C., & Gleitman, L. A study of the acquisition of language. *Language,* 1969, **45**, 322–342.

Sinclair de Zwart, H. Sensorimotor action patterns as a condition for the acquisition of syntax. In R. Huxley & E. Ingram (Eds.), *Language acquisiton: Models and methods*. London: Academic Press, 1971.

Slobin, D. Cognitive prerequisites for the development of grammar. In C. Ferguson & D. Slobin (Eds.), *Studies of child language development*, New York: Holt, Rinehart & Winston, 1973.

Snow, C. Mother's speech to children learning language. *Child Development*, 1972, **43**, 549–555.

Speech Communication, Research Laboratory of Electronics, *Quarterly Progress Reports*, 1975, No. 115.

Stevenson, H. Learning in children. In P. Mussen (Ed.), *Carmichael's manual of child psychology*, (Vol. I). New York: Wiley, 1970.

Tulkin, S., & Kagan, J. Mother-child interaction in the first year of life. *Child Development*, 1972, **43**, 31–41.

Vuorenkoski, V., Wasz-Hockert, O., Lind, J., Koivisto, M., & Partinen, T. Training of the auditory perception of some specific types of abnormal pain cry in newborn and young infants. *Quarterly Progress Report*, January 15, 1972, Royal Institute of Technology, Stockholm.

Vygotsky, L. *Thought and language.* Cambridge, Mass.: M.I.T. Press, 1962.

White, S. Some general outlines of the matrix of developmental changes between 5 and 7 years. *Bulletin of the Orton Society*, 1970, **20**, 41–57.

Woodburne, L. *The neural basis of behavior.* Columbus, Ohio: Charles, E. Merrill, 1967.

Wozniak, R. Verbal regulations of motor behavior. *Human Development*, 1972, **15**, 13–57.

5 The Etiology of Cognitive Competence: A Systems Perspective

Arnold J. Sameroff
University of Rochester

A happy, competent, intelligent society of healthy human beings has been the goal of every civilization. Every civilization has developed cultural norms designed to achieve these goals. Yet every civilization produced unhappy, ill, incompetent, and retarded individuals. What caused this gap between aspiration and achievement? Ignorance is the standard excuse. Previous civilizations did not have enough medical, psychological, and educational knowledge to achieve the goals that they had set for themselves. If they had more medical, psychological, and educational facts, they could have solved their problems.

Unfortunately, facts alone have never served this admirable function. If anything, the study of history has taught us that it is not new facts, but new conceptions that produce progress. The seminal work of Kuhn (1962) has already become required reading for every scientist. In his view, facts only serve to prove that current theories are inadequate. In themselves, they do not produce new theories or new understanding, although they may inspire them. Surprisingly, new theories may arise and be accepted even though they contradict currently accepted facts. Brush (1974) has documented a number of instances in the history of physics where this has occurred.

Do we need an understanding of the history of science to document the connections between early deviations in infants and later manifestations of retardation in cognitive competence? I would answer affirmatively. We need a perspective on the history as well as the philosophy of science. Our current view of our work can be fully appreciated only in light of past views. This becomes especially relevant when we attempt to relate biological and psychological functioning.

CAUSAL MODELS FOR DEVELOPMENT

The term *medical model* has become a pejorative phrase used to describe over simplified views of the etiology of disorder. Its attraction is derived from past medical achievements where a single entity, such as a pathogenic microorganism, was shown to be responsible for some physical disease. The history of medicine is replete with examples of such medical model successes from small-pox to poliomyelitis. The history of psychology is noteworthy for the absence of such successes. Except for general paresis resulting from syphillis, as yet no single entity has been shown to cause a specific psychological disorder.

Current understandings of cognitive development take the view that early levels of functioning become integrated through normal adaptational processes into more complex organizations of thought. Before one can grasp developmental deviances in these systems, one must first have an accurate description of the system itself. Similarly, in order to understand the transmission of abnormalities from one developmental level to another, one must understand the normal transitions from one level of functioning to another.

In sum, my position is: (a) medical model explanations that search out unitary causes for deviant behavioral development have been generally unsuccessful, and (b) behavioral problems must be viewed in a systems context that addresses the structural complexity of cognitive functioning. Each of these points is examined in detail in the following sections.

A generally accepted theoretical assumption holds that continuity exists between early and later competence. By identifying valid measures of early cognitive abilities, we should be in a better position to predict later forms of cognitive functioning.

In this paper, I approach the topic by considering criteria of later cognitive competence. Because reviewers of longitudinal studies have found little evidence of simple continuities between earlier and later cognitive abilities (Clarke & Clarke, 1976; McCall, Hogarty & Hurlbut, 1972; Sameroff, 1975), it may be more profitable to identify those variables that are known to be related to later cognitive competence. There is evidence to suggest that a variety of noncognitive aspects of both the child and the environment are better predictors of later intelligence than what would normally pass for measures of early cognitive competence (Sameroff & Zax, 1978). Once the central variables that critically influence later cognitive performance are identified then the issues of developing appropriate measures for these variables can be addressed.

UNIFACTOR DEVELOPMENTAL MODELS

The notion that a variety of pregnancy, delivery, and newborn complications cause later mental problems is currently a popular concept. It is patently obvious that if a child is born with anencephaly, there should be serious consequences for the child's mental functions. Minor anatomical defects should also have negative consequences. Gesell and Amatruda (1941) proposed a concept of minimal cerebral injury as a perinatal factor causing later learning disorders. In a series of comprehensive retrospective studies, Pasamanick and Knobloch (1961) expanded the range of deviant developmental outcomes thought to result from minor central nervous system (CNS) dysfunction caused by damage to the fetus or newborn child. Their results led them to propose a continuum of reproductive casualty. The term *reproductive casualty* refers to a range of minor motor, perceptual, intellectual, learning, and behavioral disabilities found in children. In a review of their studies, Pasamanick and Knobloch (1966) reported that five later disorders were significantly associated with greater numbers of complications of pregnancy and prematurity. These included cerebral palsy, epilepsy, mental deficiency, behavioral disorders, and reading disabilities. In the comparisons between groups of children with these disorders and control, those children having one of the most serious conditions, e.g., cerebral palsy, were more sharply differentiated from control groups in the number of obstetrical complications than were those children who had one of the milder disorders, e.g., reading disabilities.

Retrospective studies such as those of Pasamanick and Knobloch have implicated at least three perinatal factors as being related to later mental disorders: anoxia, prematurity, and delivery complications or newborn status. The major question is how these perinatal variables can play a role in producing later abnormalities. The most obvious answer, the biological possibility, was that these conditions caused damage to the brain, the most obvious being oxygen deprivation, which results in asphyxia.

Asphyxia

Little (1861) is generally credited with being the first investigator to focus on asphyxia as a cause of brain damage in the child. It seemed logical to assume that a generalized deficit in brain functioning could be related to cerebral oxygen deprivation early in development. Studies in which animals were deprived of oxygen indicated that asphyxia at birth led to learning deficits and brain damage (Windle, 1944).

Human research on asphyxia was stimulated by a report by Schreiber (1939) that 70% of a group of mentally retarded persons had histories of anoxia at birth. Although suggestive, Schreiber's study was far from definitive because it was retrospective, had no control groups, and did not differentiate anoxia from a variety of other complications of birth and development his subjects had suffered.

Moreover, retrospective approaches have serious problems of selection bias because only those subjects who have the later disorder are ever studied. Prospective research, by contrast, permits the selection of subjects with early characteristics thought to be implicated in the etiology of later disorders. The early characteristics assume the status of independent variables, and later outcomes, the status of dependent variables. In the current example, anoxia would be an experimental variable and mental retardation the outcome studied.

Despite the methodological advantages offered by prospective over retrospective designs, major problems remain (Graham, Ernhart, Thurston, & Craft, 1962). One basic problem in the prospective design, as applied to perinatal complications, is the lack of random assignment into the complicated vs. noncomplicated comparison groups. As a consequence, even if a relationship is found between the independent and dependent variable, (e.g., anoxia and mental retardation), a causal connection is still not certain because both of these conditions might be determined by a third variable not included in the study. The seriousness of this issue is evident in a later section when the effects of environmental factors are examined.

To overcome some of the selection biases in retrospective studies, researchers have often reviewed early hospital records to identify a study population on the basis of risk factors rather than outcome measures. In the case of anoxia, groups of children with known histories of anoxia can be selected and evaluated for their current functioning.

Several studies have found IQ differences between anoxic and normal control children at school age. From the birth records of 40,000 babies, Benaron et al. (1960) selected a sample of 43 seriously apneic infants who had from 12 minutes to over an hour delay in the onset of respiration. These children, all of whom were of low social economic status (SES) were matched with control children ranging in age from 3 to 19 years. The authors concluded that severe anoxia may have deleterious psychological effects. Contrary to expectation, these children were not uniformly poor in intellectual performance; they had both higher and lower IQs than did children in the control group. Schachter and Apgar, (1959) tested 8-year-old children who had different histories of birth complications. They found a mean 5 point IQ deficit in a small sample of children who were anoxic as infants. No differences on special neurological tests designed to detect brain damage were found. They noted that the magnitude of the IQ difference observed was of questionable significance.

A larger number of "prospective" studies have not found later effects of asphyxia on intelligence in children who had reached school age. Campbell, Cheseman, and Kilpatrick (1950) examined 61 children, 8 to 11 years of age, born in a 3-year period at a Belfast hospital. They found no differences in physique, hemoglobin levels, or intelligence between children who had suffered anoxia of 2 minutes or more and a control group with normal births. Usdin and Weil (1952) studied 41 12-year-old children who had an anoxic period of longer than 3 minutes and again found no IQ differences between these subjects and a group of matched controls. McPhail and Hall (1941) divided their anoxic children into those who had suffered severe apnea and those who had suffered mild apnea. Neither group was different from control children in IQ. Fraser and Wilks (1959) also divided their anoxic subjects into a moderate and severe group. The severe group included subjects who took longer than 3 minutes before their first' breath and at least 5 minutes before the onset of regular respiration. At 7.5 to 11.5 years of age, 60 moderately apneic and 40 severely apneic children were compared with control children, and no intellectual differences were found. Benaron, Brown, Tucker, Wentz, and Yacorzynski (1953) also found no IQ differences between children who had been apneic and control children when they were tested at 5 to 15 years of age. Bailey (1958), reviewing studies of the effects of oxygen deficiency at birth, indicated that if one were to arrive at any conclusions from these studies, it would first be necessary to overlook defects such as improper selection of subjects, inaccuracies of case histories in the clinical reports, or inadequate techniques.

Although prediction from early high-risk to the eventual intellectual status of anoxic infants is the major consideration, it is also of interest to determine whether any transient effects appear early but disappear by school age. Longitudinal studies of anoxic infants throw some light on this issue. Graham and her associates (Graham, Caldwell, Ernhart, Pennoyer, & Hartman, 1957) criticized most previous studies because the possible presence of subtle brain damage was poorly determined by gross, undifferentiated IQ measures. If a variety of measures including neurological, personality adjustment, and perceptual-motor tasks had been included, more differences might have been found. In many prior studies control groups had not been adequately matched, and the criteria of anoxia had not been carefully defined. Graham et al. proposed a longitudinal study beginning at birth with multiple contemporary assessments of anoxia and its effects on newborns' behavior, followed by assessments during later years.

Several hundred infants in St. Louis were seen in the newborn period (Graham, Matarazzo, & Caldwell, 1956) followed-up at 3 years (Graham, Ernhart, Thurston, & Craft, 1962), and again at 7 years (Corah, Anthony, Painter, Stern, & Thurston, 1965). As expected, when examined during the first days of life, anoxic infants were found to be "impaired" on a series of five measures that included maturation level, visual responsiveness, irritability, muscle tension, and pain threshold (Graham, Pennoyer, Caldwell, Greenman, & Hartman, 1957). When performance on these measures was compared with a prognostic score based on the degree of prenatal anoxia, postnatal anoxia, and the clinical assessment of CNS disturbance, infants with the poorest prognostic scores performed most poorly on the newborn assessments.

These same infants were seen again at 3 years of age and tested with a battery of cognitive, perceptual-motor, personality, and neurologic tests (Graham et al., 1962). The group of anoxic infants scored lower than control infants on all tests of cognitive function, had more positive neurological findings, and showed some personality differences. There were, however, no differences on tests of perceptual-motor functioning. The anoxic effect seemed to be strongest in the children with postnatal anoxia, i.e., delayed onset of respiration. Those with prenatal anoxia, inferred from disturbances of pregnancy, performed as well as children in control groups. There were small but statistically significant correlations between the degree of anoxia and the 3-year intelligence test scores. (The highest of these correlations was − .15). Thus, about 98% of the variance in the 3-year intellectual functioning of previously anoxic infants is left unexplained by the anoxia.

At 7 years of age, these children were again tested (Corah et al., 1965). Significant IQ differences had disappeared between the anoxic group and the control population. Of the 21 cognitive and perceptual measures, only vocabulary and one perceptual task seemed still to be deficient in these children. Corah et al. concluded that anoxics showed minimal impairment of functioning at 7 years and that efforts to predict current functioning on the basis of severity of anoxia were highly unreliable.

In sum, these studies show that anoxic infants did poorly on newborn measures, still showed effects of the anoxia at 3 years of age, but by 7 were performing almost as well as nonanoxic control children.

Other studies have found similar developmental patterns among anoxics (MacKinney, 1958; Stechler, 1964). In terms of personality differences, there was little evidence in the 3 year follow-up that any personality constellation could be related to early anoxia. By the 7-year follow-up, Corah et al. (1965) found no data to support the existence of a hyperkinetic personality syndrome in their anoxic group, although they did find some impairments in social competence. The anoxic subgroup with the better newborn prognostic scores were rated as more impulsive and distractible than were the control children, but, paradoxically, the subgroup having the poorer prognosis was found to be significantly less distractible than were the normal control children. Gottfried (1973), in a review of 20 studies on the long-term effects of anoxia, came to similar conclusions. Among these conclusions were (a) that the intellectual consequences of perinatal anoxia are more prevalent in infants and preschoolers than in older children and adolescents, (b) anoxic subjects as a group are not mentally retarded, and (c) whether anoxic subjects are deficient in specific intellectual abilities is not yet known. In their extensive review of the effects of anoxia, Sameroff and Chandler (1975) were even more doubtful of the negative developmental effects of anoxia.

Prematurity

Prematurity is an outcome of many complications in pregnancy and represents the most prevalent abnormality of birth that is thought to effect later functioning. Birch and Gussow (1970) suggested that it was the modal problem for assessing the effects of the continuum of reproductive casualty. In contrast to the oxygen deprivation associated with asphxia, it is less clear why the condition of prematurity alone should produce behavioral problems.

As in studies of anoxia, the data on long-term effects of prematurity do not lead to any clear-cut conclusions. Although Wiener (1962), in a review of 18 studies of prematurity, found only 1 that did not report an IQ deficit in the premature group, Parmelee and Haber (1973) argued that it is by no means clear whether the later adverse consequences associated with prematurity are a function of the prematurity itself, the accompanying low birth weight, an extended period of living in an incubator, accompanying perinatal trauma, or the social climate in which the child is raised. A gestationally premature infant who suffers no prenatal, perinatal, or postnatal trauma other than prematurity itself and is raised in an optimal home environment may, according to these investigators, be no different from a full-term infant raised under the same circumstances. Parmelee and Haber's views are consistent with those studies of prematurity undertaken by Hess, Mohr, and Bartelme (1939), who found generally good childhood outcomes for their subjects. Those premature children who did perform less well than normal children were typically those who had evidence of additional neonatal complications.

Several large studies that have followed premature infants from infancy through school age did find small intellectual deficits associated with low birth weights. Douglas (1960) reported that when compared with control children the premature children did less well at 8 and 11 years of age. In an extensive study of the effects of prematurity, Drillien (1964) found that the lighter the infant had been at birth, the greater the deficit in developmental quotient at 4 years. The mean IQ scores ranged from 107 for the full-term control group to 89 for a group of infants under 3.5 pounds at birth. A complicating factor in the interpretation of these studies is that because a birthweight criterion was used, no consideration was given to the possibility that small-for-date infants were included in the sample.

A sample of premature infants initially studied by Knobloch, Rider, Harper, and Pasamanick (1956) was followed-up with intelligence testing when they were 6 to 7 years old (Wiener, Rider, Oppel, Fischer, & Harper, 1965) and again when they were 8 to 10 years old (Wiener, Rider, Oppel, & Harper, 1968). The premature children, who at birth had weighed between 1500 and 2000 grams, scored 5 points lower at ages 6 to 7, and 6 points lower at ages 8 to 10. In another study the effects of physical defects were separated from the intellectual deficits in premature children. McDonald (1964) eliminated from her sample infants who were twins or had cerebral palsy, blindness, deafness, or IQs below 50. The resulting sample had an average IQ of 102 when tested at ages 6 to 8, no different from the national mean in Britain. Still, within her sample those infants with birth weights under 3 pounds had an average IQ 5 points less than those with birth weights between 3 and 4 pounds.

It is interesting that studies of the effects of prematurity have shown consistent, albeit small, IQ deficits, whereas studies of the effects of anoxia have not. A possible explanation is that premature infants are more easily recognized and labeled by their parent than are anoxic infants. The parents may now know if their infant had some form of asphyxia, whereas premature infants, especially lower birth weight premature newborns, are quite easily identified not only by their physical appearance but also by their initial separation from the parents, and the subsequent increased caretaking demands. As discussed later, the parent's perception can play a major role in the child's deviant development exclusive of any actual deficit that may be present.

Delivery Complications and Newborn Status

The concept that single problems such as asphyxia or prematurity should be related to later problems was generalized to a variety of other delivery complications that were thought to influence brain function. Yet, as with asphyxia and prematurity, only minimal relationships have been found between other delivery complications and later cognitive functioning (Buck, Gregg, & Stavraky, 1969; Nelson, 1968; Niswander, Friedman, Hoover, Pietrowski, & Westpahl, 1966).

Parmelee and Haber (1973) have argued that studies making use of single events or scores based on neonatal health or adjustment often sample acute variables, the effects of which may be highly transitory. They concluded that although there is some limited basis for the widely held belief that many prenatal and perinatal factors do place an infant at risk, there is little agreement about the degree of such risk or what pathological outcomes are associated with the hazards. Although large-scale investigations, such as the Collaborative Study (Niswander & Gordon, 1972), have documented the relationship between certain perinatal factors and perinatal mortality, the risk of later sequelae for infants who survive the neonatal period is still unclear. Surviving infants often become very ill, but after recovery, they typically show little residual damage. By contrast, other more chronic but less dramatic events, may lead to permanent damage that manifests itself only later in life. Combinations of pregnancy and delivery complications also appear to increase the likelihood of both immediate damage and the risk for subsequent disorder. The most successful prediction of later deviancy would then appear to result from a combined criterion of prenatal, postnatal, and perinatal events.

Another source for specific predictions of later deviancy has been aberrations in newborn behavior. Parmelee and Michaelis (1971) have provided an excellent review of the relationship between newborn neurological status and later deviancy. Although the diagnostic search for neurological signs was a successful means of identifying infants with contemporary neurological problems, there was little evidence to suggest that such signs were of any utility as predictors of later adaptational problems.

In those prognostic studies in which a variety of different items from newborn examinations have been combined, predictive validity has been shown to increase. On the basis of such multivariate predictors, Prechtl and Beintema (1964) have, for example, successfully defined four different syndromes of disorder: apathy, hyperexcitability, hemisyndrome, and coma. Schulte and his colleagues (Joppich & Schulte, 1968; Schulte, Michaelis, & Filipp, 1965), using a similar set of multiple predictors, succeeded in identifying three additional syndromes; hypertonia, hypotonia, and seizures.

In summarizing the literature on newborn neurological examinations, Parmelee and Michaelis (1971) pointed out that those diagnostic signs demonstrating the most predictive validity have typically depended less on specific neurological signs than on general indices of behavioral state, activity level, and threshold considerations. According to these authors, it is not the disturbance of some specific reflex that appears to produce later problems but rather the occurrence of some distorting influence that disrupts the more general reprogramming capabilities of the nervous system. Parmelee and Michaelis concluded that much more needs to be known about how the nervous system compensates for brain injury before early neurological signs can be effectively employed as predictors of later pathology.

The general conclusion suggested by these various research findings appears to be that the long-range effects of chronic or multiple traumas are blockage of the neural equilibratory processes that typically occur after some single insult or trauma. A more complete understanding of such complex regulations in the development of the nervous system would probably require a change in orientation from focusing upon single events or even combinations of events to focusing upon an understanding of the integrative and organizing capacities of the whole organism.

The prediction of pathological outcome based on scores combining both prenatal and neonatal variables has been used with some success in a number of studies. When, for example, Niswander et al. (1966) used combined criteria of pregnancy complications, an Apgar score of 6 or less, and an abnormal newborn neurological examination, a strong relationship was found between these predictors and deviant scores on the 8-month Bayley Scales of Mental and Motor Development and 12-month neurological examination. Using a similar set of multiple predictions, Drage and Berendes (1966) also found a relation between infants with both low birth weight and low Apgar scores, and later evidence of disorder on the Bayley and neurological examination.

Despite these encouraging beginnings and short-range successes achieved by the use of these multiple criteria, their predictive power appears to be relatively short lived and rarely goes beyond a few years. When, for example, Drage, Berendes, and Fisher (1969) retested their subjects at 4 years of age, the relationship between low birth weight and low Apgar scores that had been demonstrated previously had all but disappeared. The mother's education level and SES were much more powerful predictors of children's intellectual functioning than were any combination of measures collected in infancy.

Other results appear to run counter to this trend of poor predictability from neonatal data. Smith, Flick, Ferriss, and Sellmann (1972) used a discriminant-function analysis to predict intelligence from perinatal data in a group of 7-year-old children. They were successful in classifying about 80% of their sample in either an abnormal or normal category. On the surface, these investigators demonstrated the strength of sophisticated statistical techniques in predicting later outcome from prenatal and perinatal variables. When, however, one examines the loadings of the variables used in the discriminant function, the education and IQ of the mother had by far the greatest weights. Although Smith et al. defined mother's IQ and education as prenatal variables, they are also 1-year, 4-year, and 7-year old variables, because the mother continues to make a contribution to the child's environment during the entire period of development.

A recurrent theme that has run through much of the preceding review is that SES variables play an important role in modulating the effects of perinatal factors. In the following discussion, it will be seen that the environment may have a much greater impact in producing deviancy than any of the biological factors examined so far.

MULTI-FACTOR DEVELOPMENTAL MODELS

In the previous section data were reviewed from studies that sought to find linkages between single biological factors in the perinatal period and single effects later in life. This research found little, if any, significant linkage. What has emerged from these studies, however, was that the single-cause view is an oversimplification ignoring environmental factors that seem to play a major role in either modulating or supplementing the effects of early physical difficulties.

Parmelee, Kopp, and Sigman (1976) cogently argued that the main concern in development is the total adaptation of the infant to the environment, regardless of biological problems. Children with motor or sensory handicaps who compensate and make adequate progress in cognitive and affective development remove themselves from the risk category. In contrast, infants with similar initial biological problems who continue to do poorly remain in the high-risk category for later developmental disability.

How is the initial biological problem compensated? Parmelee et al. (1976) suggested two mechanism; either the early apparent risk factor resulted in a transient brain insult rather than permanent brain damage; or environmental factors may have a stronger influence on behavioral outcomes than do biological events. The first of these explanations cannot be dealt with here since it is a topic for physiological research; however, the second of these explanations is the core of what follows.

Birch and Gussow (1970), in an extensive review of the effects of disadvantaged environments on development, concluded that high risk for infants is associated with both depressed SES and ethnicity. The highest rates of infant loss were found among populations that are both poor and Black. Pasamanick, Knobloch, and Lilienfeld (1956) found in their sample that the proportion of infants having some complication increased from 5% in the White, upper social class strata to 15% in the lowest White socioeconomic group, to 51% among all non-Whites. These data imply that the biological outcomes of pregnancy are worse for those in poorer environments. Birch and Gussow (1970) summarized their review by noting that there are data to indicate that the developmental outcomes for poor children are also far worse.

Drillien's (1964) data on Scottish premature infants show that for the highest social grades the deficit in developmental quotient (DQ) for children under 3.9 pounds is reduced from 26 to 13 points between the ages of 6 months and 4 years; whereas for the lowest social grade, the DQ deficit increased from 26 to 32 points. When the same children were tested in school between the ages of 5 and 7, Drillien found that few children from middle-class homes were retarded, except when birth weight had been below 3.5 lbs., whereas in poor homes there was an excess of retarded children in all weight categories studied.

McDonald (1964) found that although prematurity affected intelligence in lower social groups, there were no deficits evident in the upper social-class group in her sample. Similarly, Illsley (1966), who used a large sample of wide social background in Aberdeen, Scotland, found that whereas in the lowest social class, IQ scores were seriously depressed in low birth-weight groups, little effect was noted on IQ scores in the upper social class.

One of the most ambitious and revealing of the longitudinal studies of the effects of early complications was done in Hawaii by Werner, Bierman, and French (1971). They reported on 670 children born on the island of Kauai in 1955. Because of the multiracial nature of Kauai and the variety of social classes sampled when the whole population was used, Werner et al. were able to provide ample controls for both variables.

Each infant was initially scored on a 4-point scale for severity of perinatal complications. Twenty months later these perinatal scores were related to assessments of physical health, psychological status, and the environmental variables of SES, family stability, and mother's intelligence.

At the time of the initial perinatal assessment, Werner et al. (1971) found that 56% of the children studied had no complications; 31%, mild complications; 13%, moderate complications; and only 3%, severe complications. The distribution of complication scores was not found to be related to ethnic origin, SES, age of mother, family stability, or mother's intelligence. This unusual lack of correlation between SES and complications was probably a result of a prepaid health plan that provided good prenatal care to all women on the island. Evidence of the mothers' good health was that 80% showed no chronic illness during pregnancy.

At the 20-month examination, 14% of the children were found to be below average in health status; 16%, in intellectual development; and 12%, in social development. These findings closely approximate those of other comparable studies. Increasing severity of perinatal stress was related to lower scores in the three assessment areas. There was, however, a clear interaction between the impairing effect of perinatal complications and environmental variables, especially SES. For infants living in a high socioeconomic environment, with a stable family, or with a mother of high intelligence, the IQ differences between children with and without severe complications was only 5 to 7 points. For infants living in a low socioeconomic environment, with low family stability, or with a mother of low intelligence, the difference in mean Cattell IQs between the high and low perinatal complications groups and between infants without perinatal complications ranged from 19 to 37 points.

The results of the Kauai study indicate that perinatal complications were consistently related to later physical and psychological development only when combined with and supported by persistently poor environmental circumstances. In addition, when good prenatal care was available, SES differences in the initial distribution of perinatal complications were found to disappear.

The infants in the Kauai sample were reexamined when they reached 10 years of age (Werner, Honzik, & Smith, 1968). Data from the perinatal and 20-month examinations were correlated with intelligence and school performance at 10 years of age. There was no significant correlation between the perinatal-stress score and the 10-year measures. Some significant relationships were found between the 20-month and 10-year data, especially when SES and parents' educational level were taken into consideration. Stability of intellectual functioning was much higher for those children who had IQs below 80 at the 10-year testing. All of these children had 20-month Cattell scores of 100 or less, with almost half below 80. The majority of these children had parents with little education and low SES. In general the correlation of the child's IQ with those of the parents increased across the 8-year period. The Kauai study suggests that risk factors operative during the perinatal period disappear during childhood as familial and social factors exert their potent influence.

Werner et al. (1971) noted that for every live birth in Kauai, by age 10 two-thirds of the children were functioning adequately in school with no recognized physical, intellectual, or behavior problem. The remaining one-third of the children had problems at the age of 10, but a minor proportion could be attributed to the effects of serious perinatal stress. The major impact of biological defects associated with reproductive casualty occurs in the first weeks of pregnancy when 90% of fetal losses occur in the form of spontaneous abortions. After this initial period, environment increasingly become the dominant influence. The biologically vulnerable child makes up only a small proportion of those children who will not function adequately. The authors concluded in their study that "ten times more children had problems related to the effects of poor early environment than to the effects of perinatal stress [p. 193]."

After a comprehensive review of the perinatal-risk literature summarized above, Sameroff and Chandler (1975) were led to make the following conclusions:

> 1. A continuum of reproductive casuality which was thought to be positively related to the degree of abnormality present in the course of development, that is, the greater the reproductive complication, the greater the later deviancy, has not been generally supported by the data reviewed. There is a serious question as to whether a child who has suffered perinatal trauma, but shows no obvious brain damage, is at any greater risk for later deviancy than a child who has not suffered perinatal trauma.

> 2. Abnormalities have been found in populations with specific reproductive complications, but these tend to disappear with age. Postnatal anoxia may affect newborn behavior and intellectual functioning through the pre-school period, but, by school age, IQ differences between affected and control populations have all but disappeared. When infants born prematurely were followed through school age, the deficits in their intelligence at earlier ages were greatly reduced in later years. The lowest intelligence test scores were found in groups of infants with the lowest birth weights.

> 3. In the studies reviewed, the effects of social status tended to reduce or amplify intellectual deficits. In advantaged families infants who had suffered perinatal complications generally showed no significant or small residual effects at follow-up. Many infants from lower social class homes with identical histories of complications showed significant retardations in later functioning. Social and economic status appear to have much stronger influences on the course of development than perinatal history [p. 209].

Continuum of Caretaking Casualty

The predictive failures found when using the continuum of reproductive casualty could be attributed to ignorance about missing links in the causal chains linking perinatal risk and behavioral competencies. From a more organismic perspective, one could argue that predictive inefficiency results from a lack of knowledge about the *total* developmental process. According to this view, successful predictions cannot be made on the basis of reproductive risk alone. Sameroff and Chandler (1975) proposed a continuum of caretaking casualty to incorporate the environmental risk factors leading toward poor developmental outcomes. Although reproductive casualties may play an initiating role in the production of later problems, it is the caretaking environment that determines the ultimate outcome. At one end of the caretaking continuum, supportive, compensatory and normalizing environments appear to be able to eliminate the effects of early complications. On the other end of the continuum, caretaking by deprived, stressed, or poorly educated parents tends to exacerbate early difficulties. Except for the Kauai study (Werner et al. 1968), environmental factors have generally been ignored in research efforts aimed at finding linear chains of causality between early pregnancy and delivery complications and later deviancy.

Socio-Economic Status

The data from these various longitudinal studies of prenatal and perinatal complications have yet to produce a single predictive variable more potent than the familial and socioeconomic characteristics of the caretaking environment. The predictive efficiency of the variable of socioeconomic class is especially pronounced for the low end of the IQ scale (Werner, Simonian, Bierman, & French, 1967). Willerman, Broman, and Fiedler (1970), using a sample from the Collaborative Study, compared Bayley developmental scores obtained at 8 months with Stanford-Binet IQs at age 4. For children with a high SES, there was little relationship between their 8-month Bayley scores and their 4-year scores. For children with a low SES, however, those who did poorly at 8 months continued to do so at 4 years of age. In addition, there was a cross-over effect by which the high SES children who were in the lowest quartile at the 8-month examination were performing better at 4 years than were the low SES children who scored in the highest quartile at 8 months. Willerman et al. see poverty as amplifying IQ deficits in poorly developed infants.

At the same time that perinatal influences on intellectual functioning are dissipating, environmental influences become quite prevalent. Several studies have shown that SES differences on psychological tests do not appear until the third year of life. Even when standard psychological tests are supplemented with Piagetian-type tasks or when optimal scores are used instead of standard scores, no SES differences are found until the third year (Golden, Birns, Bridges, & Moss, 1971). Sameroff and Zax (1978) tested a large group of infants at 4, 12, 30 and 40 months of age. At 4 and 12 months, no SES differences were found. By 30 months significant differences between every SES group were found and increased in magnitude by 48 months of age. These results are shown in Figure 5.1.

If SES were used as a risk predictor, the design of a diagnostic measure with high predictive validity would be greatly simplified. The data that provide the most powerful answer to this question come from the Collaborative Perinatal Project, a longitudinal study of about 40,000 children from birth

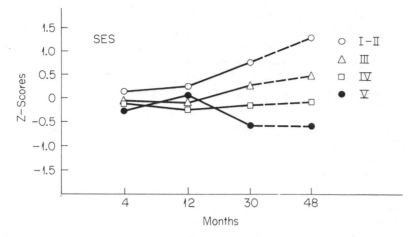

FIG. 5.1.   IQs expressed as Z scores.

to 7 years of age (Niswander & Gordon, 1972). Broman, Nichols, and Kennedy (1975) reported on the factors affecting intelligence test scores at 4 years of age. When familial and medical perinatal variables were combined in a multiple-regression analysis, only mother's educational level and SES index made major contributions to the resulting equation. For White males, White females, Black males, and Black females, the multiple Rs were .42, .42, .25, and .28 respectively. The percentage of variance explained using these two variables in the four groups ranged from 8% to 18%. No perinatal variable added more than 1% explained variance in any of the analyses. The differences in the explained variance between the samples is probably a result of the constricted range of SES and educational levels in the Black samples.

The relative importance of environmental variables demonstrated by these studies is somewhat mitigated by two important factors. The first relates to the statistical value of these variables and the second to their psychological value.

Although the statistical analysis of the data from the Collaborative Study emphasize the point that social variables are more important in the prediction of IQ than are pregnancy or birth variables, the variance explained is still quite small. Even when variables from physical assessment at age 4 months, a psychological assessment at 8 months, and a neurological assessment at age 12 months were added to the analysis, only 25% of the variance was explained for IQ scores at age 4 in the White sample, and 16% in the Black. The basic predictive problem is that many of the children from families of low SES do quite well cognitively, whereas many of the children from the higher SES groups do quite poorly. When Broman et al, (1975) attempted a discriminant-function analysis between a low IQ group whose scores were two standard deviations (SDs) or more below the mean and a normal IQ group whose scores were one *SD* below the mean, they had little success. Using data from social, perinatal, and first-year evaluations, they were able to identify only 30% of the children who actually had low IQs at age 4. In absolute numbers, over 80% of the children who were predicted to have low IQs actually had normal IQs.

The conceptual problem is that SES and mother's educational level are not behavioral variables. Why mothers with low SES and little education tend to have children with low IQs is the issue. The biological argument can be made that the connection is genetic, but such an assertion begs the question, since most of the variance in children's IQ is not explained by parental characteristics. Since parental educational level is a critical variable, how parents interact with their children is a potential explanation. If we want to explain variance and thereby improve developmental prediction of intelligence, exploration of the perimeters of the social interactions of caretaker and child are in order.

Transactional Model

The attempts to predict intelligence or retardation described above have proved inadequate when constitutional and environmental variables singly or in combination are employed. How are we to understand a situation where perinatal complications only influence later development for children raised in poor environmental conditions? These poor outcomes are clearly not the result of the delivery complications alone, because children with identical complications, raised in good environmental situations, show no negative consequences of these problems. They are also clearly not the result of the environmental situation, since children in these studies without complications raised in the same poor environments did not show the same deviant outcomes evidenced by their affected neighbors. To answer this question, Sameroff and Chandler (1975) proposed a "transactional model of development" to explain the dynamic process by which children with poor constitutions, such as those resulting from delivery complications, enter into an interaction with their environment that ultimately leads to developmental abnormalities.

Where the medical model focused only on the environment's impact on the organism, the transactional model adds the reciprocal effect of the organism on the environment. The commonsense understanding of how children are raised is that society takes them in hand through the agency of their parents or the school system and shapes them to fit current norms. But many recent studies have demonstrated that in the process of trying to shape these children, the caretakers are shaped themselves (Bell, 1968). The specific characteristics of the individual child transact with the caretaker's mode of functioning to produce an individualized ongoing miniature social system.

A clear example of this situation is found in the work of Thomas, Chess, and Birch (1968) in their New York longitudinal study. These investigators were able to classify young infants into two major categories of temperament: the difficult child and the easy child.

The mothers in the New York study were all White, educated, middle class, with normal child-rearing attitudes. However, when these supposedly "normal" mothers were confronted with a difficult infant, their behavior toward the child was negatively influenced. Most of them either became anxious over their inability to control the child's crying and irregularity or hostile through frustration. The difficult child had converted a formerly normal mother into an abnormal one. The outcome of this disturbed relationship was that nearly three times as many of the infants identified as difficult required some professional help during childhood as compared to nondifficult infants. For our present purposes, the difficult infants in the study who did not have developmental problems are of great importance. The later normalcy of these difficult infants appeared to result from their parents' ability to make allowances for their temperaments. Rather than becoming anxious or hostile, these parents treated the infants' colicky behavior as part of a passing stage. Thus, the fate of these difficult infants appeared to depend on the context in which their behavior was understood by their parents.

A second example of the transactional character of the developmental process can be found in the recent report of the 18-year follow-up of the Kauai study discussed earlier (Werner, 1975). At the 10-year follow-up (Werner et al., 1971), children who had learning disabilities, need for long-term mental health service, or need for short-term mental health service were identified and reports sent to their parents, their physicians, the local educational guidance office, and the local department of mental health. At the 18-year follow-up, these children were reexamined to determine their developmental progress during the intervening period.

The data revealed that for the overwhelming majority of children who had been diagnosed as having learning disorders at age 10, problems persisted throughout adolescence. However, for this same majority, the environment was perceived as not being supportive or understanding. Most of the learning-disorder children were loners, without close friends, who had to rely on a nonsupportive family. In contrast, the few learning-disorder children who improved did so through sustained emotional support of family and friends. In the mental health problem groups, more children showed evidence of improvement, but again the improvement appeared to be a function of environmental support rather than any difference between the children. In other words, children with a diagnosis of minimal brain damage or learning disorder raised in a nonsupportive, nonadaptive environment will continue to show the same symptoms, whereas children with the same initial diagnosis raised in an environment where both institutional and familial support are given will show little evidence of the original disorder.

What I have tried to demonstrate in the two examples above is that knowing either the characteristics of the parent alone or the child alone does not permit us to make reliable predictions of developmental outcome. In the New York longitudinal study, parents with normal attitudes were led to behave nonadaptively when confronted with a difficult child. In the Kauai study, children with learning disorders were able to improve when raised in adaptive environments. We are beginning to see the possibilities of an answer to the prediction problem, that is, why it is that some problem children show no later effects of early problems whereas others show strong signs of retardation.

ROCHESTER LONGITUDINAL STUDY

At the University of Rochester, Melvin Zax and I (Sameroff & Zax, 1973; 1976) initiated a longitudinal study of the development from birth to 4 years of a sample of about 300 infants.[1] The mothers of the children in our study came from diverse SES and racial backgrounds and included a large subsample with emotional problems. Our two goals were to identify constitutional characteristics of the infants that would be predictive of later deviancy and to determine how the social and emotional characteristics of the mother interacted with these constitutional characteristics.

Assessment Procedures

The mother was evaluated prenatally and when the child was born, both were tested and followed-up at 4, 12, 30, and 48 months. The 30-month assessment is approaching completion; the 48-month assessment is currently being carried out. The analyses discussed below are based on the first 100 infants from whom data analyses have been completed at 30 months. The measures used at the various assessment ages are listed in Table 5.1.

Prenatal. The mothers were given a clinical interview based on the Current and Past Psychopathology Scales (CAPPS) developed by Spitzer and Endicott (1969). In addition, they completed the Institute for Personality and Ability Testing (IPAT) anxiety scale (Cattell & Scheier, 1963) and the Maternal Attitude to Pregnancy Inventory (MAPI) developed by Blau, Welkowitz, and Cohen (1964). From the interview data, a social competency score was derived based on six measures similar to those used by Zigler and Phillips (1962). These included items related to friendship patterns, heterosexual adjustment, and emotional disturbance.

---

[1]Other collaborators include Fredric Jones, Ralph Barocas, Penelope Kelly, Rena Anagnostopolou, and Harry Bakow.

TABLE 5.1
Assessment Schedule and Measures
in Rochester Longitudinal Study

Age	Mother	Child	Interaction
Prenatal	CAPPS IPAT anxiety scale MAPI pregnancy attitudes Social competency score		
Obstetrical		Brazelton scales Minor physical anomalies Autonomic responsivity Obstetrical records	
4 months		Bayley Infant Scales Conditioning Social differentiation Infant temperament	Home observations
12 months		Bayley Infant Scales Conditioning Social attachment	Home observations
30 months	CAPPS IPAT anxiety scale	Bayley Infant Scales PPVT Stanford-Binet Vocabulary RABI Social-medical history	

Note. CAPPS = Current and Past Psychopathology Scales, IPAT = Institute for Personality and Ability Testing, MAPI = Maternal Attitute to Pregnancy Inventory, PPVT = Peabody-Picture Vocabulary Test, RABI = Rochester Adaptive Behavior Inventory.

Obstetrical.   The course of the mother's pregnancy, the delivery, and the condition of the newborn were assessed using the Research Obstetric Scale (ROS) developed at the University of Rochester (Zax, Sameroff, & Babigian, 1977).

The earlier review of the long-term effect of prenatal and perinatal complications had found little evidence for specific complications leading to specific risks. Parmelee and Haber (1973) have argued that the strategy of using multiple criteria combined into single scores would increase the predictive potential of perinatal variables. Prechtl (1968) devised a pregnancy scale by defining the optimal conditions for 42 pregnancy variables for a sample of Dutch women. Any deviation from the optimal range was scored as a nonoptimal condition. In Prechtl's sample, the range on nonoptimal conditions was from 0 to 15 with a mean between 3 and 4. Parmelee and associates (Beckwith, Cohen, & Parmelee, 1973) revised the Prechtl scale for use in the United States. Based on these two versions, we developed the Rochester Research Obstetrical Scale (ROS). Where the Parmelee and Prechtl versions consisted of a single score, the ROS has a total score and three-part scores based on a prenatal scale, a delivery scale, and an infant scale (see Table 5.2).

TABLE 5.2
Rochester Research Obstetrical Scale (ROS)

Scale[a]	Points
Prenatal	
1. Young mother (primigravida < 16 yrs, multigravida < 18)	1
2. Old mother (> 35 yrs)	1
3. Grant multiparity (> 6)	1
4. Abortions (> 2)	1
5. Chronic medication (exclude vitamins)	1
6. Physical disorders (chronic diseases or infections, 1 pt each)	1 2 3 4
Prenatal score	_____
Delivery	
7. C-section (planned = 1 pt, unplanned = 2 pts)	1 2
8. Induction	1
9. Premature rupture of membranes	1
10. Presentation (not vertex)	1
11. Cord (knotted, prolapsed, or tight around neck)	1
12. Placenta problem	1
13. Amniotic fluid (turbid = 1 pt, bloody = 2 pts)	1 2
14. Multiple gestation	1
15. Forceps (low = 1 pt, mid or high = 2 pts)	1 2
16. Analgesia (> 50 mg = 1 pt, > 100 mg = 2 pts)	1 2
17. Anesthesia (> local or pudental block = 1 pt, general = 2 pts)	1 2
18. Long labor (Primigravada: Stage I > 20 hrs or Stage II > 2 hrs) (Multigravida: Stage I > 20 hrs or Stage II > 2 hrs)	1
19. Short labor (Primigravada: Stage I < 3 hrs or Stage II < 10 mins) (Multigravida: Stage I < 2 hrs or Stage II < 10 mins)	1
Delivery Score	_____
Infant	
20. Birthweight low (< 2500 g) and/or premature birth	1
21. Fetal heart rate low	2
22. Neonatal heart rate (< 100)	1
23. Resuscitation necessary	1
24. Apgar at 5 min < 8	1
25. Gross physical anomaly	2
26. Fetal or neonatal death (< 30 days)	3
27. Physical disorders (1 pt each)	1 2 3
Infant score	_____
Total score	_____

The ROS consists of 27 items, 6 items in a Prenatal Scale evaluating the mother's pregnancy, 11 items in a Delivery Scale evaluating labor and delivery factors, and 8 items in an Infant Scale evaluating the condition of the newborn. The items were adjusted to United States standards of obstetrical treatment using norms derived from the Collaborative Study of 40,000 pregnancies (Niswander & Gordon, 1972).

Newborn.   During the last day in the hospital, when the infants were between 48 and 72 hours old, they were brought to a laboratory where assessments were made of autonomic functioning, i.e., heart rate, respiratory rate, and sucking; responsivity to visual stimuli; and behavioral responses using the Neonatal Assessment Scales (Brazelton, 1973), which consisted of items ranging from neurological reflexes to alertness. Using a scale developed by Waldrop, Pedersen, and Bell (1968), we examined the infants for minor physical anomalies that have been associated with chromosomal damage (Down's syndrome).

Four and 12 months.   At 4 and 12 months of age, intensive 4- to 6-hour naturalistic observations of the mother and infant interaction were undertaken in the home. Based on the work of Moss (1965), 64 variables were assessed at 60-sec intervals for the 4-month home observation; 73 variables were assessed every 20 secs at the 12-month observation. These variables described the state and position of both the infant and the mother, the background stimulation during the observation, and the spontaneous and interactive behaviors of both mother and child.

The data from each observation were summarized to provide the proportion of time the mother or infant engaged in any activity and the conditional probabilities that any combination of behaviors would occur together. For example the proportions were expressed as percentage of time that the infant smiled spontaneously or that the mother vocalized responsively, whereas the contingent relationship was expessed as a phi-coefficient reflecting the probability that both the infant's spontaneous smiling and mother's responsive vocalization occurred together. The various proportions and phi-coefficients could then be factor analyzed to search for underlying relationships among the interaction behaviors.

The child was then tested in the laboratory using the Bayley Infant Scales that produce a Mental Developmental Index (MDI) and a Psychomotor Developmental Index (PDI). In addition, the social and emotional behaviors of the infant were scored by the examiner on the Bayley Infant Behavior Rating Scale (IBR). The infant was also tested in an operant-conditioning situation in which a panel press produced a display of colored lights.

At the 4-month session, the infant was alternately confronted with a stranger and his or her mother, while gazing and smiling behavior was recorded to test for an ability at social differentiation. Afterwards, the mother filled out a temperament questionnaire developed by Carey (1970) that measured the same characteristics that Thomas et al. (1968) had assessed through extensive interviews. Carey defined a difficult child as one who was above the mean in four of the following five categories: arhythmic, withdrawal rather than approach, poor adaptability, negative mood, and high intensity of reaction.

At the 12-month session, social differentiation and maternal attachment were evaluated using the procedures developed by Ainsworth and Bell (1970) in which the mother plays with her child, a stranger enters and leaves, the mother leaves, and then returns for a final reunion episode.

Thirty months.   At 30 months no home observations were made. The mother and child came to the laboratory and were then separated, the child to be tested and the mother to be interviewed. The testing included the Bayley Scales, the Peabody-Picture Vocabulary Test (PPVT), and the vocabulary scale from the Stanford-Binet. The mother's interview included the Rochester Adaptive Behavior Inventory (RABI), which is a detailed, behavior-specific, maternal interview, and a social and medical history of the family covering the past 30 months. The mother returned alone for a second session that was a repeat of the initial prenatal clinical interview to determine if any changes had occurred in her emotional status.

Competence Criteria

For the analyses of the development of competence or its more clinically relevant counterpart, incompetence, two scores from the 30-month assessment were used as dependent criteria measures, the Bayley Infant Scales' Mental Development Index (MDI) and the Rochester Adaptive Behavior Inventory (RABI) Global Rating. The Bayley was thought to reflect cognitive competence whereas the RABI score measured social and emotional competence (Jones, 1978).

The format used for the RABI assessment is that of a clinical interview that enables the interviewer to probe and pursue related issues during the interview. Scoring of the items can be done during the interview. Interrater reliabilities of the 30-month and 48-month-old forms of the RABI have exceeded .95 (Pearson *r*). In addition to generating scalar data suitable for factor or cluster analysis, a global 5-point rating of adjustment is generated by the interviewer for each child. Interrater reliability has ranged upwards of 90% agreement for the global scores.

Path Analysis of Longitudinal Data

The typical strategy used to find differences in infant behavior is to compare groups who differ on various constitutional or social dimensions. This approach has been successful in demonstrating many differences related to SES. However, if one wants to understand why children behave the way they do, such a direct approach explains very little of the variability in target behaviors. For example, social class is a "sociological" variable that must be translated into "psychological" behaviors that directly affect the child. In addition to the translation of sociological variables into psychological ones, account must be taken of the interplay of the mothers' and infants' behaviors as they influence each other across time.

Statistical models that are adequate to interpret the complexities of developmental processes are scarce. This lack is felt particularly in developmental research where there is a need to explain changes in a variety of behaviors across time. Multivariate analysis of variance provides a basis for relating a set of independent to a set of dependent variables but does little to clarify the paths of influence between and within the two sets of variables. A more complex form of multivariate analysis is path analysis.

Path analysis is becoming widely accepted as the methodology of choice in attempting to understand relationships among longitudinal data (Duncan, 1966; Jencks, 1972). Correlation matrices provide some indications of relationships but offer no basis for judging causal relationships. In addition, the large correlational matrices necessary in longitudinal studies usually provide many serendipitous and unreplicable relationships.

Path analysis is based on a series of regression analyses that attempt to tease apart the interrelations of an array of variables. In longitudinal research a relationship between two variables at different points in time might result from a number of connections between intermediate points that would not be readily apparent. For example, in Figure 5.2, the infants behavior at 30 months could be the result of five different paths of influence:

1. C4 ≯ C30: Characteristics of the child at 30 months are the continuation of constitutional characteristics at 4 months.
2. M4 ≯ C4 ≯ C30: 30-month characteristics are the consequence of infant characteristics at 4 months that were produced by the mother at 4 months.
3. M30 ≯ C30: 30-month characteristics are related only to how the mother is treating the child at 30 months.

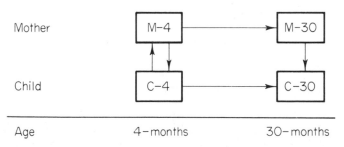

FIG. 5.2. Potential path analysis of contributors to 30-month child behaviors.

4. M4 $\gg$ M30 $\gg$ C30: Mother characteristics at 4 months influence her characteristics at 30 months that then determine the child's 30-month behavior.

5. C4 $\gg$ M4 $\gg$ M30 $\gg$ C30: This path is similar to the last except that the mother's 4-month characteristics were influenced by the infant's characteristics at that age. This last path is an example of the transactional model of development described by Sameroff (1975).

Complex developmental interactions appear to require complex data analyses. The analyses from the longitudinal study will necessarily be of much greater complexity than this simple example because of the myriads of mother and infant variables. To our knowledge, full path analyses have not been applied to data from longitudinal studies in early child development. Cross-lagged panel correlation designs (Campbell & Stanley, 1963), a simpler form of path analysis, have already produced some novel contributions (Clarke-Stewart, 1973).

Data from the on-going 30-month assessment of our sample has provided us with measures of child competency that can be used as criteria for predictions based on variables from earlier assessments of the child and mother. A set of demographic, prenatal, newborn, 4-month, and 12-month variables was selected from the data provided by 100 subjects who had completed their 30-month assessment (see Table 5.3). Demonstration path analyses were performed with the RABI Global rating of adaptive behavior and the Bayley Mental Development Index as outcome measures. Figures 5.3 and 5.4 show the results of the analyses.

Within the constraints of this paper, it would be impossible to completely explicate these complex-appearing figures nor would such an explication be worthwhile, because we have not yet reduced our complete set of variables to a size where all the assessment data could be included in these path analyses. However, in order to demonstrate both the power and possibilities of this approach, the following discussion deals with two aspects of the analysis.

The importance of path analysis is that two variables chosen from different points in time usually have not one, but a variety of ways in which they are related. The variables in Figure 5.5 are a subset of those in Figure 5.4 showing all the paths leading from the mother's educational level to the child's 30-month IQ. It can be seen that there is a direct influence at each age showing the continuing impact of the mother on her child's development. There is also a continuity in the child's behavior by which IQ is serially related from 4 to 12 to 30 months of age. As a consequence, it can be seen that the child's intelligence at each age results from a combination of prior intrinsic and extrinsic influences. As an additional factor, it can be seen that the mother's education is related to the child's temperament at 4-months, which produces an independent impact on the 30-month Bayley

TABLE 5.3
Independent Variables in Path Analyses

Assessment Age	Variable
Demographic data	Family size (gravida)
	Years of education
	Socioeconomic status
Prenatal interview	Chronicity of mental illness
	Severity of mental illness
	IPAT anxiety score
	Schizophrenia
	Neurosis
	Social competency score
Obstetrical & newborn	Sex of child
	ROS prenatal score
	ROS obstetrical delivery score
	ROS infant score
	Apgar – 1 min
	Apgar – 5 min
	Birth weight
	Brazelton summary score
4 months	Bayley MDI
	Bayley PDI
	Home Observation variables
	Mother in earshot range
	Mother in eyeshot range
	Mother caretakes
	Infant cries
	Mother lacks response
	Mother negative response
	Mother smiles
	Infant smiles
	Infant temperament questionnaire
	Difficult temperament score
	Temperament Cluster A (adaptability, approach, mood)
	Temperament Cluster B (threshold, intensity)
12 months	Bayley MDI
	Bayley PDI
	Home Observation variables
	Mother in earshot range
	Mother in eyeshot range
	Mother caretakes
	Mother lacks response
	Mother socializes
	Mother smiles
	Mother negative
	Infant smiles
	Infant cries

Note: See text for full titles of tests.

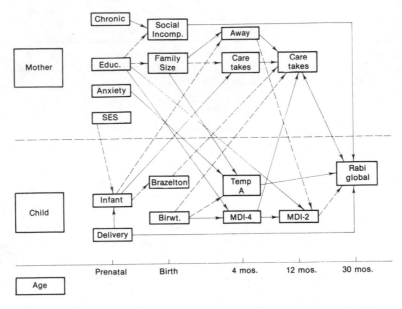

FIG. 5.3. Path-analysis summary for 30-month Rochester Adaptive Behavior Inventory (RABI) Global Rating of adaptive incompetency. (Dashed lines are negative relationships. High SES is upper status.)

Scores, i.e., good education is related to a good temperament that is related to a higher IQ and vice versa.

A second type of contribution that path analysis makes to the data analysis is in the identification of those variables that mediate between mother and infant characteristics. Table 5.4 shows the regression analysis for the RABI global rating using only the mother's initial characteristics as predictors. The mother's social incompetency, anxiety, and SES together explain (R^2) 21% of the variance in the child's behavior. Table 5.5 shows the results of the regression analysis when variables from the newborn, 4-, and 12-month assessments are added. It can be seen that anxiety and SES are no longer in the equation. Instead, they are replaced by a set of mother and infant behaviors that explain almost 50% of the variance in the criterion. The more inclusive analysis provides a more complete understanding of how children become incompetent based on the mother's actual behavior rather than her demographic description.

In the Broman et al. (1975) analysis of the Collaborative Perinatal Project described earlier, a maximum of 28% of the variance in 4-year IQ was explained using mother's education and SES, birth data, and 4-, 8- and 12-month assessments of the infant. In the Rochester study over 50% of the variance in 30-month IQ was explained when additional characteristics of the mother (e.g., social competence) and of her behaviors toward the child (e.g., home observation data) were added.

These studies emphasize that developmental assessments cannot be based on simple notions of continuity between analogous-appearing behaviors. From the child's side, the data from the Rochester study revealed a stronger connection between 4-month infant temperament scores and 30-month Bayley MDIs then between 4- and 30-month Bayley scores (Sameroff, 1978). On the mother's side, it appears that a much greater proportion of the variance can be explained using assessments of the environment than of the child in these early years.

PREDICTIONS OF COGNITIVE COMPETENCE

Finally, we get to the crux of the issue. From the general overview of theory and data, we must face the problem of utility. What can we distill from the previous discussion to improve our predictive success at identifying infants at risk for later cognitive incompetence?

The first lesson is that to make relatively accurate predictions, one must monitor both the child and environment continuously throughout development. From a cost-efficiency viewpoint, this is impossible even for small research populations. A utility analysis would have to be made to determine the maximum rate of predictive success for the minimum rate of assessment.

Although I have argued that behavioral assessments of the infant are of little utility in themselves, some approaches have been proposed that increase predictive accuracy. These are usually in the form of cumulative risk

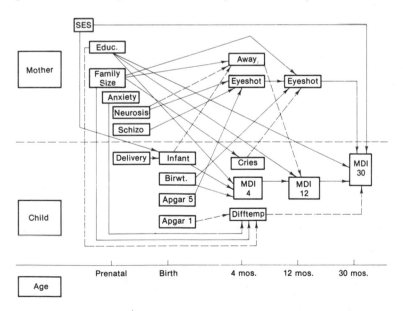

FIG. 5.4. Path-analysis summary for 30-month Bayley Mental Development Index (MDI).

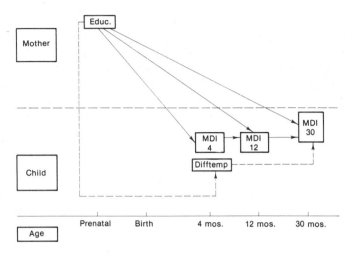

FIG. 5.5.   Paths of relation between mother's education and Bayley Mental Development Index (MDI).

indices. Parmelee et al. (1976) proposed such an index that combined risk scores derived from biological variables in the prenatal, neonatal, and early infancy periods to sort out those infants with transient brain insult from those with brain injury that remain deviant. Psychological assessments were added later in the first year when environmental events begin to have their impact. This cumulative procedure could avoid the high error rates of one-shot screening instruments.

In order to achieve a demonstrable increase in predictive efficiency, better assessments of environmental variables are necessary. The global variable of concern would be the adaptive capacity of the social setting, especially that of the immediate family. Adaptive capacity can be crudely defined as the amount of plasticity possible in the behavior of the primary caretakers to meet the needs of their developing child. These adaptive capacities are limited by economic, social, educational, and personality constraints. The economic constraints act on the family's ability to provide special attention and day-care facilities and to utilize medical and mental health care. The social constraints act on the norms which the family applies to the child in terms of expectations about progress and deviancy. Educational constraints act on the family's ability to maximize the utilization of economic resources and the understanding of social norms. Finally, personality constraints reduce the physical and emotional investment that members of the family are able to devote to the child-rearing process.

The economic and educational resources of the home environment are relatively easy to assess simply by asking a few questions. However, little

TABLE 5.5
Regression Analysis Summary of 30–month
Rochester Adaptive Behavior Inventory (RABI) Global Rating
Using Variables from All Prior Assessments as Predictors

Variable	Multiple R	R² Square	Simple R	Beta
Social incompetency	.41	.17	.41	.35
4–Month Temperament Cluster A	.51	.26	.40	.24
Delivery complication score	.55	.31	.14	.24
12–month Bayley MDI	.59	.35	−.29	−.17
12–month mother caretakes	.63	.39	.07	.21
4–month mother in eyeshot	.65	.42	−.21	−.18
12–month mother socializes	.67	.45	−.24	−.22
12–month infant smiles	.68	.47	.14	.16
Apgar at 5 mins	.70	.49	−.22	−.16

has been done to determine valid and reliable indices in the social and personality spheres. A variety of studies have investigated mother–infant interactions during the first few years of life.

Although social and personality measures have been related to cognitive functioning, little use has been made of them for predictive purposes. Caldwell and her associates (Bradley & Caldwell, 1976; Elardo, Bradley, & Caldwell, 1975) have developed a Home Observation for Measurement of Environment (HOME) inventory. In a short-term longitudinal study, HOME inventory scores taken when infants were 6 months of age were correlated with Stanford-Binet IQs at 3 years, and a strong .50 correlation was found. The subscales of the HOME are: (a) emotional and verbal responsivity of mother, (b) avoidance of restriction and punishment, (c) organization of physical and temporal environment, (d) provision of appropriate play material, (e) maternal involvment with child, and (f) opportunities for variety in daily stimulation. Subscales (c) and (d) were most strongly related to the criterion IQ score. When those infants who improved in IQ between 6 months and 3 years were compared with those infants who declined in IQ during the same period, it was found that subscales (d) and (e) were most related to increases, whereas subscale (c) was most related to decreases.

In a longitudinal study of IQ changes from 2.5 to 17 years of age, McCall, Applebaum, and Hogarty (1972) also studied the differences between groups that increased and groups that decreased in IQ. They argued that it is not constant environmental factors such as educational opportunities and rewards that are the major influences on IQ change, but rather the relation between the parents and the particular child. Although McCall et al. used a sample older than the age of children in our immediate concern, it seems clear that transactions are again at work. The conclusion that must be drawn is that children must be studied individually in their own

TABLE 5.4
Regression Analysis Summary of 30–month Rochester
Adaptive Behavior Inventory (RABI) Global Rating Using Only
Demographic and Prenatal Interview Variables

Variable	Multiple R	R^2 Square	Simple R	Beta
Social incompetency	.41	.17	.41	.23
IPAT anxiety	.43	.19	.31	.16
Socioeconomic status	.45	.21	.36	.17

context if accurate predictions are to be made, because siblings from the same family may have quite different patterns of IQ change.

PARENT'S UNDERSTANDING OF DEVELOPMENT

Data from investigations such as the Rochester Longitudinal Study appear to identify reciprocal chains of behavior between mother and child that produce a diversity of later competencies. A major factor in this diversity has been the variety of ways in which parents react to their children. If the more negative of these interactive chains could be identified early in development, it might be possible to improve the behavior of more maladaptive parents. It seems that an assessment of parental attitudes and personalitites should be of some value, yet despite a vast research literature on efforts to relate the child-rearing attitudes of parents to the behavior of their children surprisingly few relationships have been found (Becker & Krug, 1965). On the face of it, it is peculiar that the children of parents with very different attitudes turn out the same, whereas children of parents with the same attitudes will turn out very differently. The findings become somewhat less surprising when we relate them to the research on parent–child transactions discussed earlier. Predicting outcome from child-rearing attitudes of parents without knowing the characteristics of the child to be reared appears to be an empty exercise. It seems obvious that there are extremes in rearing practices that would be detrimental to any child, yet reports have appeared of cultures with normal adolescents who spent the first 2 years of their life in dark cupboards (Kagan & Klein, 1973). The typical child-rearing attitude question used in such research has focused on specific caretaking practices. Such questions as "Should children be taught about sex? or "Is early toilet training beneficial?" are commonly used. A different approach has been suggested (Sameroff, 1975) that focuses not so much on the specific practices of parents, but rather on their general understanding of the process of child development. Mothers whose understanding of children is restricted to more primitive levels of explanation may have great difficulty in dealing with what they consider to be deviant children.

For our present purposes, I only describe a few possible levels of parental understanding. At a lower level, which might be called the *labeling* level, parents are able to see their children and themselves as independent actors, such that the children's actions and characteristics are viewed as intrinsic characteristics of the child. A consequence of this objectification is that the child can be labeled. A mother who has had a successful experience with her child assigns positive labels, for example, the good child, the pretty child, or the bright child. Once labels are assigned, however, they are thought to belong to the child. Just as the 2- to 5-year-old "labeling" child thinks that the label "cup" belongs to a particular object in the same way as does its color or shape, so the "labeling" mother thinks that the child is the "good child" in the same way as he has blue eyes or brown hair. This device can be very adaptive, for when the good child occasionally acts badly, such as crying too much, breaking a few dishes, or throwing a tantrum, the mother will still think of her child as the good one. On the other hand, this device can be very maladaptive in a case where the mother, because of the negative early experiences she may have had with the child, comes to label him as the difficult child, the bad child, or the ugly one. Even though this infant may outgrow the behavior that caused him to be labeled as difficult in the first place, the perceptions and reactions of the parent who is restricted to the labeling level may continue to be dominated by the original label.

At advanced levels of understanding the child, parents are able to view their children as existing independently of the labels that they give them. For example, the behavior of the child can now be related to age: infants cry, toddlers are hyperactive, adolescents brood. The positive achievement at this higher level is that the behavior of the infant that could have resulted in a life-long label of "difficult" can be seen as age-specific and, moreover, that the child will probably behave quite differently at later ages. The parent is able to use a much broader context for evaluating the child. Beauty can compensate for brains and vice versa. No single label can typify the entire range of the child's behavior. Additional scope is provided when the parents can place their particular child and the child's caretaking situation into a hypothetical context relating all kinds of children to all kinds of caretaking situations. The specific situation of their own child is only one of a multitude of possibilities. The parents are able to see the child's behavior as stemming from its individual experience with its specific environment. If that experience had been different, the child's characteristics would be different. Deviancies in the child can be perceived as being deviancies in the relationship of a particular child to a particular environment, rather than as concrete expressions of the intrinsic nature of the child. Moreover, remediation can now be proposed through an alteration in the current experience of the child by environmental changes.

The level of parental understanding of the child clearly influences the continuum of caretaking casualty described earlier. At one end of the continuum the environment is so adaptive to the needs of the child that even the most distressed infant can achieve an adequate developmental outcome, whereas at the other extreme the environment is so disordered through emotional, financial, and social stress that even the best of infants can come to a bad end. The mother who can appreciate her child's development at a high level of sophistication is better equipped to make qualitative changes in her treatment of the child as the child's activities and requirements change with age. The mother who is restricted to more primitive levels of viewing her offspring ensnares the child at later stages in obsolete social and affective relationships formed during infancy.

The picture becomes more complex when consideration is given to the source of such constitutional factors as "difficult," "colicky," or even the delivery complications themselves. The view espoused by Thomas et al. (1968) was that infants with a random assortment of temperaments were born into environments with a random assortment of adaptive capacities. In contradiction, a number of researchers have noted that women with emotional problems tended to have not only more reproductive complications (MacDonald, 1968; Ferreira, 1969) but also more difficult infants (Carey, 1968; Sameroff, 1978). Thus, it would appear that the same mothers, who, through their emotional difficulties, tend to have the most trouble adapting to infants with caretaking problems are those most likely to produce infants with caretaking problems.

One of the major stumbling blocks to studying the separate effects of prenatal, delivery, or neonatal variables on development is the compounding of these variables in real life. The mother who begins her pregnancy under stressful emotional conditions starts the cycle that ultimately leads to a poor attachment after delivery. Her prenatal stress tends to be associated with more delivery complications and delivery complications tend to be associated with a higher incidence of difficult temperament in the offspring. Difficult temperaments place more demands on the mother's adaptive ability and caretaking skill and tend to produce reduced affection and attachment of the mother to her child. Among the major questions unanswered in this analysis are the identification of points in this negative cycle where intervention should occur and the kinds of interventions that would be the most effective.

In contrast to the stress-laden situations described above is the positive reciprocal cycle of the mother who has prepared for her pregnancy, who suffers a minimum of stress, who trains for her delivery, who requires a minimum of obstetrical intervention, who immediately begins caretaking for her good-tempered child, who feels effective in her caretaking, and who is able to enter a responsive, affectionate relationship with her infant.

CONCLUSIONS

Cognitive competence during the early years depends, for much of its continuity, not on the unfolding of innate capacities, but on environmental constraints. We can assess the contemporaneous competencies of infants on many sensory, perceptual, and cognitive dimensions. Yet these measures do little to help us determine the child's later cognitive competencies. Inefficient predictions are not the result of methodological problems but of conceptual ones. As long as one conceptually isolates children from their environments, the inefficiencies will continue. Only when development is appreciated as a complex interplay between the child's changing competencies and temperament and the changing attitudes and behavior of the important socializing agents in the environment can the prediction problem be squarely faced.

The biological model is one of continuous dynamic transactions between organism and environment, not one of simple causes and effects. An additional complicating problem is that these transactions produce new layers in the child's cognitive organization with new levels of competence that are intrinsically unrelated to former levels of competency. Children's competencies at concept attainment may have no relation to their sensorimotor competencies, whereas later developing logical competencies may be unrelated to their capacities for concept attainment. If a child is highly competent at each new level, the source of the continuity must be sought in the transacting environment rather than in some intrinsic characteristic of the child.

At first glance we may be dismayed at accepting this picture of the inadequacies of our scientific achievement. On the other hand, from a humanistic standpoint, if the maintaining environment plays such a strong role in influencing changes in cognitive competencies, than a multitude of remediation possibilities become available. What is even more pleasurable about this humanistic position is that it coincides with the actual biological case. Current attempts at genetic therapy, for example, have focused on environmental interventions to introduce chemicals that may be lacking in a deviant developmental system.

It is clear that we are not yet aware of the limits of plasticity in human development and achievement. It is important to detail the changes and consistencies in the behavior of young children, but eventually all must be related to the systems context in which behaviors occur.

ACKNOWLEDGMENTS

The research reported here was supported by funds from the National Institute of Mental Health and the Grant Foundation.

REFERENCES

Ainsworth, M. D. S., & Bell, S. M. Attachment, exploration, and separation. Illustrated by the behavior of one-year-olds in a strange situation. *Child Development*, 1970, **41**, 49–67.

Bailey, C. J. Interrelationship of asphyxia neonatorum, cerebral palsy and mental retardation: Present status of the problem. In W. F. Windle (Ed.), *Neurological and psychological deficits of asphyxia neonatorum.* Springfield, Ill.: Charles, C. Thomas, 1958.

Becker, W. L., & Krug, R. S. The Parent Attitude Research Instrument—A research review. *Child Development*, 1965, **36**, 329–366.

Beckwith, L., Cohen, S., & Parmelee, A. H. *Risk, sex, and situational influences in social interactions with premature infants.* Paper presented at the meeting of the American Psychological Association, Montreal, August 1973.

Bell, R. Q. A reinterpretation of the direction of effects in studies of socialization. *Psychological Review*, 1968, **75**, 81–95.

Benaron, H., Brown, M., Tucker, B. E., Wentz, V., & Yacorzynski, G. K. The remote effect of prolonged labor and forceps delivery, precipitate labor with spontaneous delivery, and natural labor with spontaneous delivery on the child. *American Journal of Obstetrics and Gynecology*, 1953, **66**, 551–568.

Benaron, H., Tucker, B. E., Andrews, J. P., Boshes, B., Cohen, J., Fromm, F., & Yacorzynski, G. K. Effects of anoxia during labor and immediately after birth on the subsequent development of the child. *American Journal of Obstetrics and Gynecology*, 1960, **80**, 1129–1142.

Birch, H., & Gussow, C. D. *Disadvantaged children.* New York: Grune & Stratton, 1970.

Blau, A., Welkowitz, J., & Cohen, J. Maternal attitudes to pregnancy instrument. *Archives of General Psychiatry*, 1964, **10**, 65–71.

Bradley, R. H., & Caldwell, B. M. Early home environment and changes in mental test performance in children from 6 to 36 months. *Developmental Psychology*, 1976, **12**, 93–97.

Broman, S. H., Nichols, P. L., & Kennedy, W. A. *Preschool IQ: Prenatal and early development correlates.* Hillsdale, N. J.: Lawrence Erlbaum Associates, 1975.

Brush, S. G. Should the history of science be rated X? *Science*, 1974, **183**, 1164–1172.

Buck, C., Gregg, R., & Stavraky, K. The effect of single prenatal and natal complications upon the development of children with mature birthweight. *Pediatrics*, 1969, **43**, 942–995.

Campbell, D. J., & Stanley, J. C. Experimental and quasi-experimental designs for research and teaching. In N. L. Gage (Ed.), *Handbook of research on teaching.* Chicago: Rand-McNally, 1963.

Campbell, W., Cheseman, E., & Kilpatrick, A. The effect of neonatal asphyxia on physical and mental development. *Archives of Diseases in Childhood*, 1950, **25**, 351–359.

Carey, W. B. Maternal anxiety and infantile colic. *Clinical Pediatrics*, 1968, **7**, 590–595.

Carey, W. B. A simplified method for measuring infant temperament. *Journal of Pediatrics*, 1970, **77**, 188–194.

Cattell, R. B., & Scheier, I. H. *Handbook for the IPAT Anxiety Scale questionnaire* (2nd ed.), Champaign, Ill.: Institute for Personality and Ability Testing, 1963.

Clarke, A. M., & Clarke, A. D. B. *Early experience: Myth and evidence.* London: Open Books, 1976.

Clarke-Stewart, K. A. Interactions between mothers and their children: Characteristics and consequences. *Monographs of the Society for Research in Child Development*, 1973, **38** (6-7, Serial No. 153).

Corah, N. L., Anthony, E. J., Painter, P., Stern, J. A., & Thurston, D. L. Effects of perinatal anoxia after seven years. *Psychological Monographs*, 1965, **79**(3, Whole No. 596).

Douglas, J. W. B. "Premature" children at primary schools. *British Medical Journal,* 1960, *1,* 1003–1013.

Drage, J. S., & Berendes, H. W. Apgar scores and outcome of the newborn. *Pediatric Clinics of North America,* 1966, **13,** 635–643.

Drage, J. S., Berendes, H. W., & Fisher, P. D. The Apgar score and four-year psychological examination performance. In *Perinatal factors affecting human development.* Pan American Health Organization, W.H.O., Scientific Publication, No. 185, 1969, 222–226.

Drillien, C. M. *The growth and development of the prematurely born infant.* Baltimore: Williams & Wilkins, 1964.

Duncan, O. D. Path analysis: Sociological examples. *American Journal of Sociology,* 1966, **72,** 1–16.

Elardo, R., Bradley, R., & Caldwell, B. M. The relation of infant's home environments to mental test performance from six to thirty-six months: A longitudinal analysis. *Child Development,* 1975, **46,** 71–76.

Ferreira, A. *Prenatal environment.* Springfield, Ill.: Charles C. Thomas, 1969.

Fraser, M. S., & Wilks, J. The residual effects of neonatal asphyxia. *Journal of Obstetrics and Gynecology of the British Commonwealth,* 1959, **66,** 748–752.

Gesell, A., & Amatruda, C. *Developmental diagnosis.* New York: Hoeber, 1941. .

Golden, M., Birns, B., Bridges, W., & Moss, A. Social class differentiation in cognitive development among black preschool children. *Child Development,* 1971, **42,** 37–45.

Gottfried, A. W. Intellectual consequences of perinatal anoxia. *Psycholgical Bulletin,* 1973, **80,** 231–242.

Graham, F. K., Caldwell, B. M., Ernhart, C. B., Pennoyer, M. M., & Hartman, A. F. Anoxia as a significant perinatal experience: A critique. *Journal of Pediatrics,* 1957, **50,** 556–569.

Graham, F. K., Ernhart, C. B., Thurston, D., & Craft, M. Development three years after perinatal anoxia and other potentially damaging newborn experiences. *Psychological Monographs,* 1962, **76**(3, Whole No. 522).

Graham, F. K., Matarazzo, R. G., & Caldwell, B. M. Behavioral differences between normal and traumatized newborns. II. Standardization, reliability, and validity. *Psychological Monographs,* 1956, **70,**(21, Whole No. 428).

Graham, F. K., Pennoyer, M. M., Caldwell, B. M., Greenman, M, & Hartman, A. F. Relationship between clinical status and behavior test performance in a newborn group with histories suggesting anoxia. *Journal of Pediatrics,* 1957, **50,** 177–189.

Hess, J., Mohr, G., & Bartelme, P. F. *The physical and mental growth of prematurely born children.* Chicago: University of Chicago, 1939.

Illsley, R. Early prediction of perinatal risk. *Proceedings of the Royal Society of Medicine,* 1966, **59,** 181–184.

Jencks, C. *Inequality: A reassessment of the effect of family and schooling in America.* New York: Basic Books, 1972.

Jones, F. H. The Rochester Adaptive Behavior Inventory: A parallel series of instruments for assessing social competence during early and middle childhood and adolescence. In J. Strauss, H. Babigian, & M. Roff (Eds.), *Methods of longitudinal research in psychopathology.* New York: Plenum, 1978.

Joppich, G., & Schulte, F. J. *Neurologie des Neugeborenen.* Berlin: Springer-Verlag, 1968.

Kagan, J., & Klein, R. E. Cross-cultural perspectives on early development. *American Psychologist,* 1973, **28,** 947–961.

Kuhn, T. S. *The structure of scientific revolutions.* Chicago: University of Chicago Press, 1962.

Little, W. J. On the influence of abnormal parturition, difficult labor, premature birth, and asphyxia neonatorum on the mental and physical condition of the child especially in relation to deformities. *Lancet,* 1861, **2,** 378–380.

MacKinney, L. G. Asphyxia neonatorum in relation to mental retardation: Current studies in man. In W. F. Windle (Ed.), *Neurological and psychological deficits of asphyxia,* Springfield, Ill.: Charles C. Thomas, 1958.

McCall, R. B., Hogarty, P. S., & Hurlbut, N. Transitions in infant sensorimotor development and the prediction of childhood IQ. *American Psychologist,* 1972, **27,** 728–748.

McDonald, A. D. Intelligence in children at very low birth weight. *British Journal of Preventive and Social Medicine,* 1964, **18,** 59–74.

McDonald, R. L. The role of emotional factors in obstetric complications: A review. *Psychosomatic Medicine,* 1968, **30,** 222–237.

Moss, H. A. Methodological issues in studying mother–infant interaction. *American Journal of Orthopsychiatry,* 1965, **35,** 482–486.

Nelson, K. B. The 'continuum of reproductive casualty'. In R. MacKeith & M. Bax (Eds.), *Studies of infancy.* Clinics in Developmental Medicine, No. 27, Lauenham, England: Heineman, 1968.

Niswander, K. R., Friedman, E. A., Hoover, D. B., Pietrowski, R., & Westphal, M. Fetal morbidity following potentially anoxigenic obstetric conditions. I. Abrupto placentae. II. Placenta previa. III. Prolapse of the umbilical cord. *American Journal of Obstetrics and Gynecology.* 1966, **95,** 838–846.

Niswander, K. R., & Gordon, M. (Eds.), *The Collaborative Perinatal Study of the National Institute of Neurological Diseases and Stroke: The Women and their Pregnancies.* Philadephia: Saunders, 1972.

Parmelee, A. H. & Haber, A. Who is the "Risk Infant"? *Clinical Obstetrics and Gynecology,* 1973, **16,** 376–387.

Parmelee, A. H., Kopp, C. B., & Sigman, M. Selection of developmental assessment techniques for infants at risk. *Merrill–Palmer Quarterly,* 1976, **22,** 177–199.

Parmelee, A. H., & Michaelis, R. Neurological examination of the newborn. In J. Hellmuth (Ed.), *Exceptional infant: Studies in abnormalities* (Vol. 2). New York: Brunner/Mazel, 1971.

Pasamanick, B., & Knobloch, H. Epidemiologic studies on the complications of pregnancy and the birth process. In G. Caplan (Ed.), *Prevention of mental disorders in children.* New York: Basic Books, 1961.

Pasamanick, B., & Knobloch, H. Retrospective studies on the epidemiology of reproductive causality: Old and new. *Merrill–Palmer Quarterly,* 1966, **12,** 7–26.

Pasamanick, B., Knobloch, H., & Lilienfeld, A. M. Socio-economic status and some precursors of neuropsychiatric disorders. *American Journal of Orthopsychiatry.* 1956, **26,** 594–601.

Prechtl, H. F. R. Neurological findings in newborn infants after pre- and paranatal complications. In H. H. P. Jonxis, H. K. A. Visser, & J. A. Troelstran (Eds.), *Aspects of praematurity and dysmaturity: Nutricia symposium.* Leiden: Stenfert Kroese, 1968.

Prechtl, H. F. R., & Beintema, D. J. The neurological examination of the full term newborn infants. *Little Club Clinics in Developmental Medicine,* No. 12. London: National Spastics Society, 1964.

Sameroff, A. J. Infant risk factors in developmental deviancy. In E. J. Anthony & C. Koupernik (Eds.), *The child in his family* (Vol. 4). New York: Wiley, 1978.

Sameroff, A. J. Early influences on development: Fact or fancy? *Merrill–Palmer Quarterly,* 1975, **21,** 267–294.

Sameroff, A. J., & Chandler, M. J. Reproductive risk and the continuum of caretaking casualty. In F. D. Horowitz, M. Hetherington, S. Scarr-Salapatek, G. Siegel (Eds.), *Review of child development research* (Vol. 4). Chicago: University of Chicago Press, 1975.

Sameroff, A. J., & Zax, M. Neonatal characteristics of offspring of schizophrenic and neurotically-depressed mothers. *Journal of Nervous and Mental Diseases.* 1973, **157,** 191–199.

Sameroff, A. J., & Zax, M. In search of schizophrenia: Young offspring of schizophrenic women. In L. C. Wynne, R. Cromwell, & S. Matthysse (Eds.), *Nature of schizophrenia: New findings and future strategies.* New York: Wiley, 1978.

Schachter, F. F., & Apgar, V. Perinatal asphyxia and psychologic signs of brain damage in childhood. *Pediatrics,* 1959, **24** 1016–1025.

Schreiber, F. Mental deficiency from paranatal aspyhxia. *Proceedings of the American Association of Mental Deficiency,* 1939, **63,** 95–106.

Schulte, F. J., Michaelis, R., & Filipp, E. Neurologie des Neugeborenen: I. Mitteilung Uraschen und Klinische Symptomatologie von Funktionsstorungen des Neurensystems bei Neugeborenen. *Zeitschrift fur Kinderheilkunder,* 1965, **93,** 242–263.

Smith, A. C., Flick, G. L., Ferriss, G. S., & Sellmann, A. H. Prediction of developmental outcome at seven years from prenatal, perinatal and postnatal events. *Child Development,* 1972, **43,** 495–507.

Spitzer, R., & Endicott, J. Diagno. II. Further developments in a computer program for psychiatric diagnosis. *American Journal of Psychiatry,* 1969, **125,** 12–21.

Stechler, G. A longitudinal follow-up of neonatal apnea. *Child Development,* 1964, **35,** 333–348.

Thomas, A., Chess, S., & Birch, H. *Temperament and behavior disorders in children.* New York: New York University Press, 1968.

Usdin, G. L., & Weil, M. L. Effect of apnea neonatorum on intellectual development. *Pediatrics,* 1952, **9,** 387–394.

Waldrop, M. F., Peterson, F. A., & Bell, R. Q. Minor physical anomalies and behavior in pre-school children. *Child Development,* 1968, **39,** 391–400.

Werner, E. E. *The Kauai study: Follow-up at adolescence.* Unpublished manuscript, Honolulu: 1975.

Werner, E. E., Bierman, J. M., & French, F. E. *The children of Kauai.* Honolulu: University of Hawaii Press, 1971.

Werner, E., Honzik, M., & Smith, R. Prediction of intelligence and achievement at ten years from twenty months pediatric and psychologic examinations. *Child Development,* 1968, **39,** 1063–1075.

Werner, E. E., Simonian, K., Bierman, J. M., & French, F. E. Cumulative effects of perinatal complications and deprived environment on physical, intellectual, and social development of preschool children. *Pediatrics,* 1967, **39,** 480–505.

Wiener, G. Psychologic correlates or premature birth: A review. *Journal of Nervous and Mental Diseases.* 1962, **134,** 129–144.

Wiener, G., Rider, R. V., Oppel, W. C., Fischer, L. K., & Harper, P. A. Correlates of low birth weight: Psychological status at 6-7 years of age. *Pediatrics,* 1965, **35,** 434–444.

Wiener, G., Rider, R. V., Oppel, W. C., & Harper, P. A. Correlates of low birth weight: Physhological status at eight to ten years of age. *Pediatric Research,* 1968, **2,** 110–118.

Willerman, L., Broman, S. H., & Fiedler, M. Infant development, preschool IQ, and social class. *Child Development,* 1970, **41,** 69–77.

Windle, W. F. Structural and functional changes in the brain following neonatal asphyxia. *Psychosomatic Medicine,* 1944, **6,** 155–156.

Zax, M., Sameroff, A. J., & Babigian, H. Birth outcomes in the offspring of mentally disordered women. *American Journal of Orthopsychiatry,* 1977, **47,** 218–230.

Zigler, E., & Phillips, L. Social competence and the process-reactive distinction on psychopathology. *Journal of Abnormal and Social Psychology,* 1962. **65,** 215–222.

6 Iatrogenic Retardation: A Syndrome of Learned Incompetence

Richard B. Kearsley
Center for Behavioral Pediatrics and Infant Development
New England Medical Center Hospital

In 1974, Philip Zelazo and I joined the Pediatric Department of the New England Medical Center Hospital in Boston, Massachusetts. We established the Center for Behavioral Pediatrics and Infant Development and began to examine the clinical and diagnostic utility of a set of laboratory procedures[1] used in our prior research to monitor cognitive development in normal children between the ages of 3 and 30 months (Kagan, Kearsley, & Zelazo, 1978; Kearsley & Zelazo, 1975). These procedures had revealed age-related changes in such elicited responses as visual fixation, smiling, vocalization, and heart-rate acceleration and deceleration among normal children. We believed that they might offer a more direct probe of processes associated with early cognitive behavior than that provided by neurological examinations or traditional tests of infant development. Moreover, since these measures placed minimal reliance on either gross-motor performance or productive speech, they allowed us to assess cognitive behavior in physically handicapped infants and explore the possiblity that mental and motor development, although mutually facilitating, can proceed independent of one another.

Initially, we examined the results obtained when this battery of cognitive tests was presented to infants who manifested a variety of developmental handicaps. We found that children with Down's syndrome, congenital cytomegalic inclusion disease, severe microcephaly, and uncontrolled infantile seizures showed fragmented patterns of visual fixation. They also had significant delays, relative to normal children, in age-related clusters of

---

[1]A detailed description of these procedures, together with a discussion of the theoretical issues that led to their derivation, is contained in Chapter 3.

behavioral and physiological responses that we use to infer information processing and the assimilation of sequential visual and auditory stimuli. Children with clinical and laboratory evidence of major brain damage showed age-related delays in their response patterns. However, we observed age-appropriate patterns of responses among children whose neuromotor deficits, although resulting in major physical handicaps, were apparently unrelated to their capacity to process and assimilate visual and auditory information. Repeated testings of infants with well-controlled phenylketonuria revealed response clusters that were indistinguishable from those obtained on normal children of comparable ages. We examined a 14-month-old infant with congenital absence of the right forearm, a deformed left arm, and nonfunctional lower extremeties. His pattern of responses indicated an age-appropriate level of cognitive competence and led us to predict that he would respond to a program directed towards stimulating his mental development. Two years later, this child is speaking in complex grammatically correct sentences, and demonstrates the capacity for abstract symbolic reasoning. He is presently enrolled in a class of physically handicapped, intellectually intact preschool children.

Thus, we were encouraged to believe that these procedures offered a viable alternative to conventional measures that are used to infer cognitive development during the early months of life. Moreover, they made it possible for us to assess cognitive development among children with a variety of physical handicaps who heretofore had been either considered untestable or labeled as mentally retarded.

A SYNDROME OF LEARNED INCOMPETENCE

During the course of these initial explorations, we tested a number of children who were diagnosed as having mental and motor retardation of unknown etiology. Typically, they were between 18 and 30 months of age, with developmental quotients of 60 or less based on the Bayley Scales of Mental and Motor Development or the Denver Developmental Screening Test. They had been variously labeled as "nonorganic failure to thrive," "minimal brain damage," "psycho-social deprivation," or "nonspecific congenital encephalopathy." A review of their medical records revealed a prior history of slow weight gain, small stature, and delays in both motor performance and language production. However, the results of repeated medical, neurological, and metabolic studies had failed to identify any specific organic cause for their developmental retardation.

These children presented such remarkably similar histories that it was possible to construct a prototypic exemplar of this group of developmentally retarded infants. Their histories began with an episode during the immediate perinatal period that was interpreted by parents and professionals alike as a possible cause of brain damage and subsequent mental impairment. The nature of the episode varied widely and included prematurity, prolonged difficult delivery, viral infection, perinatal sepsis, and respiratory distress. The first few months of life were characterized by fussy, colicky behavior; erratic sleep patterns; difficulty with feeding; and slow weight gain. Repeated medical evaluations eventually resulted in a diagnosis of nonorganic failure to thrive. Persistent delays in neuromotor development and the emergence of such problem behaviors as tantrumming, head banging, breath holding, and uncontrollable crying contributed to an already high level of anxiety in the minds of the parents concerning the developmental status of their child. The majority of the parents' efforts were directed towards placating the child and avoiding the imposition of demands that might lead to resistant, rebellious behavior. Finally, as the child approached the end of the second year without having acquired productive speech, the diagnosis of mental and motor retardation of unknown etiology was made on the basis of neurological evidence of delays in motor performance and failure to pass age-appropriate items on conventional tests of infant development.

The most striking finding was that the results of our cognitive testing revealed that each of these children showed patterns of behavioral physiological responses indistinguishable from those obtained on age-appropriate normal children. In spite of prior reports of difficulty in conducting neurological examinations and developmental testings, the majority of these children remained quiet and attentive during the 25 mins required to present the two visual and three auditory episodes that comprise our cognitive test battery. Because the child is neither restrained nor verbally coached during the testing, this quiet, attentive behavior and the pattern of behavioral and physiological responses suggested that the child's capacity to process and assimilate complex, sequential visual and auditory information was at an age-appropriate level.

The finding of an apparently normal level of cognitive development among this group of motorically, linguistically, and socially delayed infants whose development had taken place in an environment characterized by prolonged parental anxiety and inappropriate caretaking practices prompted the use of the term *iatrogenic retardation* to describe what we consider to be a recognizable syndrome of learned incompetence. We use the term *iatrogenic* to convey our belief that the manifestations of developmental retardation found among this group of children are the result of the manner in which they had been treated. Traditionally, the term *iatrogenic* implies an unwanted and frequently unexpected complication of what is considered to be an appropriate mode of therapy based on information derived from generally accepted diagnostic procedures. The label *iatrogenic retardation* is based on qualitatively similar criteria.

The procedures used to monitor the development of this group of infants and to infer the level of their mental abilities are generally accepted diagnostic measures. Results of such testings are widely used to influence not only the manner in which the child is treated, but also to plan for his future care. The treatment consists of parenting practices modified to accommodate a lowered level of expectation of the child's mental abilities. The fact that the course of these childrens' motor and speech development was consistent with these lowered expectations suggests that *Iatrogenic Retardation* is but another instance of the so-called self-fulfilling prophecy (Rosenthal & Jacobson, 1968).

We believe that the origins of this form of retardation can be found within the social and psychological environment that surrounds the developing organism. Thus, assuming the basic cognitive skills necessary for age-appropriate intellectual and social behavior remain intact, it should be possible to test the validity of such an assumption by exposing such children to a restructured environment that contains the requisite challenges necessary to activate cognitive potential and overcome the developmental delays used to infer their mental incompetence.

The following section of this paper is a detailed account of a patient whose prior history, presenting problems, and cognitive testing warranted the diagnosis of iatrogenic retardation. Her response to a therapeutic trial of behavioral intervention offers preliminary evidence that such children may have retained the potential for learning and are capable of acquiring age appropriate levels of speech, motor performance, and social behavior.

Case Presentation

Amy was a 950 g premature infant born at an estimated gestational age of 27 weeks, following a delivery that was precipitated by premature separation of the placenta. At birth, she was cyanotic, had an initial APGAR score of 4, and experienced repeated episodes of apnea and respiratory distress. She was placed in the intensive care nursery and during the next 3 days developed hyaline membrane disease, cardiac failure, and jaundice that required an exchange transfusion. Because of recurrent prolonged episodes of apnea, she was placed on an infant respirator and received ventillatory assistance until 10 days of age. Following this, her condition remained relatively stable, although she required repeated blood transfusions to maintain normal hemoglobin level. At 4 weeks of age, she became hypothermic, jittery, and had recurring episodes of apnea. The diagnosis of neonatal sepsis was made on the basis of positive blood cultures, and antibiotic therapy was initiated. The onset of persistent diarrhea necessitated a period of intravenous feeding; however, at 6 weeks of age she was started on breast milk and began a gradual increase in weight. She was discharged from the intensive care unit at 11 weeks of age, weighing approximately 2,000 g.

During the course of Amy's hospitalization, her mother had made repeated visits to the intensive care unit and in the days immediately preceding discharge had spent considerable time in the nursery receiving instructions and support from the nursing personnel. The anxiety and uncertainty associated with the early weeks of Amy's life had gradually subsided as her condition stabilized, and she began to show steady progress. Thus, over the several weeks that preceded discharge, the mother had become increasingly confident about her capacity to care for Amy because her first daughter, now a normal, healthy 6 year old, had also been a premature, although not of this severity.

At the time of discharge, Amy's neurological examination was considered to be within normal limits, and her parents were told that there was no evidence of major brain damage. However, because of the severity of the problems encountered during the perinatal period, the possibility that Amy might develop signs of brain dysfunction in the future could not be ruled out. Moreover, they were cautioned that in view of her extreme prematurity and the need for intermittent oxygen therapy, there was some risk for visual impairment that might not manifest itself for several months. In addition, the marked disparity between head size (75th percentile) and body size (3rd percentile) raised the possibility of her developing hydrocephalus. A schedule of follow-up visits was arranged, and the parents were instructed to obtain frequent measurements of head circumference and to report any rapid increase in the size of their daughter's head.

It is important to note the degree to which the information transmitted to the parents at the time of Amy's discharge altered the mother's belief that her daughter had managed to survive the initial period of stress without serious damage. The possibility that brain damage, blindness, and hydrocephalus might emerge at some time in the future not only resulted in a heightened level of concern about her daughter's condition, but also raised serious doubts in the mother's mind about her ability to care for her child adequately outside of a hospital setting.

Although she maintained frequent contact with her physician and received help from nearby relatives and friends, the mother experienced considerable difficulty in caring for her daughter once at home. Amy fed poorly, gained weight slowly, slept erratically, cried during most of her waking hours, and required almost constant attention. At 5.5 months, she became ill with an upper respiratory infection, lost weight, and was hospitalized following an episode of choking and cyanosis while being fed. She responded well to treatment, and a thorough evaluation failed to reveal any organic cause for her poor weight gain and slow progress. With the exception of poor head control, the neurological examination was again reported to be within normal limits, and the rate of head growth had not been excessive. However, the parents were encouraged to continue their frequent monitoring of head size and were advised that the possibility of future visual impairment and minimal brain dysfunction could not be eliminated at this time.

When Amy was 9 months old, the parents' continuing concern about her vision was increased when they noted that her left eye was turning out. She was reexamined, and the question of cortical blindness was raised. Because there was still no evidence of retinal damage, her apparent inability to focus on and follow visual targets was interpreted as indicating that higher visual centers might have been damaged. In addition, the finding of a left exotropia (the out turning of the left eye) resulted in the parents being advised to cover the right eye in order to stimulate and preserve vision in the left, a procedure that Amy refused to tolerate.

Amy was hospitalized again when she was 1 year of age in order to evaluate her continued failure to thrive. A series of studies that included an electroencephalogram, skull x-rays, an electrocardiogram, and a series of laboratory tests designed to rule out the presence of cystic fibrosis or endrocrinologic disorders all proved negative. Height and weight continued below the 3rd percentile; however, her head size appeared to have stablized, and the parents were advised that the possibility of hydrocephalus was now extremely remote. In addition, it was the opinion of the ophthalmologist that in spite of the left exotropia Amy appeared to have functional vision, although it was not possible to test her visual acuity accurately.

During the course of this hospitalization, the mother was interviewed by a social worker as part of the overall evaluation of her child's failure to thrive. Feelings of anxiety and uncertainty were identified and support was offered to assist her in dealing with Amy. Of particular concern was the recent appearance of head banging that, in conjunction with the neurologist's report of a developmental lag of 5 months, was interpreted by both parents as confirming the emergence of the previously predicted minimal brain damage.

The next 6 months were characterized by continued feeding problems, head banging, temper tantrums, and erratic sleep patterns. Following a series of recurrent ear infections, Amy was admitted to the hospital and at 18 months of age underwent an operation to remove a large mass of adenoid tissue. While in the hospital, an opthalmologic examination was attempted, but because of her extreme uncooperative behavior, an accurate assessment of her vision could not be obtained. The results of a thorough neurological and developmental examination showed Amy to be functioning at a 12-month level. She was capable of sitting by herself, stood with support, and could transfer objects from one hand to another; however, she had no productive speech and failed the majority of the items on the Denver Developmental Screening Test. A diagnosis of "congenital encephalopathy with moderate mental and motor retardation secondary to extreme prematurity" was made, and the parents were advised that although Amy would continue to develop, there was a high probability that she had suffered sufficient brain damage at birth to compromise future intellectual development.

The diagnosis of iatrogenic retardation.   At 20 months of age, Amy was seen at the Center for Behavioral Pediatrics and Infant Development for an evaluation of her cognitive development. During the pretest interview, the parents described the magnitude of the problem they had encountered in caring for their child. The anxiety and uncertainty experienced immediately following birth and at the time of her discharge from the intensive care unit had continued during the course of the first year as they watched for evidence of blindness, hydrocephalus, and brain damage. The task of raising this fretful, fussy, irritable child had all but exhausted the mother. Her attempts to feed and nurture her frail-appearing offspring had met with a recurring diagnosis of failure to thrive and the accompanying implication of inadequacy on her part. The initial unwillingness and later inability to leave Amy in the care of others had resulted in the mother having remained in almost constant attendance over the past 18 months.

Amy's failure to achieve normal developmental milestones combined with her persistent head banging and tantrumming behavior were accepted as evidence that irreparable damage sustained during the early weeks of life had rendered their daughter incapable of responding to the demands and expectations that they had imposed without question on their first child. Thus, the recent prognosis of continuing intellectual handicap had been anticipated by both parents, who viewed their major problem as that of adjusting their future plans to accommodate the care of a handicapped child.

As the testing procedures were explained, both parents expressed doubts that Amy would cooperate with any venture that required her to remain seated and quiet for more than a few minutes at a time. The fact that the interview had taken place in an atmosphere of intermittent fussing, screaming, and head banging — interrupted only when Amy was picked up and a nursing bottle place in her mouth — lent considerable credance to the parents' predictions.

The procedure that we use to assess cognitive and social development consists of three phases and requires approximately 1.5 hrs to complete. In the first phase we record the child's behavioral and physiological responses to the presentation of a series of complex, sequential visual and auditory events that comprise our cognitive test battery (see Chapter 3 of this volume). The second consists of a 15-min observation of the quality and complexity of the child's spontaneous play with a standard set of common toys. The procedure is based on our studies of functional play (Kearsley & Zelazo, 1977), defined as the child's use of toys in an adult-determined manner, and is used to index the major shift in cognitive behavior that appears towards the end of the first and the beginning of the second year of life (Kagan, 1971; Zelazo, 1975). The third phase is a 12-min observation of the quality of mother–child interaction that evolves as mother attempts to teach her child how to use three toys selected from a larger set of available play things (Kearsley & Zelazo, 1977). The manner in which the mother proceeds to sustain her child's involvement with the target toy during each of three, 4-min sequences together with the child's reactions are recorded on standardized check sheets. The results provide an informative sample of both parenting practices and the child's behavior. In addition, the episode gathers useful baseline information with regard to specific behaviors on the part of both parent and child that may require reinforcement or modification when therapeutic intervention appears warranted.

Thus, in our assessment of Amy's cognitive and social development, we attempted to obtain an estimate of her current level of cognitive functioning, as evidenced by her capacity to process and assimilate visual and auditory information; a measure of the degree to which these cognitive skills are activated and manifested in her use of simple play things; and a sample of the parenting practices and the psychological environment generated by the interaction of the mother–child dyad engaged in a task that requires the imposition of constraints and demands by the mother and accommodation and compliance on the part of the child.

The results of the cognitive test battery revealed Amy's capacity for sustained, quiet attentiveness. Her patterns of visual fixation, smiling, vocalization, pointing, and heart-rate accelerations and decelerations indicated that her ability to process sensory information and to assimilate rapdily stimulus events presented in either the visual or auditory mode was comparable to that of the normal 20-month-old child.

The quality and complexity of her play behavior was considerable less mature. Although she demonstrated several instances of functional play indicative of her capacity to generate specific ideas for specific events, the majority of the 15-min solo play episode consisted of stereotypic mouthing, banging, and waving of objects, interspersed with prolonged intervals of fussing and tantrumming behaviors. Although the results of the cognitive battery suggested a level of development sufficient to support complex, symbolic play, this underlying capacity appeared to be masked by Amy's overriding fretful behavior. Her failure to demonstrate an age-appropriate level of functional play appeared to be related more to her inappropriate behavior than to a primary deficit in her level of cognitive development.

The 12-min "teaching episode" revealed Amy's complete intolerance for being constrained as well as the mother's inability or unwillingness to impose any but minimal demands for compliance. For example, repeated attempts to teach Amy to use a toy telephone were met with fussing, crying, and head banging that resulted in the episode being terminated after 2 mins of unsuccessful attempts at instruction. Repeated efforts on mother's part to surpress rebellious behavior by hugging, kissing, or providing Amy with a nursing bottle not only demonstrated the degree to which the child's behavior controlled the interaction, but also indicated the manner in which the mother's responses served to reinforce and sustain a variety of inappropriate behaviors.

The results of the evaluation, combined with our prior experience, led to the following conclusions: (a) Amy's level of cognitive competence approximated that of the normal 20 month old and as such, was presumed to be capable of supporting both the mental and social behaviors associated with children of this age. These include the capacity for productive speech and the ability to comprehend and conform to the imposition of appropriate socialization demands. (b) Her developmental retardation was primarily experiential in origin and not directly caused by the episode of biological stress that accompanied her premature birth. (c) The primary determinants of the psychological environment within which she had developed were the day-to-day caretaking practices that had evolved as a function of her behavior and the parents' unresolved uncertainty about their daughter's mental status. (d) The major deterrent to Amy's demonstration of age-appropriate levels of cognitive, social, and motor performance was the presence of a number of learned, inappropriate behaviors that served to perpetuate a condition of social and cognitive isolation. (e) Provision of a psychological environment that demanded the exercise of her underlying cognitive skills, extinguished her disruptive rebellious actions, and encouraged compliant, socially appropriate behaviors would eliminate the manifestations of developmental retardation. (f) Any attempt to restructure Amy's psychological environment depended upon the parents' capacity to alter their perception of her mental status and to assume the primary responsibility for her treatment.

The behavioral prescription.   We began by informing the parents that on the basis of our testing, we found that Amy's capacity to comprehend the nature of events taking place in her environment and her ability to respond to the imposition of demands for age-appropriate behaviors were similar to those of a normal 20-month-old child. Thus, their first and most difficult task was to change their perception of her intellectual competence and begin to modify their own behavior as a consequence of this assumption. Second, we stressed our belief and that of others that earlier experiences do not necessarily irrevocably impair future development (Clarke & Clarke, 1976). As such, they should concentrate on the present and future development of their child rather than direct their efforts towards reliving the past. Finally, we made it clear that although we were prepared to offer advice and support, they as parents would be responsible for implementing our treatment program.

We targeted three specific behaviors: productive speech, walking, and temper tantrums. The principles of behavioral therapy were discussed and the techniques of contingent reinforcement demonstrated. The parents were provided with a written manual that describes our method for stimulating productive speech (Zelazo, Kearsley, & Ungerer, 1976), which consists of daily, 12-min language-teaching sessions during which one parent acts as teacher and the other records the child's verbal production. They were encouraged to set aside specific times during the day and encourage Amy to stand, walk with support, and finally to walk independently. In addition, they were instructed to record instances of tantrumming and fussing and to note the circumstances that surrounded these behaviors. A replay of the videotaped teaching session that was made during our initial assessment was used to identify the strengths and weakness of mother's parenting practices and to demonstrate the degree to which Amy's behavior served to control the interaction. Monthly office visits were scheduled, and the parents were encouraged to call should questions arise.

The therapeutic trial.   The initial reluctance to accept our estimate of their child's mental competence and motor ability gradually disappeared. Within 2 months, Amy was walking by herself, had produced over 40 words during one 12-min language-teaching session, and had become considerably less inclined to engage in tantrumming behavior. However, a 3-week summer vacation was followed by a recurrence of Amy's noncompliant behaviors. Productivity within the structured language-teaching sessions decreased, athough parents did report that Amy was using more words during the course of the day. Because the mother had accepted the premise that her child was capable of age-appropriate behavior, she looked upon Amy's rebelliousness as a manifestation of willfull stubborness rather than an indication of cognitive incompetence. The father, on the other hand, had recurring doubts about his daughter's underlying intellectual status because he equated the persistence of head banging, which now occurred only at night, as evidence of mental retardation. Thus, at the end of 4 months, although Amy was walking, had a recorded vocabulary of 30 different words, and was described by relatives and friends as showing improvement in her social behavior, both parents had become discouraged; the father because he believed that the persistent head banging indicated that his daughter was, in fact, retarded, and the mother because of her feelings of frustration in getting Amy to demonstrate the behaviors that she now felt her daughter was capable of producing.

Contact with the parents was increased. A staff member visited the home twice a month and maintained frequent telephone contact with the mother. The increased level of support served to restore the mother's self-confidence and increased her skill in implementing the behavioral treatment. The next 4 months witnessed the disappearance of rebellious behaviors, the elimination of nocturnal head banging, and a marked increase in Amy's vocabulary, which exceeded 80 words and included two- and three-word sentences. She now used speech as her primary means of communication. The frequency of home visits and telephone calls diminished. Both parents were satisfied that their child was cognitively intact and had become increasingly confident of their capacity to cope with the day-to-day care of their normal 30-month-old child.

An office visit 1 year after the initiation of the behavioral treatment program revealed a small, socially responsive, verbal 32-month-old child engaged in prolonged episodes of reciprocal play with her older sibling. Amy now accompanied her mother on shopping trips, visits to neighbors, and could be taken out to eat with the family, an activity that in the past had been precluded by her rebellious, tantrumming behavior. Toilet training had been accomplished during the preceeding month with minimal difficulty, and both parents appeared relaxed and genuinely pleased with their child. They had made plans to enroll Amy in a local preschool nursery program in order to increase her contact with other children.

Amy's left exotropia had responded well to intermittent patching of her right eye, which she tolerated without protest. We repeated the 15-min solo play episode and observed Amy's capacity to activate a rich set of hypotheses as she brushed the doll's hair, fed her a toy nursing bottle, and included her in a tea party, sharing cups of imaginary tea and engaging her in conversations. The 15-min session had no instance of fussing or tantrumming. The 12-min teaching episode was also repeated and revealed a series of compliant, responsive, mutually enjoyable interactions between mother and child.

Although the parents expressed some concern with Amy's future, the nature of their concern was that none of the diagnostic studies that had been conducted early in Amy's life would be used to influence her placement in the public schools. The father's comment to our secretary as the family left the office provides a suitable summary of the outcome of this case. "We don't need any more appointments."

Thus, a 20-month-old child whose development quotient of 60 had led to the diagnosis of mental and motor retardation secondary to extreme prematurity and brain damage had, during the course of a 12-month period of behavioral intervention, demonstrated that her level of cognitive skills far exceeded that inferred on the basis of earlier neurological and developmental testings. She was, in fact, capable of activating her potential for learning and had retained the capacity to acquire age-appropriate social, motor, and cognitive behaviors as the nature of the environment that had surrounded her first 20 months of life was altered to provide appropriate levels of expectation, support, challenge, and constraint.

Other Instances of Iatrogenic Retardation

We selected this case to illustrate iatrogenic retardation because of its relevance to a volume concerned with the cognitive assessment of infants whose subsequent development may be at risk because of premature birth. However, it is important to note that the nature of the initial event that can activate parental uncertainty and provide the professional community with an etiological explanation for subsequent developmental retardation is not necessarily associated with prematurity nor with the magnitude of the biological stress encountered by this child during the initial weeks of life. For example, the mother of a "developmentally retarded" 18 month old had been told following the infant's delivery that the fact that the umbilical cord had been wrapped around his neck and that he had a low APGAR score could mean that his future development might be impaired. It was. Another child experienced a transient episode of jitteriness at 1 day of age and was transfered to the special nursery for a 3-day period of observation. At the time of the child's discharge, the mother was advised that everything seemed normal, but since the cause for her daughter's jitteriness was still not known, it would be necessary to keep a close check on her development. At 24 months of age, this child was diagnosed as having mental and motor retardation secondary to congenital encephalopathy. A prolonged episode of early feeding difficulty in a child with "low set ears and abnormal facies" led at 7 months of age to the diagnosis of failure to thrive. This resulted in the mother's referral for psychiatric treatment because of her feelings of depression and inadequacy. When seen at 19 months of age, this child had been diagnosed as having developmental retardation secondary to psychosocial deprivation.

The results of our testings revealed that each of these children was capable of demonstrating age-appropriate levels of cognitive performance in spite of delays in motor development, language production, and the presence of such behavioral problems as temper tantrums and persistent crying. Without exception, these children had retained the potential to learn and the capacity to respond successfully to behavioral intervention as manifested in their acquisition of speech, the elimination of motor delays, and the extinguishing of inappropriate behaviors. These findings suggest that developmental failure among this group of children represents the organism's response to a prolonged period of "psychological malnutrition." They also support the argument that as new skills emerge during the course of early development, they must be met by a supportive and appropriately challenging environment if they are to be activated and incorporated in the child's repertoire of increasingly sophisticated behaviors.

THE GENESIS OF IATROGENIC RETARDATION

Before discussing the issues raised by this syndrome of learned incompetence, it is important to dispel the notion that we are dealing with a rare phenomenon or with isolated instances of spontaneous recovery from major developmental handicaps. We are engaged in a systematic, longitudinal study of the diagnosis and treatment of developmental retardation of unknown etiology. The fact that we are presently following 50 children, the majority of whom demonstrate age-appropriate levels of cognitive development, and continue to see new patients at the rate of 8 to 10 a month, suggests that the problem is neither trivial nor infrequent in occurence. Our finding of persistent delays in motor and speech development as well as a continuation of major problem behaviors in a group of older children who presented this same cluster of behaviors at a younger age suggests that these overt manifestations of developmental retardation may not resolve themselves simply with the passage of time. Thus, it appears warranted to adopt the position that children's inherent capacity to attain and maintain an overall state of well being requires an environment that not only makes available the essential physical and psychological nutrients, but also provides the constraints and challenges necessary for the actualization of those processes that support physical growth and psychological development.

Although the case used to illustrate iatrogenic retardation raises a number of important theoretical issues, discussion is limited to those factors that we believe are primarily responsible for the genesis of the syndrome of learned incompetence. They include the diagnostic and therapeutic practices of the professional community concerned with the care of high-risk and handicapped infants, the effects of prolonged unresolved uncertainty on the parenting practices that surround this population of infants, and the manner in which the children themselves become unwitting contributors to the factors that impede their own development.

It is impossible to undertake such a discussion without appearing to denegrate or ascribe blame to two already overally criticized groups of individuals, physicians and parents. Thus, I must state at the very beginning that neither parents nor physicians are considered to be knowingly culpable for the genesis of this disorder any more than the children themselves, whose behaviors contribute in equal measure to the unfolding of this self-fulfilling prophecy that we have labeled iatrogenic retardation. Rather, the fault lies in our incomplete knowledge of brain function, the relative immaturity of the science of behavior, and the interdisciplinary gap that presently separates behavioral scientists and physicians.

The Use of Fallible Measures of Early Development

The pathogenesis of iatrogenic retardation reaffirms much of what is already known regarding the inability of standard neurological examinations and traditional tests of early development to predict accurately the level of future cognitive competence (Fisch, Bilek, Miller, & Engel, 1975; Stott & Ball, 1965; Thorpe & Werner, 1974). Moreover, the case used to illustrate this kind of developmental retardation makes it clear that the consequences of these inadequacies extend far beyond an academic debate about the origins of intelligence or the relative merits of different theories used to explain cognitive development in human infants, because the results of these potentially fallible measures are used not only to infer current mental ability, but also to categorize infants with labels that can markedly alter their future (Hobbs, 1975).

The neurological indices used to monitor infant development and to infer the overall functional integrity of the central nervous system (CNS) are based on a model that assumes an invariant, age-specific, cephalo-caudal process of neuromotor maturation. Recent evidence suggests that such a conceptualization can result in inaccurate inferences of early cognitive development. For example, brief episodes of stimulating an infant's stepping response were found not only to perpetuate this presumably transient reflexive behavior, but also resulted in independent walking at an earlier age than that observed among infants not exposed to such stimulation (Zelazo, Zelazo, & Kolb, 1972). Moreover, cross-cultural studies have demonstrated that specific child-rearing practices can result in the precocious acquisition of supposedly age-specific, maturationally determined motor milestones, such as sitting, walking, and toilet training (deVries & deVries, 1977; Super, 1973; Warren, 1972). The behavior that was valued and, therefore, exposed to specific stimulation was the primary manifestation of advanced development in the neuromotor repertoire of the child. There was not uniform precocity, but rather the acquisition of specific motor skills associated with particular child-rearing practices. Thus, one is left with the   disquieting evidence that neuromotor indices previously regarded as the product of invariant cephalo-caudal maturational processes within the CNS are, in fact, subject to major modification as the result of specific environmental experiences. As such, the credibility of developmental protocols that use such age-related norms to infer the level of cognitive development is difficult to accept.

The explanation offered by investigators who defend the continued use of traditional tests of early development is also open to question. They argue that during the initial months of life, gross sensorimotor performance represents the substrate for mental activity and thus provides a valid index of early mental development. However, these arguments fail to accommodate the findings of normal intelligence among children afflicted with cerebral palsy or those suffering the deleterious consequences of thalidomide exposure and such congenital handicaps as phocomelia (Crothers & Paine, 1957; Kearsley & Zelazo, 1977; Koop & Shaperman, 1973). These observations, coupled with the results of animal studies that have demonstrated centrally mediated purposeful behaviors in the absence of peripheral sensory motor input (Fentress, 1973; Taub, Perrella & Barro, 1973), necessitate a reexamination of the position that early cognitive behavior is synonomous with gross neuromotor activity. In addition, they suggest that motor and cognitive development may proceed independent of one another. What is evident is the pressing need to seek out alternative measures that may offer more direct probes of early cognitive development.

The professional community responsible for the overall well being of infants and young children must become cognizent of the weight of evidence that argues strongly in favor of relinquishing the time-honored allegiance to conventional measures of early development. The consequences of the potential fallibility of these measures warrants serious concern on the part of the physician as well as those upon whom the physician relies for diagnostic and therapeutic assistance in the management of developmentally handicapped children. In Chapter 7 of this volume, Hamilton has argued persuasively that special educators and various supporting service disciplines, such as psychology and psychometry, must develop and improve assessment instruments and procedures relevant to the care of handicapped children. Similarly, those responsible for establishing guidelines for federal and state supported programs of maternal and child health care must be scientifically rigorous in their scrutiny of developmental screening instruments lest they perpetuate, by mandate, the continued use of patently unreliable diagnostic procedures.

We recognize the magnitude of the burden that this charge imposes on the clinician, for the changing demands of health care have resulted in the physician being called upon to assume an increasingly active role in the prevention, diagnosis, and treatment of social and psychological disorders encountered during early childhood. For many, these issues represent a new domain of medical practice. Traditionally, when confronted with unsolved problems of patient care, the physician has turned to biomedical scientists whose breadth of fundamental knowledge and intimate involvement in the evolution of contemporary medicine has given them a most favored position in the minds of health-care professionals. However, the social and psychological factors associated with early development have not been areas of primary inquiry among physical scientists. Although there is evidence of a "quiet revolution" within the neurosciences that may drastically alter traditional conceptualizations of brain function (Schmitt, Dev, & Smith 1976), the results of these studies continue to be couched in the tentative language of the basic scientist. Their influence on the physician's diagnostic and therapeutic practices has yet to surface. Thus, it is suggested that solutions to problems identified within this new domain of health care may be facilitated by broadening the scientific foundation from which physicians derive their support to include the practice and theory of the behavioral sciences.

The Search for Disease

The most widely used operational definition of health is the failure to find evidence of disease. Asymptomatic adults who seek a routine check up respond to a series of questions, submit to a variety of laboratory tests, and are given a thorough physical examination by their physicians. All of this is directed towards the detection of the signs and symptoms of disease. The patients receive their "clean bill of health" when the clinicians announce that they can find nothing wrong. For, in spite of a major commitment to the maintenance of health, physicians' training and practice are devoted in large measure to the diagnosis and treatment of disease.

The fact that a specific disease entity may manifest itself in a cluster of interrelated signs and symptoms has alerted physicians to seek out these often subtle deviations from the normal in order to identify a particular causal agent. Thus, such diverse findings as muscle weakness in the foot, stomach cramps, headaches, and anemia suggest the possibility of lead poisoning and initiate a series of laboratory tests to identify the presence of this toxic substance. Similarly, the recent emphasis on genetically determined abnormalities has served to heighten physicians' sensitivity to minor variations in the physical appearance of infants and to correlate such deviations with evidence of specific chromosomal abnormalities. This diligent diagnostic search is a necessary prerequisite for the identification of previously recognized or new genetic syndromes. Yet, it often results in directing the parents' attention to minor variations in their child's physical appearance that were considered of sufficient importance by the physician to initiate a series of diagnostic tests.

The fact that such tests may prove negative does not necessarily resolve the doubt created in the parents' minds that there may be something wrong with their child. We found in reviewing case histories of children subsequently diagnosed as having iatrogenic retardation that with few exceptions the hospital records contained such observations as unusual facies, low set ears, prominent nares, spade like hands, wide-set eyes, extremely fine or course hair, partial webbing of the toes, short neck, or unusually shaped head. For example, one 26-month-old child was described as having unusually fine blonde hair, prominent eyes, and a short nose with upturned tip and prominent nares. She was not walking, had only a two-word vocabulary, exhibited a number of autostimulating behaviors, and had a developmental quotient of 65. These physical findings, coupled with her delayed development and "infantile behaviors," were used to establish the diagnosis of a genetically determined, although unspecified, form of mental retardation. The results of our testing indicated an age-appropriate level of cognitive development. Following an 8-month period of behavioral intervention, she was walking, had a recorded productive vocabulary in excess of 150 words, used three-and four-word sentences, engaged in complex functional play, and was toilet trained. The physical findings that previously had been used to infer some underlying genetically determined syndrome associated with mental retardation were still present; however, they now described a small, blonde, bright-eyed, pug-nosed child whose speech, although containing numerous misarticulations, characterized her as an engaging, loquacious, socially responsive 3 year old. The elimination of those indices used to infer mental retardation not only altered the manner in which her physical appearance was perceived, but also changed the way in which she was treated. This child was tested by the Neuropsychology Laboratory at the New England Medical Center Hospital when she was 52 months old, and was reported to have an age equivalent score of 51 months on the Stanford-Binet Intelligence Test; 62 months on the Vineland Social Maturity Scale; and 50 months on the Carrow Test for Auditory Comprehension of Language.

The physician involved in the care of infants and young children must be cognizant of the potential side effect of an overly diligent search for evidence of disease (Morrow, 1975). In the majority of cases, minor physical deviations such as those described are not associated with an underlying genetic disorder nor are they in any way directly related to delays in the child's cognitive development. Yet, by being unduly emphasized or used to infer the possible presence of some obscure syndrome, they may contribute to the parents' belief that they have an abnormal child and thus need to modify their caretaking practices to accommodate a lowered level of expectation.

Obviously, physicians cannot ignore the signs and symptoms that enable them to diagnose and treat disorders that affect children. Neither can they afford to ignore the degree to which their actions may be interpreted by parents as indicating the presence of disease when, in fact, none exists.

The Hanging of Crepe

We stated earlier that the pathogenesis of iatrogenic retardation can be traced to an event or series of events that occur either during gestation or shortly after birth. The nature of the event is such that it is construed as posing an actual or potential threat to the CNS and thus, to the subsequent course of the child's overall development. It is an anxiety-provoking experience for the parent and can serve as a nidus of unresolved uncertainty about the child's current and future intellectual status. It is apparent in the case that has been presented that the magnitude and the duration of the problems surrounding Amy's birth were sufficient to justify a high level of concern; however, she survived the initial period of stress and at the time of discharge was found to have no demonstrable retinal injury or neurological damage. Thus, one would anticipate a gradual diminution in the level of parental anxiety and a resolution of the uncertainty surrounding the possibility of brain damage. The reason that this did not take place becomes apparent when it is recalled that just prior to her discharge, the parents were advised that Amy might develop hydrocephalus, visual impairment, and evidence of brain damage. Moreover, they were told that only the passage of time and the results of repeated observations of her development could resolve the questions raised about the presence or absence of these not uncommon sequelae of extreme prematurity.

In this case, as in other instances of iatrogenic retardation, the maintenance of parental anxiety can be attributed in large measure to the manner in which the physician responsible for the child's care adjusts the prognosis to accommodate the possibility of an unfavorable outcome. It is a practice that has been described as "crepe hanging" and reflects the fact that the physician remains a practitioner of an uncertain art. In spite of the science and technology that support contemporary medicine, physicians frequently find themselves in the position of having to make a decision based on what they recognize to be incomplete or inadequate information and to offer an opinion concerning the outcome of a condition whose eventual resolution is neither clear nor certain. It is a perilous circumstance that necessitates balancing the weight of available evidence and clinical experience against patients' right to be informed and their ability to tolerate the burden of the information. Nor is the decision made easier by the fact that physicians' value is, in large measure, a function of their ability to establish and maintain a position of trust and credibility in the eyes of their patients. It is for these reasons that prudent clinicians' prognosis for the outcome of a particular disorder reflects their tendency to adopt the most conservative estimate of what the future holds. Thus, their prediction usually includes the possibility of an unfavorable outcome. Although they may emphasize that things are going as well as can be expected, they nevertheless make it clear that given the information available and the uncertainty that characterizes the patients' response to disease, it is impossible to rule out an unfavorable termination of the illness.

It is a practice that places physicians in a "no lose" situation. If, in fact, the worst does materialize, their prognostic acumen is confirmed. On the other hand, if a favorable outcome is achieved, it can be attributed to the therapeutic skills that they command. Yet, when prudently exercised, the "hanging of crepe" serves the best interest of patients and physicians alike, for it represents an honest sharing of the uncertainty that surrounds a particular illness and its eventual effects on the individual. In the case of a physical disease (e.g., phenumonia), the issue is usually resolved within a reasonably short period of time and the attending anxiety, although burdensome, does not in and of itself markedly affect the eventual outome of the disorder. However, I believe that the "hanging of crepe" is a major factor in the genesis of iatrogenic retardation. For by emphasizing the possibility that brain damage, although not presently apparent, may become manifest at some time in the future, physicians establish a nidus of unresolved uncertainty in the minds of the parents. It is this anxiety that can exert a profound and continuing negative influence on parenting practices that are modified to accommodate the predicted status of their child. The consequences of this lowered level of expectation may result in the child's failure to achieve those neuromotor landmarks used by the clinician to document normal and to infer delayed cognitive development. Yet, these neuromotor landmarks have been shown to be modifiable on the basis of specific intervention (Zelazo, et al., 1972) and particular child-rearing practices (deVries & deVries, 1977; Super, 1973; Warren, 1972). Thus, delays in Amy's sitting, crawling, and walking were viewed by her parents and her physician as evidence of CNS impairment. The later appearance of such deviant behaviors as tantrumming and head banging, her lack of speech, and failure to comply with the demands imposed by conventional scales of mental development served to confirm the prediction made shortly after birth that the consequences of her extreme prematurity might compromise the structural and functional integrity of her CNS. We recognize that the neuromotor sequelae of a traumatic birth are often delayed in their appearance. What we seek to emphasize is that neuromotor indices are subject to major variation as a function of child-rearing practices and are of limited value in predicting the level of cognitive functioning.

Thus, physicians concerned with the care of high-risk infants must recognize and come to accept the fact that their prognosis of future mental impairment may in itself represent a major hazard to normal development. Of equal importance, they and others concerned with developmental diagnosis must begin to seek out alternative assessment procedures that make it possible to document more accurately the current status of infants' cognitive development.

THE EFFECTS OF MALADAPTIVE PARENTING PRACTICES

It is tempting to attribute the early difficulties encountered by Amy's mother in caring for her child to an initial period of prolonged maternal separation. Failure to provide an opportunity for close physical contact between mother and infant immediately following birth is considered by some researchers to represent a major impediment to the subsequent establishment of a normal nurturant relationship between mother and child (Klaus & Kennell, 1976). However, the quality and intensity of the mother–child relationship that presently exists suggests that the stress imposed on this psychological bond during the early months of life resulted in neither permanent estrangement nor did it interfere with the emergence of what is now an apparently normal emotional tie between mother and child. Rather than pursuing an ethological explanation of maladaptive parenting, I share the view held by others (see Chess & Thomas, 1973; Sameroff, Chapter 5 of this volume) that it is more productive to examine the consequences of the continuing dynamic interaction between parent and child.

The effect of a fussy, colicky, difficult infant on the mother's child-rearing practices and her perception of her caretaking abilities may represent a more potent threat to normal parenting than either transient or prolonged periods of maternal separation. Even in the absence of any perinatal problems, the kind of temperament exhibited by Amy cannot help but raise a recurring question of parental inadequacy on the part of the mother. However, in this case, we are dealing not with a naive parent, but with a mother who had successfully coped with the early care of her first born, also premature at birth, who is now a normal, happy 6-year-old child. Thus, it is reasonable to assume that Amy's mother had experienced a degree of parental effectiveness sufficient to sustain her during the daughter's transition from the intensive care unit to the home.

Let us set aside, for a moment, the anxiety-provoking effect of being told that Amy might become blind or develop hydrocephalus and later evidence of brain damage and examine the nature of the criteria that mothers use to judge the adequacy of their caretaking practices during the early months of life. Although there are many variations in child-rearing practices as a function of cultural values and social norms, two criteria appear to be common to many societies: the ability to sooth and quiet the crying infant and the capacity to provide nourishment adequate to promote a normal rate of physical growth.

In spite of this competent mother's continuing efforts to nurture her infant, the diagnosis on nonorganic failure to thrive was first entertained following Amy's hospitalization at 5.5 months and subsequently confirmed after the exhaustive physical examination that accompanied her second hospitalization at 1 year of age. The diagnosis of nonorganic failure to thrive implies psychosocial deprivation either through wanton neglect or because of major psychiatric or social problems within the family or because of parents' anxiety about the course of the child's development. Moreover, it serves to shift the diagnostic focus from a search for pathology within the child to a search for pathology or at least inadequacy among those responsible for the care of the child. Therapeutic intervention in such cases is based on presumptive evidence of developmental (cognitive) retardation and is directed towards either the identification and treatment of psychopathology or the provision of guidance to parents in working through feelings of guilt and inadequacy that are often associated with the care of developmentally delayed infants. Obviously, such help is valuable in assisting parents of truly mentally retarded children to face the reality of their situation; however, in the case of a child whose fundamental cognitive processes remain intact, such support serves to sustain lowered expectations and encourages parenting practices that accommodate the restricted range of behaviors associated with the retarded infant. As such, they perpetuate a psychological environment that fails to provide the challenges and constraints needed to actualize the child's cognitive potential and eliminate those behaviors used to infer intellectual incompetence.

Amy's temperament, however difficult, might not have been sufficient to compromise the mother's perception of her child and her own competence in dealing with problems associated with her day-to-day care. Fussy, colicky behavior during the first few months of life is not an uncommon occurrence nor it is often associated with subsequent evidence of mental and motor retardation. However, the initial "hanging of crepe" combined with inferences drawn from conventional measures of early motor and mental development, and the use of a linear, cause–effect model of disease to explain a deviant pattern of psychological development resulted in an intolerable burden of uncertainty. The dissonance created by the fact that her best efforts to nurture and care for her child had failed to eliminate the manifestations of developmental retardation led to Amy's mother's acceptance of the validity of earlier professional predictions that her child had been damaged by an accident of birth and was incapable of manifesting a normal pattern of physical and psychological development. As a consequence, appropriate parenting practices that had been used in raising the first child were replaced by a class of behaviors that reinforced Amy's tantrumming and head banging and interfered with her acquisition of age-appropriate motor and language skills. Thus, iatrogenic retardation can be viewed as an undesirable outcome of the child's having been treated in a manner consistent with the results of generally accepted measures of early development that were interpreted by the physician and parent alike as confirming earlier predictions of future impairment. Given the body of knowledge and the technology presently available within the behavioral sciences, iatrogenic retardation may be a preventable disease.

THE LEARNING OF INCOMPETENCE

We have characterized this form of retardation as a syndrome of learned incompetence. Further, we have suggested that the child contributes significantly to the psychological environment that serves to foster and perpetuate those behaviors used to identify developmental retardation and to infer varying degrees of brain dysfunction. Let us examine how this incompetence can be acquired in the presence of an underlying potential for normal development and the manner in which it interferes with the child's acquisition of age-appropriate levels of social and cognitive behaviors.

Without exception, each of the children that we have diagnosed as being iatrogenically retarded presented a history of delays in major motor milestones. Failure to sit, crawl, stand, and walk at appropriate ages could be documented in medical records as well as in parent reports. When questioned as to whether attempts had been made to stimulate such activities, parents replied that they expected these behaviors would emerge spontaneously as part of the normal process of development, a belief that is shared in large measure by the professional community. Thus, delays in or failure to manifest these motor landmarks were interpreted as indicating a fundamental neurological deficit. In those instances where Amy's parents had attempted to encourage standing or walking, persistent protests and tantrumming behavior were accepted as evidence that she was incapable of accomplishing these acts and that continued pressure was not only useless, but unfair given the assumption that they were dealing with a developmentally handicapped child. Yet Amy, and others like her, demonstrated the capacity to acquire age-appropriate levels of motor skills following a relatively brief period of behavioral intervention that was implemented by the parents. The mother's willingness to tolerate the burden of carrying her 20 month old who simply refused to walk indicates the degree to which the child's behavior not only conformed to the mother's expectations, but also perpetuated the delay in motor development used to infer her underlying neurological deficit.

Similarly, each of the children that we have identified as being iatrogenically retarded have shown major delays in productive speech. However, without exception they were capable of communicating their needs and wants by pointing and gesturing and their dislikes and displeasures by tantrumming and rebellious behaviors. Although Amy's parents were convinced that their daughter understood much of what was said, they were reluctant to provoke outbursts of screaming and rebellious behavior that accompanied efforts to encourage her use of words. Because Amy was capable of obtaining what she wanted or refusing what she did not want, her parents' reinforcement of gesturing and other nonverbal modes of communication surpressed her acquisition of productive speech. Thus, Amy's failure to pass conventional tests of early development that are heavily weighted with verbal items during the second and third years of life served to confirm the earlier inferences based on major motor delays and substantiated the diagnosis of mental retardation in a child whose basic cognitive skills were subsequently shown to be sufficient to support the use of speech. When the environmental contingencies were altered to reinforce the use of words and extinguish nonverbal communicative behaviors, Amy not only demonstrated the capacity to produce words, but also to use speech as a means of communicating her thoughts.

The initial phase of assisting this child to replace gesturing and tantrumming with speech was difficult and required the use of structured behavioral therapy. However, oncc having acquired the disposition to use words to communicate, the acquisition of more complex linguistic skills appeared to follow a normal developmental pattern that emerged spontaneously and did not require formal instruction. I do not believe that the language teaching sessions taught this child the complex rules of syntax and grammar. Rather, the initial behavioral intervention served as a temporary, effective, efficient means for extinguishing behaviors that interfered with speech, fostered the use of words, and facilitated the activation of her underlying linguistic potential. The formal language-teaching sessions sensitized the parents to the importance of encouraging and rewarding Amy's use of words during their daily interactions. As such, they served as an effective mode of therapy for the child and as a valuable teaching vehicle for the parents.

In addition to motor and speech delays, children with iatrogenic retardation exhibit a variety of behavior problems that not only interfere with their cognitive development, but also serve to perpetuate a condition of social isolation. One of the major developmental tasks that confronts the child during the second and third years of life is the transition from a self-centered, demanding infant to a socially responsive, integrated member of the family. It requires the imposition of constraints and demands on the part of the parents for learning a set of culturally determined, socially acceptable behaviors on the part of the child. Since Amy's parents perceived such behaviors as tantrumming and head banging, screaming and crying as evidence of their child's underlying mental incompetence, their acceptance and reinforcment of these responses served to sustain and increase the likelihood of their occurrence. Of equal importance, these learned behaviors interfered markedly with Amy's opportunity to engage in reciprocal play with her older sibling and other children. Much of the learning that takes place during this phase of development is accomplished within the informal social interchanges between the child and other individuals in the environment. Amy was denied access to this important source of social and cognitive stimulation. The negative atmosphere created by her non-compliant, rebellious behavior not only interfered with her becoming an integrated member of the family, but rendered her contact with peers almost nonexistent. Moreover, Amy's problem behavior resulted in her being kept in the home rather than accompanying her parents on visits to neighbors, nearby shopping centers, restaurants, and other environments that expose young children to new experiences and expands their understanding of the world in which they live.

It is this aspect of the child's behavior that perpetuates a state of social and cognitive isolation and sustains a barren psychological environment devoid of those environmental inputs that support normal development. Amy, in a sense, became a prisoner of her own behavior, guarded by well-intentioned parents who, unsure of their child's mental competence, shielded her from the demands and expectations necessary to activate her underlying potential and by doing so gain access to the world around her.

SUMMARY AND RECOMMENDATIONS

The tendency of physicians to seek out the abnormal and to anticipate an unfavorable outcome, however appropriate to the diagnosis and treatment of
relatively short-term physical disorders, is of dubious merit when used to influence the care and predict the future development of high-risk infants. Not
only does it create a nidus of continuing uncertainty in the parents' minds,
but it fails to recognize the plasticity of the infant's CNS and the discontinuity
that characterizes cognitive development during the early months of life.
However, the major contribution of the professional community to the
genesis of iatrogenic retardation is the continued reliance on insensitive, fallible measures used to infer the status of the infant's mental development. It is
this major deficit in the clinician's diagnostic armamentarium that must be
addressed because an increasingly large component of the care of high-risk infants is the diagnosis and treatment of developmental disorders.

Procedures described elsewhere in this volume are representative of those
presently used by behavioral scientists to monitor manifestations of mental
activity during the early months of life. Their potential value as clinical
measures is obvious. For example, it is possible to record accurately visual-
scanning behavior in newborns and observe age-related changes in the manner in which infants gather visual information over the first 6 to 8 weeks of
life. Moreover, the finding that infants are capable of manifesting stimulus-
specific response patterns as well as demonstrating the capacity for learned
behavior during the first few weeks of life suggests that physicians have
available the means for probing the functional integrity of processes concerned with these kinds of early cognitive behavior. Procedures that use
such elicited responses as visual fixation, scanning patterns, smiling,
vocalization, and changes in heart-rate acceleration and deceleration to infer
infants' capacity to process sensory information are presently being used in
a clinical setting. They appear to offer a more direct probe of infants' mental ability than that provided by neurologic examinations or traditional
psychological tests of infants' cognitive development. Thus, it is suggested-
that measures of cognitive behavior exist that may be sufficiently sensitive
to identify very early and subtle deviations from normal patterns of
development as well as to document the fact that the cognitive potential of
high-risk infants may not have been compromised by a biological insult sustained during the first few days of life.

The availability of such information would be of vital importance to the
clinician in evaluating the efficacy of those procedures presently used to sustain life within the intensive-care nursery. Of equal importance, it would

allow clinicians to define more accurately the status of childrens' mental development and, where appropriate, alleviate parental uncertainty and anxiety. I believe that the professional community involved with the care of premature and other high-risk infants and their families has much to gain by entering into a truly collaborative relationship with the behavioral sciences.

I have stated earlier that the manner in which children are perceived and treated by their parents creates a psychological environment that may lead to iatrogenic retardation. The origins of their misperceptions and inappropriate parenting practices have been discussed. However, it is important to reaffirm our position that the parents, although directly involved in the genesis of this disorder, are the primary therapeutic resource available to the children to overcome their developmental handicap. Unfortunately, the professional community has tended to underestimate the parents' capacity to assume this role. Yet, in the case that we presented, as in other instances of iatrogenic retardation, parents have demonstrated the capacity to modify their perception of their child's intellectual status, implement a program of behavioral intervention, and restructure the psychological environment that surrounds their child. We have shown that this can be accomplished after 20 months of continued uncertainty and inappropriate parenting practices. It seems reasonable to assume that if such information had been provided earlier, it could have produced comparable effects, and the probability for normal development might have been markedly increased.

Obviously, knowledge of the child's underlying cognitive potential is not in and of itself sufficient to eliminate the anxiety and stress imposed by a difficult, fussy infant or the normal concern that attends the rearing of children. However, the opportunity to eliminate doubt within the parents' minds regarding the mental status of their child should contribute to the preservation of the parents' sense of self-confidence and effectiveness that in the case we presented disappeared when the diagnosis of failure to thrive was accompanied by that of mental and motor retardation.

There is a traditional reluctance within the medical profession in general and the psychiatric community in particular to focus on the treatment of symptoms rather than seeking out the root cause of the disorder. Yet, the elimination of the signs and symptoms used to infer mental retardation not only served to convince Amy's parents that their child's underlying cognitive competence was intact but, moreover, eliminated those behaviors that were interfering with her intellectual development. The major qualitative change in the nature of the psychological relationship between Amy's parents and their child before and after the elimination of problem behaviors and developmental delays argues strongly for the use of symptomatic therapy in the management of iatrogenic retardation. It is doubtful that assisting these parents in working through feelings of guilt, inadequacy, anger, and hostility would have resulted in the cognitive and social gains shown by their child after 12 months of behavioral intervention that they themselves implemented, for the primary premise upon which these parents' feelings were based, namely, the presence of a developmentally retarded child, would have been preserved and reinforced.

We lack the information necessary to document the initial months of Amy's cognitive development. As such, it is not possible to establish whether those processes that support early cognitive behavior were temporarily impaired or emerged relatively intact in spite of the biological stress associated with her extreme prematurity. Neither is our clinical experience sufficient at this time to warrant a detailed discussion of the variables that may influence the reversability of this syndrome of learned incompetence. We have found that the behaviors of older children are more resistant to change and that the psychological, social, and economic resources of the family exert considerable influence on the parents' ability to assume the role of primary therapist in the treatment of their child. The failures that we have encountered to date have involved children older than 27 months from single parent or economically disadvantaged homes or whose parents showed evidence of major psychological disorders. Although we have demonstrated that iatrogenic retardation is a treatable and perhaps a preventable disorder, its successful resolution may require both early detection and the provision of varying degrees of external support to the family.

The primary purpose of this paper has been to identify a category of developmental retardation that may seriously compromise the lives of a significant number of infants considered to be at risk. There is evidence within the literature that the so-called medical model, however useful it has been in elucidating the etiology of physical disoders, is inadequate to accommodate the variables associated with social and cognitive development, particularly during early childhood (Eisenberg, 1977; Engel, 1977). If nothing else, the syndrome of iatrogenic retardation illustrates the potential fallacy of regarding subsequent manifestations of deviant development as the natural sequelae of specific perinatal events. Rather, it is the continuing dynamic interaction of the biological heritage that accompanies the child's entry into the world with the physical, social, and psychological environment that provides the conceptual framework needed to examine the phenomena associated with the process of development.

ACKNOWLEDGMENTS

As Codirector of the Center for Behavioral Pediatrics and Infant Development, Philip Zelazo shared equally in the initial recognition of the syndrome that we labeled *iatrogenic retardation* as well as in the derivation of the diagnostic and therapeutic procedures used in the management of this disorder. I thank "Amy's" parents for their permission to allow their daughter's case history to be presented and their willingness to share with parents and physicians the problems they encountered and the success they achieved in caring for their child. The sensitivity and skill of Noreen Carey, "Amy's" home visitor, is gratefully acknowledged. Finally, the capacity of Mary Anne Glennon to tolerate retyping "one more draft" made it possible to complete this chapter, almost on time, while the diligence of Maryann Collins and Kathleen Kurowski in preparing the subject index preserved the editors' psychological well-being.

REFERENCES

Chess, S., & Thomas, A. In *Individual differences in children.* J. C. Westman (Ed.), New York: Wiley, 1973.

Clark, A. M., & Clarke, A. D. B. *Early experience: Myth and evidence.* The Free Press, New York, 1976.

Crothers, B., & Paine, R. S. *The natural history of cerebral palsy.* Cambridge, MA: Harvard University Press, 1957.

deVries, M. W., & deVries, M. R. The cultural relativity of toilet training readiness: A perspective from East Africa. *Pediatrics,* 1977, **60**, 170–177.

Eisenberg, L. Psychiatry and society: A sociobiologic synthesis. *New England Journal of Medicine,* 1977, **296**, 903–910.

Engel, G. The need for a new medical model: A challenge for biomedicine, *Science, 1977,* **196**, 129–135.

Fentress, J. C. Development of grooming in mice with amputated fore limbs. *Science,* 1973, **179**, 704–705.

Fisch, R. O., Bilek, M. K., Miller, L. D., & Engle, R. R. Physical and mental status at 4 years of age of survivors of the respiratory distress syndrome. *Journal of Pediatrics,* 1975, **86**, 497–503.

Hobbs, N. *Issues in the classification of children,* Vol. II. Washington, D. C.: Jossey-Bass, 1975.

Kagan, J., Kearsley, R. B. & Zelazo, P. R. *Infancy: its place in human development.* Cambridge, MA: Harvard University Press, 1978.

Kagan, J. *Change and continuity in infancy.* New York: Wiley, 1971.

Kearsley, R. B., & Zelazo, P. R. *The emergence of functional play in infants: A cognitive landmark.* Paper presented at the annual meeting of the Ambulatory Pediatric Association, San Francisco, April 1977.

Kearsley, R. B., & Zelazo, P. R. *Intellectual assessment during infancy and early childhood.* Paper presented at the meeting of New England Pediatric Society, Boston, March 1975.

Kearsley, R. B., & Zelazo, P. R. *The identification of maladaptive parenting practices.* Unpublished manuscript, New England Medical Center Hospital, 1977.

Kearsley, R. B., & Zelazo, P. R. *The documentation of normal cognitive development in a physically malformed infant.* Unpublished manuscript, New England Medical Center Hospital, 1977.

Klaus, M., & Kennell, J. H. *Maternal infant bonding.* St. Louis: C. V. Mosby, 1976.

Koop, C. B., & Shaperman, J. Cognitive development in the absence of object manipulation during infancy. *Developmental Psychology,* 1973, **9**, 430.

Morrow, G. Iatrogenesis imperfecta. *Pediatrics,* 1975, **55**, 453–455.

Rosenthal, R., & Jacobson, L. *Pygmalion in the classroom: Teacher expectation and pupils' intellectual development,* New York: Holt, 1968.

Schmitt, F. O., Dev, P., & Smith, B. H. Electronic processing of information by brain cells. *Science,* 1976, **193**, 114–120.

Stott, L. H., & Ball, R. S. Infant and preschool mental tests: Review and evaluation.

Monographs of the Society for Research in Child Development, 1965, (30, No. 101).

Super, C. M. *Infant care and motor development in rural Kenya.* Paper presented at the meeting of the International Association for Cross-Cultural Psychology, Ibaden, Nigeria, 1973.

Taub, E., Perrella, P., & Barro, G. Behavioral development after forelimb deafferentiated on day of birth in monkeys with and without binding. *Science,* 1973, **181,** 959–960.

Thorpe, H. S., & Werner, E. E. Developmental screening of preschool children: A critical review of inventories used in health and education programs. *Pediatrics,* 1974, **53,** 362–370.

Warren, N. African infant precocity. *Psychological Bulletin,* 1972, **78,** 353–367.

Zelazo, P. R. *The year old infant: A point of major cognitive change.* Paper presented at the conference on "Dips" in Learning and Developmental Curves: Organization for Economic Cooperation and Development, St. Paul-de-Vence, France, March 1975.

Zelazo, P. R., Kearsley, R. B., & Ungerer, J. *A manual for the acquisition of speech,* Boston: Center for Behavioral Pediatrics and Infant Development, 1976.

Zelazo, P. R., Zelazo, N. A., & Kolb, S. Walking in the newborn. *Science,* 1972, **176,** 314–315.

7
Assessment in Mental Retardation: Toward Instructional Relevance[1]

James L. Hamilton
Bureau of Education for the Handicapped
U.S. Office of Education

The field of education in the United States is presently in the throes of a right-to-education movement. Important milestones in this long-awaited movement are embodied in two recent court decisions. In the first, a decision was rendered in a suit brought by the Pennsylvania Association for Retarded Children that made it mandatory that free public school education be provided for all school-age mentally retarded children (Creamer, 1971). The implications of this right-to-education consent agreement were expanded by the *Mills v. Board of Education of the District of Columbia* case, which provided that all handicapped children, not just mentally retarded children, have an equal right to education. The spirit of the *Mills* decision has been included in guidelines issued by many state legislatures and in the recently passed (1975) Education For All Handicapped Act (Public Law 94-142).

The impact of the right-to-education movement is widespread and pronounced. Probably the most affected groups, other than the parents and guardians of handicapped children and the children themselves, are the special educators and the various supporting service disciplines such as psychology and psychometry. The various requirements of the Education For All Handicapped Act (such as the provision of nondiscriminatory testing, placement of the child in the least restrictive educational setting, and the development of individualized educational plans) predict that the testing and measurement community will come under increasing pressure to develop and improve assessment instruments and procedures relevant to the

[1]This chapter was written by the author in his private capacity. No official support or endorsement by the U.S. Office of Education is intended or should be inferred.

education of handicapped children.

It is axiomatic to many special educators that typical psychoeducational evaluation has contributed little toward solving the educational problems of handicapped children. For example, in the area of mental retardation, the diagnosis of most cases is not difficult. Administration of an intelligence test to moderately, severely, or profoundly retarded children is generally superfluous and typically provides little educationally relevant information. By the time an intelligence test is given to a child thought to be mildly retarded, that child has usually demonstrated some degree of failure in school-related tasks. The test results merely confirm the more important criterion information already obtained in the classroom (Haywood, Filler, Shifman, & Chatelanat, 1975) and do not provide information that can be used by a teacher to plan a child's education (Filler, Robinson, Smith, Vincent-Smith, Bricker, & Bricker, 1975).

Although the detection of mental retardation is not meant to be over-simplified here, particularly with reference to children of preschool age (Gallagher & Bradley, 1972; Meier, 1973) and children who are culturally different (Mercer, 1973), it is nevertheless evident that the testing community must begin to proffer substantially more information to those charged with the responsibility of providing an appropriate educational program. In short, until assessment instruments and procedures are available that are beneficial in designing and improving curriculum and instruction for children classified as mentally retarded, the attitude expressed in the phrases "teach, don't test" and "develop potential, don't predict it" will go unaltered among many special education personnel.

My purpose in this chapter is to summarize some alternative approaches to the intellectual assessment of school-age mentally retarded children. As a preface to exploring these alternatives, the following section contains a brief review of the kinds of research and professional opinion that have suggested the limitations of using conventional intelligence tests with this population and that may have been instrumental in motivating a search for alternative approaches.

CONVENTIONAL MEASUREMENT MODEL

A useful conceptualization of standard intelligence tests (such as the Peabody Picture Vocabulary Test, the Stanford-Binet Intelligence Scale, and the various Wechsler tests, each of which is commonly used with mentally retarded persons) is to consider them as general achievement tests that indicate what the children have previously learned outside the test situation (Dyer, 1961; Jensen, 1963). The traditional approach to estimating children's intelligence, then, requires the measurement of their achievement relative to age norms; that is, children are compared with respect to their relative mastery of the products of prior learning (Haywood et al., 1975). Such an approach makes a number of assumptions that are rarely satisfied when testing mentally retarded children:

1. The children being compared have had an equal opportunity to learn similar skills and acquire similar information.
2. They are equally motivated to learn the information and skills.
3. They are equally motivated to exert themselves in a test situation and equally familiar with the demands of the test situation.
4. They are equally free of emotional disturbances and anxieties that might interfere with their performance.
5. They are equally free of biological dysfunctions and organic difficulties that might interfere with their test performance (Mercer, 1973).

Thus, the degree to which one or more of the above assumptions are violated may correspond directly with the measurement of factors other than the children's intelligence. For example, it can be hypothesized that violations of Assumptions 1 and 5 would yield an IQ reflecting the inadequacy of the children's past experiences as well as the extent to which ancillary handicapping conditions interfered with the assessment of their intelligence.

The penalizing nature of standardized tests used with mentally retarded children was implied in a study by Fair and Birch (1971). Using intellectually normal children matched on chronological age (CA), grade level, and IQ with intellectually normal physically handicapped children, the investigators found that the provision of a rest period between the two sections of the Advanced Stanford Achievement Test significantly increased the physically handicapped children's scores. Rest did not have a facilitating effect for the physically normal children. Although the study was conducted with intellectually normal children, the implications are particularly relevant for the moderately, severely, and profoundly retarded population, a population replete with multiple handicapping conditions.

O'Connor, Justice, and Payne (1970) investigated the statistical expectations of physical handicaps of institutionalized retarded persons (N = 17,893). Using the Tarjan, Dingman, and Miller (1960) model, they found that (a) the number of handicapping conditions was inversely related to CA and IQ, and (b) 50 to 100% of young, moderately, severely and profoundly retarded persons (CA less than 20 years) can be expected to have speech handicaps. The latter finding is particularly important when one considers that the Stanford Binet, which requires many verbal/language skills, has been rated the best single test for severely retarded persons (Johnson & Capobianco, 1957) and has been reported as the most widely used test within state institutions for mentally retarded persons (Silverstein, 1963).

The utility of standard tests is further questioned by their single administration format. Studies of discrimination learning in moderately and severely retarded children and mental age (MA) matched normal children have shown that the retarded subjects need several trials to attend to the relevant stimuli. Both the retarded and normal children demonstrate similar learning-acquisition curves, but the retarded children are slow to start learning (Zeaman & House, 1963).

A study reported by Barrett (1965) further suggests the need for repeated assessments. Investigating the acquisition of operant differentiation and discrimination among institutionalized retarded children (CA range 7 to 20 years; IQ range 33 to 81), she found that "a child's initial pattern and rate of change do not predict the course or final state of his performance [p. 876]."

A number of investigators have demonstrated that after practice many mildly retarded children perform at levels overlapping children of average ability on simple motor tasks (Clarke & Clarke, 1958) and paired-associate learning tasks (Jensen, 1963). Further, in a study of the evaluation of the vocational potential of mildly retarded young adults, Tobias (1960) concluded that "proper evaluation of the retarded seems to require a form of testing that permits observation of more than single-trial learning [p. 123]." He further concluded that performance after a period of practice and instruction was a better predictor of vocational and social adjustment than was an IQ score.

Several investigators have questioned the value of standard intelligence test scores as predictors of learning performance. In the previously mentioned study, Barrett (1965) found that neither CA, IQ, verbal facility, nor duration of institutionalization accurately predicted individual performance.

In a study of word learning in a group of 100 retarded persons (mean MA 8.4; mean CA 24.8), McCullock, Reswick, and Weissman (1955) found that the relationship between initial performance on the word-learning task and IQ was greater than the relationship between learning scores and IQ. They concluded that predictions of learning scores from intelligence test scores are especially precarious.

Despite the limitations of conventional tests as applied to mentally retarded persons, it is evident that some of these shortcomings rest with the test givers and test users (Dyer, 1973). However, it is also apparent that the test development community has been extremely reticent in designing assessment procedures that go beyond classification and selection purposes. Six alternative assessment approaches are presented that attempt to provide some further information regarding a person's intellectual abilities.

SOME ALTERNATIVE ASSESSMENT APPROACHES

Although several nontraditional assessment approaches have been developed (e.g., Haeussermann, 1958) or proposed (e.g., McClelland, 1973), the techniques reviewed in this chapter are confined to those that measure a person's response to instruction. Prior to presenting an overview of the more recent studies, it may be useful to point out some of the earlier thinking in this area. Haywood et al. (1975) have cited Rey (1934) as observing that psychometrists seem to be more interested in adaptive responses than the process of adaption itself. This focus on what persons have previously learned, as reflected in a global score on an intelligence test, becomes problematic unless one knows whether the persons have been exposed to developmentally facilitating situations. For example, a similar prognosis may be contraindicated when two persons have similar intelligence test scores but disparate experiential backgrounds.

Penrose (1934) suggested that the measurement of a person's response to instruction would be the ideal paradigm for the study of mental dificiency. Also in 1934, Vygotsky (1934/1962) indicated that:

> Most of the psychological investigations concerned with school learning measured the level of mental development of the child by making him solve certain standardized problems. The problems he was able to solve by himself were supposed to indicate the level of his mental development at the particular time. But in this way only the completed part of the child's development can be measured, which is far from the whole story [p. 117].

He further states that:

> Studying child thought apart from the influence of instruction . . . excludes a very important source of change and bars the researcher from posing the question of the interaction of development and instruction peculiar to each age level [p. 117].

More recently, Luria (1961) and Gordon (1965) have made similar suggestions to incorporate instruction within an assessment procedure so that one might ascertain a person's potential for learning. Following are summaries of six rather different approaches to applying this suggestion.

Budoff and Associates

Over the past decade, Budoff and his associates have investigated the use of a test-train-test procedure for the intellectual assessment of mentally retarded persons. Although there were several factors motivating a search for an alternative procedure, the arguments and findings of two investigators seem particularly salient to Budoff's approach.

Jastak (1949) argued that a radically different assessment procedure is warranted when a child comes from adverse social circumstances and/or is suffering from the long-term effects of a personality disturbance. Jastak further argued that low global IQ scores, in the presence of good achievement on some tests or test items, may indicate deficiencies in environmental experiences or the presence of personality defects that must be considered independent of the ability the person has demonstrated.

A second investigator lending support to Budoff's approach was Jensen (1963), who reported that when procedures that sought to clarify the response required on a paired-associate learning task (using geometric forms as stimuli) were introduced into the experimental procedure, some mildly retarded subjects performed at a level similar to that of children of average, and even gifted ability. Prior to these clarifying procedures, the mildly retarded children were uniformly poor learners. Further, Jensen (1964) reviewed the literature in the areas of early experience, perceptual development, environmental deprivation, and laboratory studies of verbal learning and argued that it is the verbal deficit to which much of the lower class disadvantage can be attributed.

The assumption of Budoff's approach to assessment of mentally retarded persons is that some mildly retarded children are more capable of learning and reasoning than the verbally biased intelligence score indicates. To test this assumption, a task was chosen that was not related to school work, yet required a large component of reasoning for its successful solution. Initially, the task chosen was the Kohs (1923) Block Design Test, which was modified for the learning potential assessment procedure.

In the initial study in the series (Budoff & Friedman, 1964), the subjects were 32 institutionalized adolescents with IQs ranging from 42 to 78. From this pool, pairs of subjects were matched on CA and Stanford Binet IQ within a low-ability group (IQs 42 to 57) and a high-ability group (IQs 63 to 78). One member of each pair was randomly assigned to the experimental condition of coaching; the other served as the control. The subjects were tested with the modified Kohs block designs on three occasions (initially, after 1 week, and after 1 month). Given that the learning potential assessment approach is based on a conceptualization of intelligence that stresses trainability (or the ability to profit from learning experiences), a coaching session was provided to the experimental subjects. This training session, during which nontest items were used, was administered on the day prior to the second testing session. Coaching consisted of three basic components; first, demonstrating to the subjects the separateness of the blocks making up the design; second, encouraging the subjects to check their work by pointing from match to sample (blocks to picture of blocks) in a block-by-block manner; and third, emphasizing the process of making a stripe with two-colored blocks. The results of this study supported the contention that the experimental subjects, as a group, significantly improved their performance after a systematic learning experience (coaching). More importantly, however, an examination of individual scores revealed that several subjects, after coaching, solved designs comparable in difficulty with Wechsler Adult Intelligence Scale designs at the normal intellectual level. Others, however, did not manifest this improvement.

Similar results were obtained in a later study by Budoff (1967). After pooling the subjects in both investigations, differences were examined between the subjects who significantly improved after coaching (gainers) and those who did not (nongainers). Several subjects who solved difficult designs on initial testing (high scorers) were included in the gainer category. Analyses revealed that (a) there was a greater relationship between initial Kohs scores and performance-type IQs (e.g., Raven's Progressive Matrices) than between initial Kohs scores and verbal-based scores (e.g., Stanford Binet), (b) CA was unrelated to performance on the Kohs measures, (c) the relationship between the Kohs measures and length of institutionalization was negligible, and (d) gainers performed significantly better than nongainers on two related problem-solving tasks (a double alternation task and a paired-associate learning task).

Much of the more recent work using the learning potential assessment procedure has focused on exploring other nonverbal measures that could be cast in a test-train-test format. These have included Raven's Progressive Matrices (Budoff & Hutton, 1971) and an instrument developed by Babad (Corman & Budoff, 1973) called the Series Learning Potential Test. The latter instrument is a nonverbal reasoning task that requires the child to determine the missing element in a series of stimuli in one of four concept classes (semantic content, size, color, orientation) as in the following example: large, small, small; large, small, small; _____, small, small. As with the Kohs measure, training procedures have been developed for the Raven's Progressive Matrices and the Series Learning Potential Test. Several studies have been conducted using these instruments. Budoff (1973) suggested that the Raven Learning Potential Test is potentially the best instrument for measuring learning potential because it is highly reliable, interesting to children, a good test of general reasoning, and can be successfully administered to groups.

A second focus of Budoff's recent work has been to determine further the correlates of children's performance on the learning potential assessment procedure. As an example, Budoff, Meskin, and Harrison (1971) examined the predictive validity of learning potential status (gainer, nongainer, high scorer) against the criterion of performance on a classroom laboratory science program in electricity. The hypothesis was that high-able subjects by the learning potential criterion (high scores and gainers) would learn more about electricity than the low-able learning potential subjects (nongainers) when the curriculum and evaluation instruments made minimal verbal demands. The results of the study supported the hypothesis and provided further evidence that response to training on the learning potential assessment procedure is not task-specific but relates to several areas of children's functioning that are not tapped by conventional intelligence tests.

Although most of Budoff's work has concentrated on mildly mentally retarded children, two studies were recently completed that applied the learning potential assessment paradigm to moderately, severely, and profoundly retarded persons. In the first of these studies (Hamilton, 1972; Hamilton & Budoff, 1974), a downward extension of the Kohs (1923) block designs was constructed so that more severely retarded persons could successfully construct the easiest items. To determine whether the learning potential assessment procedure was measuring important abilities, the coached subjects were administered a related test, a modified version of the Knox Cube Test (Arthur, 1947), and the subjects' teachers were given a questionnaire requesting that they classify each subject as a gainer or nongainer with reference to their experience with the subject in a teaching situation. As predicted, the subjects demonstrated differential responses to training that were not predicted by IQ. Further, response to training (gainer, nongainer) correlated significantly with teacher ratings and performance on a modified version of the Knox Cube Test. The researchers concluded that the learning potential assessment procedure measured important abilities among these adolescents that the Peabody Picture Vocabulary Test failed to measure. Because performance on the PPVT has been found to be highly correlated with performance on the Stanford Binet among institutionalized mentally retarded persons, (Budoff & Purseglove, 1963; Koh & Madow, 1967), Hamilton and Budoff (1974) hypothesized that the Stanford Binet would also fail to predict learning scores on the learning potential assessment procedure.

The purposes of the second study (Budoff & Hamilton, 1976) were to (a) obtain further validity estimates for the learning potential assessment procedure with this population and (b) compare the performance of these persons on two learning potential formats: when training is presented during a separate session (test-train-test) vs. when training is embedded within the testing procedure (train-within-test). The reason for exploring the train-within-test format was that during the first study (Hamilton & Budoff, 1974), the experimenters observed that some subjects could correctly solve nontrained instances of Kohs problems during or immediately following training but failed to apply the strategy to similar items durii.g the posttest session on the following day. They apparently understood the problem during training because they solved it successfully with a minimal lapse in time, but they had difficulty retaining and/or spontaneously invoking it after a 1-day interval. Because the intent of the learning potential assessment is to ascertain persons' ability to learn and apply problem-solving principles under optimal conditions, the train-within-test procedure was developed and employed in two different measures: Raven's Coloured Progressive Matrices and the Leiter International Performance Scale (Arthur, 1952). The general procedure in the train-within-test format consisted of providing a correction and training procedure immediately when a person made an error on a test item. After the training, the subject was given a maximum of three trials to complete the item correctly. If the subject missed the item on any of the following trials, the correction and training procedure was repeated. The results of the study provided further support for the conclusion that a learning potential approach to the assessment of abilities of moderately, severely, and profoundly retarded persons provides a fairer estimate of their capabilities than traditional intelligence measures. The high intercorrelations among the Kohs learning potential scores (test-train-test format) and the weighted Leiter and Raven's scores (train-within-test format) suggested that both formats were equally effective when evaluated against the various predictive criteria.

The investigations conducted by Budoff and his associates have provided substantial evidence supporting the use of a learning potential assessment procedure with persons classified as mentally retarded. At a minimum, the results of administering the learning potential assessment provide significantly more information and frequently promote a different estimation of the person's capabilities than that supplied by traditional intelligence tests. (See Budoff [1974] for a synopsis of the various studies.)

Feuerstein and Associates

Conceptually similar to Budoff's measurement approach is the work reported by Feuerstein (1968, 1970). Characterized as a dynamic rather than a static approach to measurement, this approach was designed to assess the hidden potential of adolescents who have been described as mildly mentally retarded, culturally deprived, or socially disadvantaged.

In Feuerstein's (1968) words:

> The [traditional] psychometric approach limits itself to the establishment of an inventory of existent information, knowledge and various perceptual and cognitive skills as the sole criterion of the individual's level of intelligence. The major assumption is that intelligence reflects itself only in test results achieved spontaneously by the individual, disregarding his experiential, educational and motivational background [pp. 562–563].

He goes on to assert that

> This static goal may be justified only if one considers the intellectual characteristics of the individual as constant and unmodifiable. That this is a major assumption of psychometric tests is reflected in the enormous investment made by these methods to reach a high rate of predictability. This emphasis on predictability may be legitimate in the psychotechnical field since it is isomorphic with the economic goals involved in selection. However, it is inappropriate and leads to unjustified pessimism when applied to educational or clinical aims, where the object of search should be the *modifiability* of the individual and the optimal conditions for such a change [p. 563].

Although he recognizes the variety of etiological factors in cognitive deficiency, Feuerstein (1970) contended that the most active etiological factor is inadequate, and insufficient "mediated learning experience," that is defined as "the interactional process between the developing human organism and an experienced adult who, by interposing himself between the child and external sources of stimulation, mediates the world to him by framing, selecting, focusing and feeding back environmental experience in such a way as to create appropriate learning sets [pp. 358-359]." Thus, Feuerstein views the cause of retarded intellectual development among mildly retarded persons as inadequate or insufficient *instruction,* given a definition of instruction that is not limited to formal education but, rather, includes instruction that may occur in the home and other settings.

The deficient learning sets are viewed as affecting three phases of cognitive operations: an input phase, an elaborational or processing phase, and the output of the processed data. Feuerstein and his colleagues (cited in Haywood et al., 1975) have listed 28 different skills that may be lacking or deficient in children with a deficit in mediated-learning experience.

To facilitate the development of appropriate learning sets, Feuerstein first attempts to assess the specific deficiencies to be modified through the use of the Learning Potential Assessment Device (LPAD) (Feuerstein, 1968). The structure of the LPAD is based on three dimensions: degree of novelty and complexity of the task; the symbolic modality of presentation (e.g., figural, pictorial-concrete, verbal, numerical); and the variety of cognitive operations the task represents (e.g., classification, analogy).

The structure of the LPAD consists of a series of tasks, each of which has several variations of the initial task. The child is taught the underlying cognitive principle on the first instance and is then presented with variations of the initial task. From this procedure, the examiner may derive a number of measures: (a) the capacity of the child to grasp a given principle, (b) the amount and quality of investment required to teach the principle, (c) the extent to which the principle can be used by the child in progressively new situations, and (d) the preference modalities (e.g., pictorial-concrete, numerical) of the child. This structure is designed to enable the examiner not only to measure the degree of modifiability of the child but also identify points of resistance in one or another area of functioning.

The primary changes in the examination situation include: using the child's failure as a starting point for a focused learning process aimed at uncovering the learning potential of the child; reducing the emotional distance between examiner and child by helping the child when errors occur; providing feedback to the child and attempting to induce inferential thinking and insight processes; and attempting to isolate the relevant from the irrelevant factors (e.g., impulsive behavior) in the test situation.

The interpretation of the LPAD results is different from the usual methods. Although with traditional assessment interpretation, a single, unusually intelligent response from a child would tend to be discounted,

Feuerstein feels that the isolated successful response points to the true potential of a child and may predict modifiability more efficiently than the usual test responses. Thus, the examiner not only takes notice of unusual responses, but actively attempts to elicit them by arranging the test situation in the most conducive way. It is through such arrangement that a useful estimate of an individual's ability to profit from the most optimal situation available can be obtained.

The LPAD consists of four types of tasks used to obtain the information needed for planning an intervention program. The tasks are generally nonverbal in nature. (See Haywood et al. [1975] for further information.)

The first instrument is Organization of Dots, developed by Rey and Dupont (cited by Haywood et al. [1975]), and modified for the LPAD. The child's task is to recognize geometric structures suggested by the organization of dots and to construct these structures by drawing straight lines connecting the dots.

This task requires that both maturational and cognitive developmental variables interact to create the necessary schemes. The skills measured by the task include: the ability to conserve the structure of the geometric forms when the orientation in space is modified; the ability to analyze and segregate the relevant from the irrelevant dimensions; and the ability to delay responding and plan ahead prior to attempting a solution, because there is only one correct solution. The task is increased in difficulty by an increased number of geometric structures to be discovered and a decrease in the distance between the dots.

The second instrument, the Plateaux Test, was developed by Rey (cited by Haywood et al. [1975]) and consists of four plates, each with nine buttons arranged in three parallel rows of three buttons each. This task requires that the child learn and retain which one (and later, two) of the buttons on each plate is not removable. The child attempts to remember the correct position(s) of this fixed button(s) for each plate and, without touching the plates, points them out correctly to the examiner. The first phase of this task measures simple concept formation, such as right–left and top–bottom as well as the child's ability to approach systematically a multifaceted problem. The task is increased in difficulty by (a) moving from a three-dimensional problem to two-dimensional drawings, (b) increasing to two the number of fixed buttons on each plate, and (c) rotating the plates through 90 (and later, 180) degrees in the presence of the child.

The third instrument, the LPAD Matrices Test, consists of several problems from the Raven's Progressive Matrices plus several variations. The child's performance indicates ability to transfer operations across various stimulus properties of the problem. Training focuses on three different operations: (a) recognizing and organizing the relevant features of the problem, (b) the reasoning requirements of the problem (e.g., analogy, permutation), and (c) inhibiting impulsive responses.

The final instrument is the Representational Stencil Design Test developed by Arthur (1930). This test consists of 20 stencils, each of which has a unique design characteristic. The child's task is to view a model design, which has been constructed by superimposing two or more stencils, and indicate the stencils and order of position required to produce the model design. Although originally designed as a manipulative, trial-and-error task, the procedure has been modified so that the child must indicate verbally the solution to the problem. The abilities measured by the task include (a) discriminating the model design characteristics and the design characteristics found among the stencils and (b) creating a mental representation of the various stencils and imagining the design that would result from superimposing the various individual stencils.

Although the LPAD procedure includes a certain amount of training when the child errs, the training is not designed to induce lasting modification. Rather, the administration of the LPAD is designed to indicate the type and amount of training or mediated learning that may be necessary. A program of intervention has been developed (Feuerstein & Hamburger, cited by Haywood et al. [1975]) that consists of approximately 200 hours of instruction and exercises that can be administered over 1 school year. The program focuses on the operations and information-processing strategies identified as deficient by the LPAD (Feuerstein, 1970).

Haywood and Associates

Haywood and his associates have studied the ability of mildly retarded persons to form verbal abstractions. The basic intellectual problem in forming verbal abstractions is to group and classify isolated events into a common category and assign an abstract label. For example, *orange, apple,* and *plum* can be grouped into a common category and assigned the abstract label *fruit.*

Rather than provide extensive verbal-abstraction instruction to mildly retarded persons, Haywood's procedure is to provide stimulus enrichment (additional exemplars) and note the effect on the person's ability to form abstractions. This rather simple adjustment is based on the premise that a person's apparent deficiency may be the result of a secondary deficiency in information-input capacity, rather than a deficiency in the ability to form abstractions (Haywood et al., 1975).

Gordon and Haywood (1969) administered similarities tests under two conditions to organically retarded and cultural-familially retarded persons. In one procedure, items in the similarities test were given in the same manner as they are given in the Wechsler scales: "In what way are an orange and a banana alike?" In the second (enriched) procedure, each item had five exemplars: "In what way are an orange, a banana, a peach, a plum, and a pear alike?'' These procedures were used subsequently with a group of nonretarded children matched with the retarded children on mental age. On the similarities test using two exemplars with each item, the retarded children in both groups scored lower than the nonretarded children. Under the five-exemplars procedure, however, the verbal-abstracting scores of the cultural-familially retarded group were (a) significantly higher than were their scores on the two-exemplars test, (b) significantly higher than the five-exemplars scores of the organically retarded group, and (c) not significantly different from the five-exemplars scores of the nonretarded group. Thus, giving verbal enrichment in the form of an increased number of exemplars of each concept improved the abstracting performance of cultural-familially retarded persons but not that of organically retarded persons nor that of nonretarded persons. The investigators concluded that cultural-familially retarded persons are not necessarily deficient in the ability to form verbal abstractions but do have an information-input deficit that can be overcome by enriching the amount of information available to the person. Several other studies by Haywood's associates have corroborated these findings (Call, 1973; Foster, 1970; Tymchuk, 1973).

Haywood and Switzky (1974) investigated the extent to which providing enriched verbal input to intellectually normal children and mildly retarded children would generalize to subsequent nonenriched items. They found that enriched verbal input raised the performance of the retarded children on subsequent nonenriched items (a learning-set like phenomenon), but enrichment had no discernible effect on the performance of the intellectually average children.

The basic phenomenon observed in this series of studies has led to the conclusion that mildly retarded persons, particularly those whose retardation is associated with cultural deprivation, have significantly more ability to form verbal abstractions than is characteristically revealed on a standard intelligence test (Haywood et al., 1975). By observing the person's response to information enrichment, one can clarify the nature of the deficiency and plan intervention accordingly.

Schucman

Schucman (1960) described the development of an educability index for moderately, severely, and profoundly mentally retarded persons. Her basic hypothesis was that "the child's educability can be inferred from his responses to learning situations which require abilities on which education depends, namely, to learn from instruction, to transfer the training, and to retain the learning [p. 1]."

The subjects were 114 noninstitutionalized mentally retarded children (CA range 5 to 12 years) with IQs ranging from 8 to 55. After several pilot studies, a battery of five tests was constructed: imitative ability and memory, size discrimination, brightness discrimination, shape discrimination, and another test of brightness discrimination. The children were tested individually. After the initial tests, each subject was trained to the correct responses and retested to evaluate the gains following training. Different test forms were used to evaluate transfer, and retention was measured by retesting at various later dates. The test battery was administered on nine occasions--the first three yielding pretraining, posttraining, and transfer scores, respectively. The fourth and fifth tests measured retention under different conditions and at different times; and the last four administrations, given after an interval of 7 weeks, were repetitions of the first four.

Schucman (1960) found that the group as a whole learned, transferred, and retained learning to a significant extent on all tests. Intelligence (IQ) positively correlated with all test scores but correlated most highly with pretraining performance. Schucman concluded that learning performance was significantly more stable and more consistent than pretraining performance. Transfer and retention performance were the most sensitive measures of differences in ability.

In a later report, Schucman (1968) presented similar results based on performance of 300 moderately and severely retarded children, with a mean age of 95.16 months (standard deviation $[SD]$ = 23.48) and a mean IQ of 36.18 (SD = 12.01). Schucman concluded that initial test performance is generally misleading as a predictor of later performance and "that tests which are administered only once may fail to identify abilities fundamental to the education of the [mentally retarded] child [p. 572]."

Beery

Although he writes primarily about children with learning disabilities, Beery's (1968, 1972) approach to assessment appears to be pertinent to the assessment of mentally retarded persons as well. Termed *remedialdiagnosis,* Berry's procedure for determining an optimal remedial (educational) program is to measure the child's actual response to remediation. Although this procedure may appear to be similar to other approaches, there is an important difference in orientation. Rather than an observation of a child's response to one or even two instructional approaches, the remedial-diagnostic approach includes measuring the child's response to several likely remedial approaches. The purpose of remedialdiagnosis is to determine the instructional strategy that results in the most efficient learning by the child.

With reading, for example, the remedialdiagnostician might administer the Learning Methods Test (Mills, 1955). This test was designed to aid the remedial-reading teacher in determining the child's ability to learn new words under four different teaching procedures: visual, phonic or auditory, kinesthetic or tracing, and a combination of all three. The procedure makes use of word cards that the examiner administers as a pretest to identify a pool of words not known to the child. From this pool, 40 words are selected at random and arranged into four sets of 10. Using any one of the four teaching methods, the examiner spends exactly 15 mins teaching the first set of 10 unknown words. At the termination of the teaching period, the examiner administers an immediate recall test followed a day or so later by a word-retention test. On subsequent days, the other sets of 10 words are taught and tested in a similar manner, except that the other teaching methods are employed in turn. After the four methods have been used, and the child's response to each has been recorded, the scores obtained after each teaching session are compared to determine the relative efficiency of each instructional method for each child.

The remedialdiagnostic approach to assessment is not designed to measure a person's intellectual abilities. Rather, the approach focuses on the assessment of instructional methods as indexed by the person's response to those methods. Although the general premise underlying remedialdiagnosis is appealing and has been suggested by others (Shepherd, 1970; Tenorio & Raimist, 1971) as a valid departure from conventional tests, the approach requires further empirical evidence to support its use.

Behavior Analysis

Although not generally characterized as an assessment approach per se, behavior-analytic methods are directly applicable to assessing the abilities of mentally retarded persons and have been suggested as an alternative to intelligence tests (Bricker & Bricker, 1973). If one accepts the proposition that criterion information (current observable behavior) is preferable to predictor information (presumed correlates of future behavior), then behavior analysis represents one of the most extreme attempts to secure the criterion information.

In a recent review, Barrett (1977) defined behavior analysis as "a methodology that identifies and manipulates environmental conditions that are actively affecting a person's behavior [p. 141]." Because the variables of this analysis are behavioral and environmental events, behavior analysis may be considered to be an abbreviated form of behavior–environment analysis.

Descriptions of this procedure and the basic methodology are presented by MacMillan (1973), Reese (1966), and Sulzer and Mayer (1972). Barrett (1977) offered the following:

> The first business of behavior analysis is to determine which observable aspects of the environment a person *is* interacting with. Behavior analysis begins with an operational description of what the person is doing or is supposed to do, the conditions that should or may serve as initiating signals for the behavior, the observable changes in

the environment following the behavior and how often and when these environmental reactions occur. It then proceeds to determine the functionality of each physical component by systematically changing one at a time and observing the effect of every change on the measured frequency of the selected behavior ... Identification of a defective component for a given person in a given environment constitutes behavioral "diagnosis." A defective component is one that is not currently functional in relation to the desired behavior, or one that is supporting an undesirable behavior. Manipulation of various parameters of a defective environmental component until its measured effect demonstrates the desired function for the desired behavior is the process of behavior-analytic habilitation. The *environment* is modified until the appropriate behavior-generative and behavior-supportive effects are shown in measured and durable behavior change [p. 145].

The primary task of behavior analysts is to identify those environmental events that exert, or could exert, control of the person's behavior. The identification *and* manipulation of specific environmental events that affect a person's behavior suggests the logical and practical integration of assessment and treatment using behavior-analytic methods (Kiernan, 1973).

Behavior analysts argue that "intelligence" is essentially descriptive rather than causal and that the administration of an intelligence test merely provides an opportunity to observe a highly restricted sample of behavior, which is finally summarized as a numerical score (Filler et al., 1975). This numerical score is then translated into a noun (intelligence) rather than an adjective (intelligent behavior from a restricted sample of behavior), which more accurately describes the outcomes of the intelligence test situation (Skinner, 1953).

To behavior analysts, individual variations in behavioral competencies across people result directly from diversity in organismic and environmental factors rather than from deficiencies in mediating processes. Mental retardation is denoted by the detection of limited repertoires of behavior that result from atypical variations in a number of historical factors conceived as independent variables and assumed to underlie all development (Filler et al., 1975). As Bijou (1963) has noted, "a retarded individual is one who has a limited repertory of behavior evolving from interactions of the individual with his environmental contacts which constitute his history [p. 101]." Congruent with this conceptualization of mental retardation, Lindsley (1964) has stated: "Children are not retarded. Only their *behavior* in average environments is sometimes retarded. In fact, if is modern science's ability to design suitable environments for these children that is retarded [p. 62]." Moreover, Barrett (1977) indicated that "failures in applying behavior-analytic methods are ... attributable not to hypothetical characteristics such as 'intelligence,' 'defective ego strength' or 'brain damage,' but to inadequate design of a habilitating environment [pp. 145-146]."

The behavior-analytic methodology does not ignore biological factors nor does it deny the value of biological research. Biological factors are seen as "setting" conditions that change the probability of a large number of events (Bijou & Baer, 1961). What is critical, however, is that an analysis of retarded behavior does not have to await a knowledge of biological functioning. Through behavior analysis, the functional relationships between behavior and environmental variables may be revealed and changes in behavior brought about in many instances despite a biological condition (Kiernan, 1973).

Two points should be noted regarding the assessment component of the behavior-analytic approach. First, behavior analysis does not prescribe behavioral goals nor does it suggest when particular behaviors should be developed or altered. The application of behavior-analytic procedures is usually made within the context of existing curricula, child development theory (see Filler et al., 1975), or after the identification of a task, skill, or outcome considered to be important for the person's general adaptation (Davies, 1973). Second, although behavior analysts tend to view behavioral events, environmental events, and their interaction as a system, each of these components can be viewed separately for the purpose of assessment. Behavior analysis requires that precisely defined behaviors be continuously recorded during frequent intervals in a reliable manner (Birnbrauer, Burchard, & Burchard, 1970). Thus, it permits an educator to assess objectively the person's behavior and experiment scientifically with different teaching methods (Hall, 1971; Hall, Hawkins, & Axelrod, 1975). Rather than assessing static levels of performance and inferring behavioral ceilings from one-shot tests, behavior analysts continuously monitor the effects of environmental arrangements that may yield increasingly efficient learning. By measuring the effect of various environmental arrangements on an individual's behavior, behavior analysts can assess a variety of instructional conditions and then select the conditions that maximize the individual's learning opportunities. Although differing in methodology, this procedure appears to be conceptually similar to Beery's remedialdiagnosis and would appear to be particularly warranted for use with mentally retarded persons (see Baer, Wolf, & Risley [1968], Barrett [1977], Bricker [1970], Bricker & Bricker [1973], Gardner [1971], Skinner [1953]).

TOWARD IMPROVING INSTRUCTION

The common theme of these alternative approaches involves measuring the person's response to instruction, with instruction defined as purposefully manipulating the environment in such a way as to evoke, or attempt to evoke, higher functioning from the individual. The approaches differ, however, on a number of dimensions, including the extent to which curriculum content is prescribed from the assessment, the degree to which the assessment approach parallels school-related tasks, the relative emphasis on cognition vs. observable behaviors, the extent to which instructional strategy is inferred or prescribed from the assessment, the emphasis placed on evaluating the child vs. evaluating the environment or instruction, and the relative emphasis placed on revising the estimation of a person's intellectual capabilities. Nevertheless, insofar as it provides additional, more accurate, or more relevant information than that obtained from the traditional testing approach, each of the alternative approaches described holds some promise for improving educational programming for mentally retarded persons.

For educators, who must decide what to teach (content) and how and when to teach that content, each of the alternative assessment approaches provides some additional information on which to make decisions. It is evident, however, that none of the approaches prescribes the timing of instruction (when to teach), and only one approach (Feuerstein's) prescribes some curriculum content (what to teach). It is also apparent that measuring a person's response to instruction, regardless of the number of instructional methods used, is in part, an evaluation of the adequacy of the instructional method(s) chosen. Thus, those alternative assessment approaches that evaluate the effects of several different instructional strategies appear to have much potential for improving instruction for a given child. Indeed, the identification and implementation of teaching methods that yield the most efficient learning for a particular child correspond to most educators' concept of individualized instruction. Improving instruction for a child by testing empirically alternative teaching methods assumes that among available teaching methods there is one or more that will result in optimal learning for a specific child. Congruent with Beery's approach and the behavior-analytic approach, the responsibility for learner performance rests with the instructional method, and the assessment is focused on the relative effectiveness of given instructional procedures in exerting a positive effect on learner behavior.

Such an approach assumes that once teachers have discovered an instructional procedure that "works," they may proceed to evaluate other strategies that may provide for even greater learning efficiency. Shepherd (1970) has suggested the establishment of a "diagnostic classroom" within a school to serve this type of assessment function. The classroom teacher would inform the diagnostic teacher that a particular curriculum objective has been identified for a given child and request that the diagnostic teacher determine an appropriate teaching method. The diagnostic teacher would then expend the time and effort with the child necessary to generate an efficient instructional procedure that could be implemented by the classroom teacher. Implementation of this model assumes that the diagnostic teacher has both a thorough knowledge of the child's class and classroom as well as information regarding the classroom teacher's capabilities and the constraints under which this teacher may be working. Implementing the model also assumes that there are few or no teacher/method interactions that may serve to attenuate the effectiveness of the method identified.

Those alternative assessment approaches that do not employ multiple instructional methods also provide information that can lead to improved instruction. Haywood's approach is diagnostic in nature and, to a certain degree, prescribes a general strategy for overcoming informational deficits of particular children. Budoff's learning potential assessment also prescribes a general instructional strategy (e.g., methods making minimal verbal demands) that can be used successfully with specific children. Both approaches provide information beyond that yielded by conventional tests and both procedures may alter the estimate of a child's abilities, which may then lead to more appropriate expectations and educational placement.

With the possible exception of the behavior-analytic approach, however, none of the alternative assessment procedures described in this chapter is well known or widely applied in educational settings. The reasons for these phenomena may relate to a number of factors: (a) each approach is clinical in nature and requires an additional expenditure of time and resources; (b) the approaches may not be seen as providing significant information beyond that supplied by the usual methods; (c) the approaches may not be viewed as sufficiently developed or sufficiently transportable; (d) other methods of improving instruction, such as aptitude-by-treatment interaction research (see Reynolds & Balow, 1972; Ysseldyke, 1973), and careful sequencing of curriculum content (see Resnick, Wang, & Kaplan, 1973), may be viewed as holding more promise; and (e) the educational community may simply be unaware of the alternative techniques.

Nevertheless, it is the contention of the author that assessment procedures that measure the person's response to instruction hold great promise for improving instruction for mentally retarded persons. Hunt, Frost, and Lunneborg (1973) have suggested that "[we need] measuring instruments which are diagnostic, in the sense that they tell us how the institution should adjust to the person, instead of simply telling us which people are already adjusted to the institution [p. 120]." The assessment techniques reviewed in this chapter suggest that we may have taken an important step in that direction.

REFERENCES

Arthur, G. A. *A point scale of performance tests. Vol. 1. Clinical manual.* New York: Commonwealth Fund, 1930.

Arthur, G. A. *A point scale of performance tests.* New York: Psychological Corp. 1947.

Arthur, G. A. *The Arthur adaptation of the Leiter International Performance Scale.* Washington: Psychological Service Center Press, 1952.

Baer, D. M., Wolf, M. M., & Risley, T. R. Some current dimensions of applied behavior analysis. *Journal of Applied Behavior Analysis,* 1968, **1,** 91–97.

Barrett, B. H. Acquisition of operant differentiation and discrimination in institutionalized retarded children. *American Journal of Orthopsychiatry,* 1965, **35,** 862–885.

Barrett, B. H. Behavior analysis. In J. Wortis (Ed.), *Mental retardation and developmental disabilities* (Vol. IX). New York: Bruner/Mazel, 1977.

Beery, K. E. *Remedialdiagnosis.* Sioux Falls, S. D.: Adapt Press, 1968.

Beery, K. E. *Teaching triads.* Sioux Falls, S. D.: Adapt Press, 1972.

Bijou, S. W. Theory and research in mental (developmental) retardation. *Psychological Record,* 1963, **13**, 95–110.

Bijou, S. W., & Baer, D. M. *Child development.* New York: MacMillan, 1961.

Birnbrauer, J. S., Burchard, J. D., & Burchard, S. N. Wanted: Behavior analysts. In R. H. Bradfield (Ed.), *Behavior modification: The human effort.* San Rafael, Calif.: Dimensions Publ. Co., 1970.

Bricker, W. A. Identifying and modifying behavioral deficits. *American Journal of Mental Deficiency,* 1970, **75**, 16–21.

Bricker, W. A., & Bricker, D. Behavior modification programmes. In P. J. Mittler (Ed.), *Assessment for learning in the mentally handicapped.* London: Churchill Livingstone, 1973.

Budoff, M. Learning potential among institutionalized young adult retardates. *American Journal of Mental Deficiency,* 1967, **72**, 404–411.

Budoff, M. *Learning potential and educability among the educable mentally retarded* (Progress report, Grant No. OEG-0-8-080506-4597 from the Bureau of Education for the Handicapped, U. S. Office of Education, DHEW). Washington, D. C., 1973.

Budoff, M. *Learning potential and educability among the educable mentally retarded* (Final report, Grant No. OEG-0-8-080506-4597 from the Bureau of Education for the Handicapped, U. S. Office of Education, DHEW). Washington, D. C., 1974.

Budoff, M., & Friedman, M. Learning potential as an assessment approach to the adolescent mentally retarded. *Journal of Consulting Psychology,* 1964, **28**, 434–439.

Budoff, M., & Hamilton, J. L. Optimizing test performance of moderately and severely mentally retarded adolescents and adults. *American Journal of Mental Deficiency,* 1976, **81**, 49–57.

Budoff, M., & Hutton, L. The development of a learning potential measure based on Raven's Progressive Matrices. *Studies in learning potential.* Cambridge, Mass: Research Institute for Educational Problems, 1971.

Budoff, M., Meskin, J., & Harrison, R. H. An educational test of the learning potential hypothesis. *American Journal of Mental Deficiency,* 1971, **76**, 159–169.

Budoff, M., & Purseglove, E. M. Peabody Picture Vocabulary Test: Performance of institutionalized mentally retarded adolescents. *American Journal of Mental Deficiency,* 1963, **67**, 756–760.

Call, R. *Verbal abstracting performance of low SES children: An exploration of Jensen's theory of mental retardation.* Unpublished doctoral dissertation, George Peabody College for Teachers, 1973.

Clarke, A. M., & Clarke, A. D. B. (Eds.). *Mental deficiency: The changing outlook.* London: Methuen, 1958.

Corman, L., & Budoff, M. The Series Test as a measure of learning potential. *Studies in learning potential.* Cambridge, Mass: Research Institute for Educational Problems, 1973.

Creamer, Attorney General J. S. *Pennsylvania Association for Retarded Children v. Commonwealth of Pennsylvania:* U. S. District Court for the Eastern District of Pennsylvania order, injunction and consent agreement on the right of any mentally retarded child to access to a free public program of education and training, Civil Action No. 71-42. Philadelphia, U. S. District Court, 1971.

Davies, I. K. *Competency based learning: Technology, management, and design.* New York: McGraw-Hill, 1973.

Dyer, H. S. Is testing a menace to education? In *New York state education,* XLIX, October 1961, 16–19.

Dyer, H. S. Recycling the problems in testing. In *Assessment in a pluralistic society: Proceedings of the 1972 invitational conference on testing problems*. Princeton: Educational Testing Service, 1973.

Fair, D. T., & Birch, J. W. Effect of rest on test scores of physically handicapped and nonhandicapped children. *Exceptional Children*, 1971, **38**, 335–336.

Feuerstein, R. The learning potential assessment device. In B. W. Richards (Ed.), *Proceedings of the first congress of the International Association for the Scientific Study of Mental Deficiency*. Reigate, Surrey, England: Michael Jackson, 1968.

Feuerstein, R. A dynamic approach to the causation, prevention, and alleviation of retarded performance. In H. C. Haywood (Ed.), *Social-cultural aspects of mental retardation*. New York: Appleton-Century-Crofts, 1970.

Filler, J. W., Robinson, C. C., Smith, R. A., Vincent-Smith, L., Bricker, D. D., & Bricker, W. A. Mental retardation. In N. Hobbs (Ed.), *Issues in the classification of children*. San Francisco: Jossey-Bass, 1975.

Foster, M. *The effects of different levels of enriched stimulus input on the abstracting ability of slow learning children*. Unpublished master's thesis, George Peabody College for Teachers, 1970.

Gallagher, J. J., & Bradley, R. H. Early identification of developmental difficulties. In I. Gordon (Ed.), *Early childhood education*. Chicago: National Society for the Study of Education Yearbook, 1972.

Gardner, W. I. *Behavior modification in mental retardation*. Chicago: Aldine-Atherton, 1971.

Gordon, E. W. Characteristics of socially disadvantaged children. *Review of Educational Research*, 1965, **35**, 377–388.

Gordon, J. E., & Haywood, H. C. Input deficit in cultural-familial retardation: Effect of stimulus enrichment. *American Journal of Mental Deficiency*, 1969, **73**, 604–610.

Haeussermann, E. *Developmental potential of preschool children*. New York: Grune & Stratton, 1958.

Hall, R. V. *Behavior modification (Vol. 1), The measurement of behavior*. Lawrence, Kan.: H & H Enterprises, 1971.

Hall, R. V., Hawkins, R. P., & Axelrod, S. Measuring and recording student behavior: A behavior analysis approach. In R. A. Weinberg & F. H. Wood (Eds.), *Observation of pupils and teachers in mainstream and special education settings: Alternative strategies*. Minneapolis: Leadership Training Institute/Special Education, University of Minnesota, 1975.

Hamilton, J. L. *Application of the learning potential paradigm to severely mentally retarded adolescents*. Unpublished doctoral dissertation, University of Missouri, Columbia, 1972.

Hamilton, J. L., & Budoff, M. Learning potential among the moderately and severely retarded. *Mental Retardation*, 1974, **12**, 33–36.

Haywood, H. C., Filler, J. W., Shifman, M. A., & Chatelanat, G. Behavioral assessment in mental retardation. In P. McReynolds (Ed.), *Advances in psychological assessment*. (Vol. 3). San Francisco: Jossey-Bass, 1975.

Haywood, H. C., & Switzky, H. N. Children's verbal abstracting: Effects of enriched input, age, and IQ. *American Journal of Mental Deficiency*, 1974, **78**, 556–565.

Hunt, E., Frost, N., & Lunneborg, C. Individual differences in cognition: A new approach to intelligence. In G. H. Bower (Ed.), *The psychology of learning and motivation* (Vol. 7). New York: Academic Press, 1973.

Jastak, J. A rigorous criterion of feeblemindedness. *Journal of Abnormal and Social Psychology*, 1949, **44**, 367–378.

Jensen, A. Learning ability in retarded, average and gifted children. *Merrill-Palmer Quarterly*, 1963, **9**, 123–140.

Jensen, A. *Social class and verbal learning*. Unpublished manuscript, University of California, 1964.

Johnson, G. O., & Capobianco, R. J. Research project on severely retarded children (Special report to the New York State Interdepartmental Health Resources Board). In J. H. Rothstein (Ed.), *Mental retardation*. New York: Holt, Rinehart, & Winston, 1961.

Kiernan, C. C. Functional analysis. In P. J. Mittler (Ed.) *Assessment for learning in the mentally handicapped*. London: Churchill Livingstone, 1973.

Koh, T. H., & Madow, A. A. Relationship between PPVT and Stanford-Binet performance in institutionalized retardates. *American Journal of Mental Deficiency*, 1967, **72**, 108–113.

Kohs, S. C. *Intelligence measurement*. New York: MacMillan, 1923.

Lindsley, O. R. Direct measurement and prosthesis of retarded behavior. *Journal of Education*, 1964, **147**, 62–81.

Luria, A. R. An objective approach to the study of the abnormal child. *American Journal of Orthopsychiatry*, 1961, **31**, 1–14.

MacMillan, D. L. *Behavior modification in education*. New York: MacMillan, 1973.

McClelland, D. C. Testing for competence rather than for "intelligence". *American Psychologist*, 1973, **28**, 1–14.

McCullock, T. L., Reswick, J., & Weissmann, S. Studies of word learning in mental defectives, II. Relation to scores on digit repetition, the Stanford-Binet, M, and the WISC Verbal Scale. *American Journal of Mental Deficiency*, 1955, **60**, 140–143.

Meier, J. *Screening and assessment of young children at developmental risk*. Washington, D. C.: The President's Committee on Mental Retardation, 1973.

Mercer, J. R. *Labeling the mentally retarded*. Berkeley: University of California Press, 1973.

Mills, R. E. *Learning Methods Test*. Ft. Lauderdale, Fla.: The Mills Center, 1955.

O'Connor, G., Justice, R. S., & Payne, D. Statistical expectations of physical handicaps of institutionalized retardates. *American Journal of Mental Deficiency*, 1970, **74**, 541–547.

Penrose, L. S. *Mental defect*. New York: Farrar & Rinehart, 1934.

Reese, E. P. *The analysis of human operant behavior*. Dubuque, Iowa: William C. Brown, 1966.

Resnick, L. B., Wang, M. C., & Kaplan, J. Task analysis in curriculum design: A hierarchically sequenced introductory mathematics curriculum. *Journal of Applied Behavior Analysis*, 1973, **6**, 679–710.

Rey, A. Dún procedé pour évaluer l'éducabilité (quelques applications en psychopathologie). *Archives de Psychologie*, 1934, **24**, 297–337. Cited by Haywood, *et al*, Behavioral assessment in mental retardation. In P. McReynolds (Ed.), *Advances in psychological assessment. Vol. 3. San Francisco: Jossey-Bass, 1975.*

Reynolds, M. C., & Balow, B. Categories and variables in special education. *Exceptional Children*, 1972, **38**, 357–366.

Schucman, H. Evaluating the educability of the severely mentally retarded child. *Psychological Monographs*, 1960, **74**, (Whole No. 501).

Schucman, H. The development of an educability index for the trainable child. In B. W. Richards (Ed.), *Proceedings of the first congress of the International Association for the Scientific Study of Mental Deficiency*. Reigate, Surrey, England: Michael Jackson, 1968.

Shepherd, M. J. Assessment and placement. In W. J. Younie & I. I. Goldberg (Eds.), *Special education administration in the residential setting*. New York: Columbia University Press, 1970.

Silverstein, A. B. Psychological testing practices in state institutions for the mentally retarded. *American Journal of Mental Deficiency*, 1963, **68**, 440–445.

Skinner, B. F. *Science and human behavior*. New York: MacMillan, 1953.

Sulzer, B., & Mayer, G. R. *Behavior modification procedures for school personnel*. Hinsdale, Ill.: Dryden, 1972.

Tarjan, G., Dingman, H. F., & Miller, C. R. Statistical expectations of selected handicaps in the mentally retarded. *American Journal of Mental Deficiency*, 1960, **65**, 335–351.

Tenorio, S. C., & Raimist, L. I. A noncategorical consortium program. *Exceptional Children* 1971, **38**, 325–326.

Tobias, J. The evaluation of the vocational potential of mentally retarded young adults. *Training School Bulletin,* 1960, **56**, 122–135.

Tymchuk, A. J. Effects of familiarization vs. stimulus enhancement on verbal abstracting in institutionalized retarded delinquent boys. *American Journal of Mental Deficiency,* 1973, **77**, 551–555.

Vygotsky, L. S. *Thought and language.* Cambridge, Mass.: MIT Press, 1962. (Originally published, 1934.)

Ysseldyke, J. E. Diagnostic-prescriptive teaching: The search for aptitude-treatment interactions. In L. Mann & D. A. Sabatino (Eds.), *The first review of special education* (Vol. 1). Philadelphia: JSE Press, 1973.

Zeaman, D., & House, B. J. The role of attention in retardate discrimination learning. In N. R. Ellis (Ed.), *Handbook of mental deficiency.* New York: McGraw-Hill, 1963.

8

Application of Research to Psychoeducational Treatment of Infants at Risk

Irving E. Sigel
Educational Testing Service

One of the more pressing challenges facing practitioners and researchers is how to identify, communicate, and apply the large body of relevant knowledge that has accumulated during recent years. The issue is of particular importance in the case of behavioral and medical sciences. Although there is a growing awareness of the need to increase the level of interaction between these two professional groups, there is still a significant communication gap that hinders true collaborative efforts. The application of new knowledge in the field of infant development to the care of infants at risk is the case under discussion. The reasons are many, and it is not our intention to detail the historical background that has contributed to this interdisciplinary separation. Perhaps it is sufficient to point out that in the last two decades increased attention by behavioral scientists to infant development has resulted in a great output of research findings while at the same time there has been a comparable knowledge explosion within the medical and biological fields. These two considerable bodies of literature have developed increasingly technical and specialized vocabularies. The surge of such information, particularly the technical and vocabulary specialization, creates a difficult task for the practitioner and the researcher to keep abreast of information within one's own discipline that can be appropriately assimilated, let alone become cognizant of relevant findings in related fields of practice and research.

Because it is unreasonable to expect either group of professionals to become experts in the fields of the other, the task of reducing the communication gap becomes one of identifying those initial points of contact that may be most helpful, not only in enhancing the quality of medical practice but also in providing the criteria for identifying those areas that require continued exploration and further research.

The area I have selected is intellectual development, because that is and continues to be a high priority for high-risk infants. Given that infants have achieved the competence for biological survival, they now have to acquire the necessary competencies to survive socially, i.e., master necessary academic and self-help skills (e.g., learning how to communicate, care for themselves, etc., and, eventually, to read). Central to achievement of such competencies is the *development of intelligence,* the ability to adapt to the social and physical environment. Heretofore, evaluation of the intellectual competence of young children in the first year of life has been inadequate. The tests psychologists have constructed have tended to be modifications of intelligence tests used with older children. Thus, the Bayley or the Gessell or other traditional measures of development tend to evaluate particular manifestations of the child's achievements. They provide descriptive statements of the state of the child's current knowledge rather than identifying the processes the child can use in the service of solving problems and coping with novel situations. In other words, the tests that have been and are being used currently, although standardized and normed, are limited to descriptions of how the child functions at a particular point in time. Further, the tests only describe strengths and deficiencies, with no indication of the underlying processes involved. Without knowledge of *how* the child thinks or reasons, prognosis or suggestions for treatment is difficult because it is the process involved that needs remedial help. Hence, identification of the qualitative aspects involved would be of considerable value in setting directions for therapy. Of greater concern, these tests have been used to predict later performance for infants, yet have been found to have relatively little predictive validity. The reason for these failures is that the data so obtained are descriptive of the current status of the individual and do not specify the relationship of such findings to subsequent behaviors. This is because the relationship between the competencies assessed during infancy and later childhood are very different; e.g., motor behaviors comprise a larger portion of tests during the first year of life, but not at age 4. Yet the scores of such motor tasks are used to predict mental ability at the later age. This is a problem not only of measurement, but of conceptualization of relationships between behavior at one period and that at another.

Hamilton's discussion in Chapter 7 of this volume of Budoff's model illustrates an alternative approach to assessing learning competence that, in a sense, creates situations to observe how the child does, in fact, solve problems, think, and reason. This is a shift in emphasis from static assessment to an understanding of processes underlying intellectual performance. The trend to identify the specific prerequisites for subsequent performance is increasing. For example, all tests require the children to follow directions. If, in fact, children are unable to follow directions, then they will fail on the test items. There is no way of knowing whether the children do not know the content of the specific item or whether they just do not comprehend the instructions. If the instructions were changed, then it is possible that the children could solve the problem. In effect, we are often testing the instructions not the children. An example of this problem is the test that asks children to tell whether there is "more" or "less" of a quantity. If they understand the concepts of "more" and "less" then they can answer; if they do not, then they may not be able to demonstrate what they know about quantity. On the other hand, if the children are asked when presented with two different sized groups which they would rather have, then they might be able to answer the question and demonstrate that they can differentiate between "more" and "less." The point is relevant to all developmental assessments, and the task is to be certain that the children do, in fact, understand the nature of the task that they are expected to perform. The quality of performance on the test item may be more useful, for it must be remembered it is the total response to the item on the test that is the important piece of information.

This leads to a second important issue. Children's performance on any type of behavioral measure should not be interpreted in isolation of the investigator's conceptualization of behavioral development. This is a critical issue because it defines not only how the behavior is interpreted, but also the type of instrumentation that is selected to monitor change over time. The way a problem is approached, be it for diagnosis or treatment, is influenced by the way professionals conceptualize the specific instance in the context of their general view of human development. If one believes that children's development is determined by biogenetic factors, then one would be inclined use procedures to search for such factors, assess them, and suggest treatments in accordance with this perspective. If, on the other hand, one were oriented towards an environmental perspective, then the practitioners or researchers would be more inclined to focus on social and environmental features of the situation as sources of the difficulty as well as components of the treatment program. In each case, one might miss factors that are the result of the interaction of both. Trite as this may sound, it is a point that is often overlooked and, even when not overlooked, minimized. The papers in this volume aptly demonstrate the issue (see Chapters 1, 2, and 3 for examples).

As the effort is made to communicate research findings or recommendations for practice, the conceptual framework of the reader also is a critical factor in determining receptivity of the results or recommendations. Readers of this volume should be sensitized to this issue by now, since they have been reading the results of investigations derived from different theoretical and methodological perspectives. These types of differences often confuse the nonbehavioral scientists, because the behavioral sciences have many perspectives, each of which is supported by staunch adherents all proclaiming the truth. I believe that, at this stage in the development of our respective fields, especially in the area dealing with high-risk infants, one should be cautious about rejecting an approach simply because it violates a preexisting perspective of development. It is this issue that I wish to address next.

There is first the choice of accepting a model of human growth and development, one that fits one's experience and temperament. Some current models, such as the learning model of Skinner and other behaviorists, have appealed to individuals who prefer precise systematic operational statements. There is some validity to that point of view when one observes the consequences of training children, especially retarded children, to learn simple and at times even complex tasks by using behavior-modification strategies. For some investigators and practitioners, this is the be all and end all of the behavioral approach. On the other hand, there are those who would reject behavior modification and operant-conditioning models because of their narrowness. Such professionals might be more inclined to accept the broader model that incorporates a more inferential approach to the study of human behavior, for instance a Freudian or Piagetian perspective. These conceptualizations employ hypothetical constructs, i.e., mechanisms explaining behavior that are not directly observable, and that are thought to be mediators between behavioral inputs and outputs. This point of view, then, could lead investigators to function quite differently. Zelazo's discussion of schema (see Chapter 3) is an example of such conceptualization, whereas, Lipsitt's approach (see Chapter 1) is more concerned with a behavioral orientation. Obviously, individuals who can accept a broader perspective are willing and able to tolerate more ambiguity and more inpreciseness in evaluating events. Then, as was indicated earlier, a model for development can be essentially biological, with behavioral outcomes perceived on the basis of predetermined biological or genetic factors, leaving environmental experiences a small role to play in effecting outcomes.

Such an orientation is not as infrequent as one might suppose. Often, the child's parents are told that in view of certain biological givens the infants is not going to develop beyond a particular level. The assumption of the potency of biological factors speak to the salience given to the power of predetermined biological conditions and the relative impotence of environmental features. To be sure, these examples are extreme, yet typical of the dominant conceptualizations that prevail to date. It should be made clear that they are not presented to derogate a particular position, for data and evidence abound to support each and every one. Of course, rarely, if ever, is the same data base used by advocates of different conceptual positions to support their own position. Date are frequently ignored or devalued when presented from the opponent's perspective. Thus, the difficulty in using information derived from these various points of view is not that they are necessarily incomparable but not addressed. Thus, discussions among individuals varying in perspective often result in individuals talking past each other.

Is there a solution to the problem? The answer is possibly, but it requires a shift in commitment. Readers have to accept the basic premise that no one perspective encompasses the totality of the information available within the field. Obviously, the congenital status of children is relevant for subsequent performance. Cerebral palsy children with hand involvement are not going to be as competent in hand–eye activities as are children without such involvement. These are realistic givens. Assessment of learning capability might well include what children already have in their repertoire, because this is a piece of data that is of value. Thus, to reject standardized tests solely because of their emphasis on descriptive measures may result in the loss of important information. In effect, what we need is a type of logical and relevant integration where the problems at hand define the kinds of information that are necessary. In this way, the problem under consideration becomes an important determinant guiding the diagnostic efforts of practitioners and identifying unsolved issues for researchers. To be sure, this does not preclude theoretical bias rearing itself, but it does raise the possibility that the individuals concerned are aware of their position as a "bias." Focusing on the problems under study with an awareness of bias may clarify points of difference.

Let us explore this matter further. The first issue for working with infants at risk is to define the risk elements. The criteria for survival subsumes one set of risk elements. We have some sense of what is required for biological survival of the infant and what kinds of support systems are necessary to minimize these risk elements. Thus, within the intensive care unit incubators and various life-support systems are used to monitor various physiologic systems and to insure survival of the child. The state of the art is such that we can identify with increasing accuracy the support systems necessary for biological survival. Once the biological integrity of the organisms is assured, attention can be directed towards psychological survival. Psychological survival implies, as was stated above, the capability to adapt to our kind of society, a society that imposes varying intellectual, social, and economic demands on individuals during the course of their development. Our particular concern with young infants is intellectual survival, the acquisiton of those basic cognitive skills required to read, write, compute, and communicate in symbolic systems. The psychological processes prerequisite to thse achievements constitute an area of continuing basic research as to the conditions within which such intellectual accomplishments flower. What we *do now is the best we can with what we now know.* What we know comes from scientific research as well as the accumulated wisdom of clinical practice. There is no reason to denegrate the experiences of astute practitioners, for such knowledge often provides the basis for more rigorous scientific inquiry. As such, clinicians should be open to new information derived from systematic research: to this end, this volume.

The reports in this volume tend to follow the canons of current scientific rules of evidence. The experiments that are reported, as well as the survey data presented, meet the constraints of the contemporary research paradigm. There are those who would argue that this research paradigm is of limited validity because, frequently, experiments are conducted in artifical settings and employ procedures that isolate the phenomenon in question from its naturally occurring context. Haith's studies in visual behavior of infants (see Chapter 2) lend themselves to such commentary, whereas Sameroff's chapter (5) addresses the reality of the broader psychological environment. Haith, however, does approach the problem in a matter comparable to that of a medical examination. A particular aspect of behavior is assessed with the assumption that what is discovered makes a statement concerning the ability of the individual to function under a particular set of circumstances. Thus, the functional capacity of that particular variable is determined. Infants under given conditions do respond to various stimuli in a predictable manner when certain conditions prevail. This could be viewed as a diagnostic index and, as such, is informative regarding the functional status of the individual at that point in time.

Sameroff's discussion indicates that the outcome of early child behaviors are functions of an array of interacting factors, each of which must be considered. He argues that the predictive validity of outcomes requires that a host of environmental and constitutional features must be identified and employed in the analytical paradigm. The strategies of Haith and Sameroff are in no way contradictory, rather they can be viewed as complimentary. The identification of the index of a particular piece of behavior speaks to the existence and its occurence under controlled conditions; the degree to which that behavior appears in the broader social context and its function will be better understood if a more complex paradigm is employed. The blending of the two strategies can enhance practitioners' ways of looking at the phenomenon under question. To be sure, not all of the variables under discussion have or will be put to the test of applications within a broader social environment. But alert practitioners can begin to ask questions that will yield some clinical insights into the relationship between an isolated laboratory finding and its behavioral manifestation functioning in the natural setting.

This type of interrelationship can provide some understanding of performance in the here and now. However, we are also interested in the developmental aspects of children. Working with infants at risk necessitates a consideration of how the child will develop. Status considerations are important, but mostly to the degree that they will predict subsequent performance. This may appear obvious, but it is fair to say that the issue is generally assumed. An estimate of age-appropriate behavior is the usual way that children's progress is monitored. The more relevant problem of how to conceptualize development is not a simple task. To identify age as the criterion of development is to take a static approach. A 2-week-old infant is expected to perform in a way different from a 12-week-old infant. Age, however, is an arbitrary score based on the calendrical system that is also arbitrary. Chronologically based indices neither describe nor explain the process of development. They merely offer a static statement of the correlation between the postnatal age and some measure of performance.

Let us analyze the "age concept." What does age represent? It represents experience and a definition of biological and psychological time arbitrarily stated in terms of a chronology that begins at birth. The age of individuals is comparable because it can be fixed, but it does not identify (a) how the individual progresses from one chronological epoch to another (age differences), (b) what factors influence the course of the development, nor (c) that individuals necessarily pass through time at the same biological rate, and (d) that stage-like sequences seem to exist, varying even within age groups.

Age can provide a framework useful in following developmental change that occurs as a function of biological factors interacting with varying environmental experiences. Biological changes have one set of determinants: nutrition, neurological maturity, genetic factors, and endocrinological functions. Experiences are assimilated to and accommodated as a result of the individual's biological capability to deal with such experiences. Hard-of-hearing children, blind children, or children with impaired motor control will be limited to those kinds of experiences available and the types of interactions possible. Yet the experiences of blind children will vary as a function of other options in their environment. The degree to which caretakers interact and the quality of that interaction will differentially influence the children. Thus, the blind child with a parenting figure who is tuned to the child's limitations as well as strengths will foster a different set of developmental experiences that the parent who is either insensitive to or denies these limitations. Irrespective of age, such children will differ in cognitive competence. Thus, any diagnostic picture of a child that relies heavily on age and uses age-normed material may misjudge the child's capability or the source of the child's functional impairment. It is arguments of this type that lend credence to Sameroff's plea for a multifacted approach that includes environmental features.

EXPLORATION OF DEVELOPMENTAL CHANGE

As one considers development, then one must also consider what accounts for developmental change. Zelazo (Chapter 3 of this volume) suggests that the discrepancy hypothesis is one way of acccounting for developmental change. This point of view emphasizes the interactional approach because discrepancy is, in part, a function of children's biological status and experience. As these two interact, they create a degree of psychological conflict. The children attempt to resolve this conflict by incorporating discrepant experiences into their existing repertoire and, in so doing, move ahead cognitively. This is one theoretical statement of how children develop. If one accepts this orientation, then a number of questions follow. The first is, what conditions can facilitate such attention (assuming of course, that the hypothesis is valid)? Do children respond to discrepancies in the environment? If not, why not? Zelazo provides one set of methods to identify responses associated with discrepant events. Other types of assessments are also possible; for example, using Menyuk's description of children's language development (see Chapter 4) it is possible to construct verbal statements to assess this comprehension of linguistic discrepancies. Riddles and simple contradictory statements provide this type of language discrepancy. As children grapple with such discrepancies, they reveal their potential for problem solving. The degree to which parents engage in this behavior with their children may reveal the type of environmental stimulation that is available.

Implicit in the discrepancy resolution idea is that children are active organisms rather than passive recipients of stimulation. If children do, in fact, seek out stimulation, then the opportunity to engage them in actions that are discrepant becomes possible. Traditionally, I would suspect, infants at risk are viewed as less actively involved with their environment and as relatively immobile receivers rather than initiators of interactions. If the shift in viewing children as active rather than passive occurs, it would then suggest that engagement of children with their environment would be generated by the caretaker. The implications of this shift in perspective of high-risk infants are considerable. This means parents and caregivers, as well as medical personnel, would be alerted to this capability of children. In chapter 6, Kearsley speaks to this issue most clearly when he demonstrates how a neuromotor model of child development influences clinical judgments of children's overall development. If children are, indeed, outreaching organisms and if children, even though at risk, are able to process information and seek out stimulation, then those who influence the nature of the children's environment should allow for these possibilities. Mobiles for example, would be as appropriate for high-risk infants as for intact children as would verbal engagements and the use of questions. In other words, children should be treated in a way that takes into account the use of the relevant modalities through which actions and interactions may occur. For deaf children, the use of visual stimulation can provide cognitive stimulation in the absence of verbal interaction whereas for blind children the use of auditory activity would be more appropriate. In each case, children are treated as active participants, capable of producing as well as receiving environmental input.

Diagnostic procedures commonly applied to children irrespective of category or disorder employ a clinical model or a psychometric model of assessment. The clinical approach most commonly uses a medical model that attempts to identify the children's deficits. Psychological tests are given. If certain items cannot be solved, the children are classified as deficient. In addition, clinicians usually rely heavily on their own experiences. The areas tapped in the traditional clinical approach may be ones that are presumed to be most significant, e.g., language comprehension and space orientation. The choice of areas of focus or the method used in the evaluation are highly subjective, despite claims of objectivity. This is an unfortunate consequence of the state of the art rather than any particular bias on the parts of clinicians. To compensate for such potentially subjective evaluations, some behavorial instruments have been proposed, such as the Brazelton Neonatal Assessment Scales, the APGAR Score and the Denver Developmental Screening Test, that presume to be objective, yield normative data, and allow clinicians to make comparative statements about a particular child. These tasks are in the domain of psychometric models of assessments and should, if used, fit the generally accepted requirements of this model.

The usual criteria for determining the quality of a psychometric instrument are standardization, reliability, and validity. The standardization sample is especially important in working with high-risk children because there is so much variance among these children that it is difficult to assume that the larger, normative sample is in fact representative of high-risk populations. In view of this, it is important that the examiner, when using any test that is *norm referenced,* (i.e., claims standardization with a large and representative sample) should be certain that the child being assessed represents the standardization sample.

The next question addresses the test reliability where reliability refers to the consistency of a test. Two serious measurement problems that arise for consistency may not be as much a function of test as of the respondent. Children are notoriously inconsistent in their behavior — not necessarily because of the test, but because of their highly variable moods, attention spans, and motivation, each of which influences test performance. Other nontest variables which can impinge on children's performance range from the sensitivity of the examiner to the children's moods to fatigue and motivation. Because performance can be attenuated by any of these factors, it is important to keep them in mind when using any instrument, despite the claims of the test makers. To be sure, initial selection of the test will first be done by looking at its reliability score, but then when used it should still be interpreted with caution.

Validity, which refers to the test measuring what it purports to measure, poses another set of problems for the high-risk population. First, tests are impure because all test items are, in fact, multidimensional, not pure measures of any attribute or characteristic. Thus, the majority of tests have items that measure many factors. Asking children to count or to point out a difference asks not only their knowledge of the items (recognition), but also whether they comprehend the directions or even attend to the instructions. Each of these components is involved in a single, seemingly simple inquiry. Although validation is usually reported in tests by showing how the particular test relates to another test, this kind of information, *correlational validity,* is not always the most useful. Instead, it might be more advantageous to have *predictive validity,* i.e., how well the test accurately predicts to a set of future events that are relevant to the measurement being taken. For example, if the children are given a test of language comprehension, do they, in fact, demonstrate that they can comprehend language in another setting? Unfortunately, predictive validity is rarely presented in test manuals. This is not to argue that the correlational validity coefficient based on correlations of a particular test with another is not worthwhile; it is relevant data, but should not mislead the user. It can be just the compounding error. An example of this is the correlating of a new intelligence test with the Stanford-Binet. Even through the two tests may be highly correlated, it does not mean that either of the two tests measures intelligence. The Stanford-Binet, however, does predict school performance. Hence, the Stanford-Binet has predictive validity for school performance. Does this mean that the Stanford-Binet is a valid test of intelligence? The answer is yes if one considers school performance as intelligence. This line of reasoning suggests that the Stanford-Binet does not test intelligence if one uses the predictive validity concept, unless one argues that success in school is an index of intelligent behavior. What gives the Stanford-Binet credibility is that by definition it seems to tap intelligence, i.e., the ability to think in abstractions. If it is agreed that this is the case, then the Stanford-Binet manifests *construct validity,* i.e., agreement that the construct measured is, in fact, judged as being measured. The complexities of this issue are beyond the scope of this paper. Some of the issues are discussed by Hamilton in chapter 7 of this volume. The important point is that the users of tests must be careful to evaluate the criteria for validity, reliability, and standardization populations that are presented in test manuals.

Finally, in assessing the results of any test, it is important to consider another form of analysis, namely, the analysis of errors that the child made on particular test items. Usually, the only responses considered of value are those that are correct. My argument is that children's so-called wrong answers are valuable pieces of data; in fact, they often are more informative than correct answers. Children approach a test from the point of view of what they know and how they perceive reality. If they give an answer that is "wrong," this may well be their judgment of what that reality is. First, just giving an answer indicates that the child knows that something is expected. Second, what is expected by the examiner is a correct response. Children produce answers that they believe are correct. Identifying the errors instead of ignoring them may reveal much about how the children think and reason. If children are asked to count and give a number much too large or too small, then it is clear that they understand something of numbers, but not cardinality. Too often our tests prevent us from obtaining sensitive statements of children's competence. Hamilton deals with many of these issues in the context of retarded children. The issues are not limited to this group. In his presentation, Hamilton states principles and considerations that could well form the basis for evaluating any test for any group.

ROLE OF AFFECT OR EMOTIONALITY

The entire discussion in this volume has focused on diagnosing children's cognitive development; however, this emphasis minimizes the significant role affect or emotional development plays in the lives of children. Important as the ability to perform on cognitive tasks may be, the level of performance may be influenced by children's level of anxiety, or their attitude towards self and others. For very young infants, the important affect features may be anxiety about abrupt changes in the environment or sensitivity to strangers and other caretakers. As they get older, this significance of attitudes towards self and sense of competence may begin to play a significant role. In work with underprivileged children, I found that the manner in which the examiner in an intelligence test situation interacted with the child, did in fact influence the child's performance.

For those readers who are unacquainted with intelligence testing, it should be pointed out that the methods of administering the tests are very specifically stated, and examiners are trained not to deviate from the procedures described in the manuals. The rationale for such constraints is that such instructions were used in developing and standardizing the test. Thus, if deviations occur, it upsets the standardization procedure. In effect, the test makers work with the same model as chemists or laboratory technicians would in testing for some impersonal chemical substance. I think it is naive to think that children's intelligence can be tested like a chemical substance in a blood sample. The aim of the test is not to test the test or to see how well the children perform relative to the situation, but, rather, the purpose of the test is to discover what the children's intellectual status is. It may be necessary, then, to modify some procedures in order to make the children feel comfortable or minimize handicaps.

Thus, some liberties have to be taken with the testing procedure. When this is done, children often perform better. In a sense, I believe that the test is more valid in terms of assessing children's competence when appropriate adjustments are made. This is especially true with those handicaps that involve sensory or manual capability. To be sure, it would be better if tests were constructed that were deliberately geared to certain classes of handicapped children, and, in fact, some of the standard intelligence tests are modified to take these limitations into account.

Perhaps it would be more beneficial if the tests were constructed so as to allow greater flexibility on the part of the examiner to make necessary changes to meet children's limitations for performance. This is not to say that the tests would be constructed so as to preclude getting anything about the children's performance level. Rather, it is saying that the test should obviously attempt to minimize inadequate performances by encouraging latitude in administration. To follow that recommendation necessitates another, namely, the quality of training of psychological examiners. They have to be not only knowledgeable about the test, but about children. Thus, psychological examiners cannot be at the level of X-ray technicans who know a lot about X-ray technology but not about the nature of the organism. Rather, psychological examiners have to know as much about the psychology of children as physicians know about their biology, and over and above that, psychologists must know a lot about measurement and assessment. An example would be for children who are color blind to use items that involve color or for cerebral palsy children who have motor involvement to use tasks which require manual dexterity. Obvious as they may appear, clinicians sometimes do use such tests without acknowledging the particular limitation that may reduce the children's level of performance. In other words, the test is not truely testing the children. This brings us full circle to the emotional aspect, because these kinds of tasks do frustrate the children and do depress performance, not only because of some particular physical involvement, but also because of the emotional aspects of the situation.

Thus, in considering assessment, it is critical to recognize that emotional aspects play an important role in the examination. It is known that young infants do respond to changes in physical environment and in handling. Thus, it is naive to believe that infants are, in fact, not aware of social and physical stimuli. These types of sensitivities might well account for some of the low performance scores. Evaluation of the cognitive competence of *any child* must include the role of non-cognitive features of the situation as potential sources of influence on performance. Indeed, it should be made clear that the influence of noncognitive features may be positive as well as negative, positive in the sense of enhancing performance, negative in the sense of depressing performance.

CONCLUSIONS

Many of the procedures in this volume are presented with the purpose of showing not only what has been done in some critical research areas but also to indicate potential for clinical use. The chapters by Haith, Sameroff, Zelazo, and Lipsitt, for example, indicate that their procedures may well be adapted to clinical purposes. Unfortunately, such modification may be difficult at this time because of the expensive nature of laboratory equipment as well as their pioneering status. Nevertheless, in the long run, practitioners should be able to look towards researchers for just this kind of help. For example, some of Haith's visual apparatus may eventually be adapted for clinical purposes to test visual skills once it is clear how responses on his procedures do, is fact, identify quality of performance. Another example of this approach is manifest in Kearsley's paper. His clinical procedures do derive from research and have been adapted for diagnostic purposes. By instituting them as part of a clinical procedure, he has not only set in motion a broader based diagnostic battery, but also is collecting data that in time may provide him with a basis for judging the predictive validity of his material. Thus, it is hoped that one contribution of this volume is to show what techniques are or will become available. The demand for their modification will depend, in part, on the value of their data in meeting the clinical needs of high-risk infant populations. It is their potential for improving patient care, rather than their apparent complexity, that should command clinicians' attention. If the readers can gain this from these pages, then the effort will have been worthwhile.

Author Index

Numbers in *italics* refer to pages on which the complete reference is listed.

A

Ainsworth, M. D. S., 95, 97, *110,* 136, *148*
Albutt, M. G. V., *47*
Andrews, J. P., 118, *148*
Anglin, J., 93, *110*
Anmatruda, C., 117, *149*
Anthony, E. J., 119, 120, *148*
Antonova, T. G., 12, *20*
Apgar, V., 118, *151*
Arthur, G. A., 188, 192, *199*
Axelrod, S., 197, *201*

B

Babigan, H., 133, *151*
Baer, D. M., 197, *199,* 200
Bailey, C. J., 119, *148*
Bailyn, B., *80*
Baker, K., 103, *111*
Ball, R. S., 49, *82,* 166, *179*
Balow, B., 199, *202*
Bamborough, P., *47*
Barnard, K. E., 13, *20*
Barrett, B. H., 184, 196, 197, *199,* 200

Barro, G., 167, *180*
Bartelme, P. F., 121, *149*
Barton, S., 35, *47*
Bateson, M., 97, *110*
Baudonniere, P. M., 33, *47*
Bayley, N., 49, 50, 54, 66, *81*
Becker, W. L., 144, *148*
Beckwith, L., 133, *148*
Beery, K. E., 194, *200*
Beilin, H., 100, *110*
Beintema, D. J., 123, *150*
Bell, R. Q., 130, 135,
Bell, S. M., 95, 97, *110,* 136, *148*
Bellugi-Klima, U. 88, *110*
Benaron, H., 118, 119, *148*
Berendes, H. W., 123, 124, *149*
Berges, J., 87, *110*
Bergman, T., 41, *47*
Bever, T., 88, 95, 96, 99, *110*
Bierman, J. M., 125, 126, 128, 131, *151*
Bijou, S. W., 196, 197, *200*
Bilek, M. K., 166, *179*
Birch, H. G., 40, *48,* 121, 125, 131, 135, 146, *148, 151*
Birch, J. W., 183, *201*

Subject Index